Aliens in America

ALSO BY JODI DEAN

Solidarity of Strangers:

Feminism after Identity Politics

Aliens
in America

Conspiracy

Cultures

from

Outerspace

to

Cyberspace

Jodi Dean

Cornell University Press

Ithaca and London

For information, address
Cornell University Press,
Sage House,
512 East State Street,
Ithaca, New York 14850.
First published 1998 by
Cornell University Press
First printing, Cornell Paperbacks, 1998
Printed in the United States of America
Cornell University Press strives to use
environmentally responsible suppliers and
materials to the fullest extent possible in
the publishing of its books. Such materials
include vegetable-based, low-VOC inks
and acid-free papers that are recycled,
totally chlorine-free, or partly composed
of nonwood fibers. For further information,
visit our website at
www.cornellpress.cornell.edu.

PAPERBACK PRINTING
10 9 8 7 6 5

Library of Congress
Cataloging-in-Publication Data
Dean, Jodi, b. 1962
    Aliens in America : conspiracy cultures
from outerspace to cyberspace /
Jodi Dean.
      p.   cm.
    Includes bibliographical references
(p.   ) and index.
  ISBN-13: 978-0-8014-8468-1 (pbk. : alk.
paper)
    1. Human-alien encounters—Social
aspects—United States.   2. Alien abduction—Social aspects—United States.
I. Title.
BF2050.D43   1998   97-44509
306.4—dc21

For my father,

DAVID F. DEAN,

on his 60th birthday,

April 1997

I have described something I myself witnessed, and
I have reported something which I was told by someone
else, but someone I believed as thoroughly as if I had
witnessed the scene myself. I will now add something which
I have read about.

Augustine of Hippo,

The City of God

I realize *I don't know what to believe!* How does
one explain the similarities in the abductees' stories—
the consistence of detail, structure, scenario? What
would prompt a woman to make up a story about an
extraterrestrial creature trying on her high-heeled
shoe?

C. D. B. Bryan,

Close Encounters of the Fourth Kind

Contents

Acknowledgments

Countless people have watched television, tabloids, and the skies for signs of alien life. They have kept me supplied with clippings and cartoons, ever on the alert for something I may have missed. Many people have told me their personal stories, some of whom have requested that their names not be used. More have given me their opinions on aliens, abductions, and cover-ups. Thanks to Walt Andrus, Hubertus Buchstein, Claudette Columbus, Bette Jo Runnels Dean, Dave Dean, David Dean, Brenda Denzler, Iva Deutchman, Leslie Feldman, Dawn Feligno, Joey Feligno, Dahn Dean Gandell, Rachel Gandell, Mindy Gerber, Robert Girard, Judith Grant, David Halperin, Alan Hill, Budd Hopkins, Bill Hudnut, Debra Jordan Kauble, Marty Kelly, Bill Kenyon, Sue Kenyon, John Mack, David Ost, Craig Rimmerman, and Dave Stainton.

E-mail conversations with the members of Alan Hill's UFO movement discussion list kept me up to date, stimulated, and supported as I worked on this project. Faculty research grants from Hobart and William Smith helped to fund fieldwork and supply hard-to-find research materials. Students and faculty from the colleges were helpful audiences for the early presentations that became chapters of this book. Critical feedback from participants in the 1996 and 1997 Prague Conferences on Philosophy and the Social Sciences challenged me to clarify and sharpen my arguments.

I am fortunate to have had the excellent volunteer research assistance of two William Smith students. Kim Crocetta helped me on the astronaut chapter, persistently contacting the NASA History Office and poring through back issues of *Life*. Ayesha Hassan was the backbone of the abduction research. Her interviewing skills were invaluable at the 1996 Mutual UFO Network (MUFON) symposium, and her diligent and creative interpretative work proved invaluable.

I give special thanks to people who supported this project in its early stages. Without their encouragement, this project would have not been possible. Thomas Dumm, whose beautiful writing and provocative work at the intersection of political and cultural theory provided a powerful ideal, contributed valuable suggestions and advice. Lee Quinby taught me about apocalypse, accompanied me to lectures by abduction researchers, and gave me crucial advice on every chapter. Elayne Rapping, whose detailed review of the manuscript was unrelenting, pushed me to pay greater attention to the significant work done in media studies and talked me through point after point. Thanks also to Maura Burnett and Ken Wissoker for their interest in the project and to William Connolly, Bruce Robbins, Thomas DiPiero, and Michael Shapiro for their responsive recommendations on the proposal, Chapter 1, and Chapter 5, respectively.

Alison Shonkwiler has been a wonderful editor. She believed in this project (if not in the aliens) from the beginning, both taking a book about aliens to a press more likely to be associated with Carl Sagan (indeed, Cornell published a critical collection on UFOs edited by Sagan in the 1970s) and realizing that this was more than a book about aliens. Alison also provided meticulous, insightful, and immediate responses throughout the project. Often, after reading her suggestions and rereading my original words, I wondered what I could have been thinking. No doubt many of the faults that remain are the result of my failure to heed all of her advice.

Shane Kenyon was and continues to be the source and inspiration for my thinking on the various networks of the contemporary present (and for much, much more). Kian Runnels Kenyon-Dean, coincidentally (?) born nine months after UFOs were sighted over Albany, New York, reminded me of the resemblance between aliens and fetuses, especially after I first saw the sonogram of what became Kian. Both prevent my world from being a totally alien place.

A draft of Chapter 5 was previously published in *Theory and Event* as "The Familiarity of Strangeness: Aliens, Citizens, and Abduction."

The art used on pages 47, 106, 128, and 159 was provided by Jeff Westover, himself an experiencer. He can be contacted by E-mail at jeff.westover@mailexcite.com.

Geneva, New York   JODI DEAN

Aliens in America

Introduction
Alien Politics

Earth vs. the Flying Saucers

Aliens have invaded the United States. No longer confined to science fiction and Elvis-obsessed tabloids, aliens appear in the *New York Times*, the *Washington Post*, and the *Wall Street Journal*, at candy counters (in chocolate-covered flying saucers and as Martian melon-flavored lollipops), and on Internet web sites. Aliens are at the center of a battle at Harvard, caught in the university's furor over the psychologist John Mack's work with alleged abduction experiencers and its attempt to revoke the Pulitzer Prize–winning professor's tenure. Aliens have been seen in credible company at MIT. There, at the 1992 Abduction Study Conference, psychiatrists, abductees, ufologists, and professors in sociology, religion, and physics seriously discussed the possibility that aliens are abducting people from bedrooms and cars and using their sperm and ova to create a

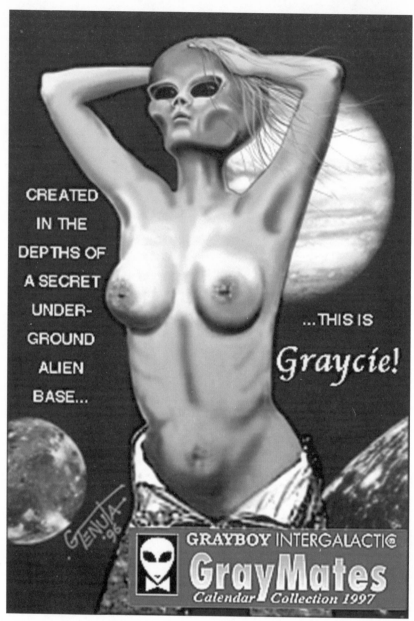

Graycie (Gary Tenuta)

hybrid human-alien species.[1] In Nevada, a stretch of interstate near the secret military base and alleged crashed-disk hiding place Area 51 was re-named the Extraterrestrial Highway. Attending the dedication ceremony were Nevada government officials, the stars, directors, and writers from *Independence Day*, and county, state, and national directors from the Mutual UFO Network.[2] Walt Disney World added a new attraction, the Extra-TERRORestrial Alien Encounter. Disney invited abductees to Orlando to promote it.[3]

Aliens have been used to market AT&T cellular phones, Milky Way candy bars, Kodak film, Diet Coke, Stove-Top Stuffing, T-shirts, Rice Krispies, air fresheners, toys, abduction insurance, skateboard accessories, and the backlist at MIT Press. Titled "Subliminal Abduction," the catalog, with its "totally alien prices," features the typical big-eyed gray alien and the alien's remarks on various books. For example, about Thomas Mc-Carthy's *Ideals and Illusions*, the alien says "Item 120 explicates earthling delusions with grace, wit, and savage sarcasm. A must read!" Fox Network's popular show, *The X-Files*, with its focus on abductions, conspiracies, and the search for truth, has generated its own line of products (mugs, hats, books, T-shirts, comic books) as well as a lively discussion group on Amer-ica OnLine. CompuServe features a closed abductee discussion forum. Ab-ductees Anonymous has a site on the World Wide Web where abductees and experiencers (those who feel more positive about their alien encoun-ters) recount and interpret important events in their lives. A special section is reserved for abductee problems, such as spontaneous involuntary invisi-bility. *Entertainment Tonight* says that ETs are one of the most accessed subjects on the Net, second only to sex.[4] The *Penthouse* site, promoting the September 1996 issue, features both: it displays photos that publisher Bob Guccione claims come from the "real autopsy" of the alien who crashed in Roswell, New Mexico, in 1947 (as opposed to the fake alien autopsy broad-cast by the Fox Network first in 1995 and frequently thereafter). The pho-tos are actually of the model alien body used in the Showtime movie *Roswell* and on display at the town Roswell's International UFO Museum.

Word on the Net is that former *Entertainment Tonight* host John Tesh is an alien. The tabloids claim that twelve U.S. senators are space aliens. Scott Mandelker says that 150 million Americans are aliens.[5] (At least they have political representation.) A Roper poll suggests that at least one in fifty Americans has been abducted by aliens.[6] A Gallup poll says that 27 percent of Americans believe space aliens have visited Earth.[7] The *Penthouse* site raises the number to 48 percent. A *Time*/CNN poll says 80 percent of its respondents believe the U.S. government is covering up its knowledge of the existence of aliens. Sixty-five percent believe a UFO crashed in Roswell in 1947.[8]

The *Weekly World News* says that an alien has visited Newt Gingrich. Reporting on the alien's exchange with the Speaker, the tabloid quotes the spokesman Tony Blankely: "I can assure you that no extraterrestrial that comes to this country from outer space would be eligible for welfare benefits of any kind."[9] *MAD* magazine asks why the aliens don't take Newt.[10] The opera singer Maria Ewing feels she's been overtaken by the Internet: "The Internet is like aliens landing on the planet and we can do nothing about it. I don't like that at all."[11] It is an age of aliens, an alien age when alien images and alien copies and copies of aliens appear unpredictably and unannounced in places they shouldn't, in places we can't understand, in multiple, contradictory, alien places.

Take, for example, this insertion of alien imagery into the history of the space program: "UFO Rescued Apollo 13," the headline for a cover story in the *Weekly World News*. Compared to the tabloid's coverage of the vampire baby ("Bat Child Found in Cave!" and "Bat Child Escapes!"), the alien report is tame, an unabashed attempt to link into the success of the film *Apollo 13* in the summer of 1995. The tabloid does more than capitalize on a popular film, however. The story of the UFO's rescue of the beleaguered American spacecraft accents the failure of the *Apollo 13* mission at a time when the movie and most popular media emphasized the safe and triumphant return of crew and capsule. Stressing the human vulnerability of the astronauts, the tabloid relocates NASA's story of success to an alien domain. In the *Weekly World News* account, the situation was too dire, humans and technology too weak, ignorant, and ill-prepared to cope with disaster. While mainstream media blurred the boundaries between the film and the mission — Tom Hanks not only played Jim Lovell but also brought the astronaut with him when he accepted an award — the tabloid wedges an alternative history between them. This alternative tabloid history offers a challenge — however credible or incredible — not only to the truth of *Apollo 13, the movie*, but to the original *Apollo 13* mission, itself created for a television audience.

The tabloid, in its wild possibility, rejects the idea that outerspace is empty, vacant. It disrupts the fantasy that three white men, heroically venturing out into a new frontier, encounter no one at all, no one to colonize, nothing to appropriate. It reminds us, in other words, that in space, "we" (if those who get there can be said to represent any of us) are the aliens. The tabloid story of a UFO saving the American space program challenges the illusions of technology, power, and agency created in the American theatrics of space. With hints of conspiratorial secrets, the tabloid lands in an alien space of virtual truth.

This is a book about alien space, about following and creating links from cultural images of the alien to tales of UFOs and abduction, to computer and communication technologies, to political passivity and conspiracy thinking in the contemporary United States. By examining changes in the metaphor of outerspace that accompany the shift from outerspace to cyberspace, we can traverse webs through U.S. society at the millennium and better understand American paranoia. To this end, I read accounts of and reactions to the officially produced space program of the 1960s. Like the tabloid, I situate America's space program in an alien domain. I consider the witnesses, and the witnessing, of launches of manned spacecraft and of alien intrusions into women's bedrooms and bodies. I look at the discredited and stigmatized knowledge of aliens and at what this knowledge might hold for mainstreams in American culture. Abduction, I suggest, is more than an alien story. It's a symptomatic or extreme form of what is widespread in everyday life at the millennium.

Windows 2000

Thoughtful analyses by scholars in religious studies have asked about the function of flying saucers in the belief systems of UFO aficionados and "cultists."[12] My questions are different. (I'm concerned less with UFO belief than with aliens in everyday life.) How is it possible that American popular cultures in the last decade of the twentieth century are so taken with, so interested in, so inscribed by aliens? People all over the world report UFOs and claim to see their occupants, but aliens are embedded in America. They have a history in American folklore, a present in Hollywood films. They are part of the cultural moment of the millennium. Stories of aliens and alien abduction appear in the most unlikely places, like the speeches of Louis Farrakhan, gay fiction, the *New Yorker*.[13] Why? Interpreting these texts won't tell us. For this we need a broader, more multilayered and interdisciplinary analysis. We need an interrogation of the connections between cultural artifacts and social and political life.

Understanding the aliens in contemporary America requires attention not only to the stories some of us tell, but to the practices and technologies that enable the stories to be told. We have to consider how the knowledge of the alien is produced. So while I look at the tabloids, testimonials, TV documentaries, and Web sites that transmit knowledge of aliens, I also take up the networks of power and information that enable these transmissions to occur. This latter concern, leading me as it does from television to televisuality, involves thinking about the conditions of democracy as it is practiced in the techno-global information society that is America at the millennium.

My focus is on those familiar alien themes and images that escape UFO subcultures to appear in a variety of contemporary media and in easily accessible locations in popular cultures. Langdon Winner says that although genetic engineering and life in space "call into question what it means to be human," science fiction is the primary site of speculation about such radical changes in the human condition.[14] He's right, up to a point. Science fiction is important. But I'm interested in the more mundane aliens that populate alternative science, that come to us from a branch called ufology. Popular practices of science such as ufology are fields of knowledge devoted to exploring and expanding, often quite beyond belief, the scope of human experience of the real.

Alternative sciences like ufology are compelling because they claim to be true. Like mainstream sciences, their truth claims take a variety of forms. Indeed, they insert themselves into the interstices of medicine, psychology, biology, religion, astronomy, and ecology. Because of their claims to truth, alternative sciences have political interconnections and repercussions, particularly in democratic societies that claim to value open discussion or in scientific circles that credit themselves with being objective, interested only in evidence.[15]

Ufology is political because it is stigmatized. To claim to have seen a UFO, to have been abducted by aliens, or even to believe those who say they have is a political act. It might not be a very big or revolutionary political act, but it contests the status quo. Immediately it installs the claimant at the margins of the social, within a network of sites and connections that don't command a great deal of mindshare, that don't get a lot of hits. UFO researcher Robert Dean (no relation) has experienced this firsthand. He sued his employer for discriminating against him because of his UFO beliefs. Dean won. It is this stigma attached to UFOs and UFO belief that enables the alien to function as an icon for some difficult social problems, particularly those located around the fault lines of truth, reality, and reasonableness. And it is also what makes aliens and UFOs interesting for critical social theory, not whether or not they are real, not whether the claims about them are true. That some people believe UFOs are real and true affects our concepts of politics and the political.

Images of outerspace throughout popular culture give us access to social and political anxieties accompanying the information revolution. They

political aspects of ufology

give us a window to changes in the cultural imaginary during the late twentieth century. William Connolly writes: "The acceleration of speed and the multiplication of border crossings in late-modern life create distinctive possibilities and dangers simultaneously."[16] Connected as they are with fantasies about the future, with time traveling and border crossing, aliens link into the hopes and fears inscribed in technologies. At the moment of globalization, of networked opportunities and communications transcending the local and national, they provide an extraterrestrial perspective.

So although aliens appeared in American popular culture at the last fin de siècle, and although most societies tell stories about otherworldly visitors, I concentrate on what the details of space stories tell us about American society today. Narratives of abduction and conspiracy are uniquely influential in the current technological context, a context where information travels at the speed of light and everything is entertainment. They tell about particular ways of being human that, as they describe experiences beyond belief and control, reach out from the lives of UFO abductees to suggest an abduction of a completely different sort. They tell about ways of being human that transform the representations of agency and spectatorship found in space imagery up through the seventies. Narratives of abduction reconfigure the present's acceptance of passivity, suspicion, paranoia, and loss as, themselves, forms of action.

My argument is that the aliens infiltrating American popular cultures provide icons through which to access the new conditions of democratic politics at the millennium. The conditions are new in that — despite the thematics of space, technology, and millennium deeply embedded in American self-understandings — the increasing complexity of an age brought about by networked computers and information, on the one hand, and the inscription of American politics within a televisual public sphere, on the other, have created a situation where political choices and decisions are virtually meaningless, practically impossible. Faced with gigabytes of indigestible information, computer-generated special effects, competing expert testimonies, and the undeniable presence of power, corruption, racism, and violence throughout science and law, voters, consumers, viewers, and witnesses have no criteria for choosing among policies and verdicts, treatments and claims. Even further, we have no recourse to procedures, be they scientific or juridical, that might provide some "supposition of reasonableness."[17]

Popular media are filled with examples of the undecidability of contemporary political issues. Elaine Showalter, in her book *Hystories*, attempts to treat some of these issues, such as Gulf War syndrome and, yes, alien abduction, as part of a new epidemic of hysteria. In so doing, she misses a fundamental point. What is at stake is the question of truth. No expert analysis can decide the matter, can convince a "public" of its rightness. Globalization and the Internet destroy the illusion of the public by creating innumerable networks of connection and information. By their introduction of disagreement, confrontation, and critique, they have always already displaced any possibility of agreement. Showalter writes that "it will take dedication and persistence to counter sensational news reports, rumors, and fear"—as if there were one truth available that simply needs to be discovered.[18] As if we can know the difference.

In contrast, I am convinced that many contemporary political matters are simply undecidable. My particular interest is in those, like ufology and abduction, that not only turn on questions of evidence, but involve charges of conspiracy and are in conflict with what is claimed as "consensus reality" or "common sense."[19] Although the crash and investigation of TWA Flight 800, the bombing at the Atlanta Olympics, and the arrest of Timothy McVeigh come readily to mind here, the O. J. Simpson trials are the most obvious example. During and after Simpson's criminal trial, a large percentage of African Americans, as well as others, were persuaded that Simpson was the victim of a racist, evidence-tampering conspiracy on the part of the Los Angeles Police Department. DNA evidence entered by the prosecution was not as compelling as what, for many, was a personal experience of discrimination and harm.

Given the political and politicized position of science today, funded by corporations and by the military, itself discriminatory and elitist, this attitude toward scientific authority makes sense. Its impact, moreover, is potentially democratic. It prevents science from functioning as a trump card having the last word in what is ultimately a political debate: how people will live and work together. Skepticism toward experts, authorities, and a technology that has made virtuality part of everyday life means, increasingly, that more people find it likely that technology is used to deceive us rather than benefit or protect us.

We have moved from consensus reality to virtual reality. Politics itself must now be theorized from within the widespread dispersion of paranoia that has supplanted focused targets such as "Jim Crow" laws, Richard Nixon, and the Vietnam War. Insofar as its practioners can link together varieties of disparate phenomena to find patterns of denial, occlusion, and manipulation, conspiracy theory, far from a label dismissively attached to the lunatic fringe, may well be an appropriate vehicle for political contestation.[20] Some government agencies, as well as some researchers and journalists, have already been thinking and acting in ways that might have been dismissed as "conspiratorial" under traditional politics. As Grant Kester explains in his compelling analysis of federal information policies during the Reagan administration:

> With the growing use of computer networks the government is faced with the problem of an information blizzard — a lascivious and potentially threatening intermingling in which memos, affidavits, invoices, receipts, bank statements, and other documents combine and recombine themselves to produce dangerous new constellations of meaning. In this scenario the threat doesn't lie with a single piece of damaging information that "leaks out" and exposes government malfeasance, but with the possible interconnections that might be made among dozens of different bits of information; bits that might mean little or nothing by themselves, but that, when assembled by the researcher into a particular narrative form, could prove extremely damaging.[21]

To reiterate, my claim is not that people who think they have been abducted by aliens threaten to destroy democracy. It is not that UFO believers are irrational.[22] Rather, being unable to judge their rationality points to the lack of widespread criteria for judgments about what is reasonable and what is not: ufological discourse upholds the very criteria for scientific rationality that mainstream science uses to dismiss it. "Scientists" are the ones who have problems with the "rationality" of those in the UFO community. "Scientists" are the ones who feel a need to explain why some people believe in flying saucers, or who dismiss those who do so as "distorted" or "prejudiced" or "ignorant."

Such dismissals, handed out ever more frequently as science increasingly impacts on our lives, contribute to the mistrust that pervades contemporary democracy. Those in positions of power deploy terms like "reasonable" and "rational." Previously, the victims of this deployment, the "unreasonable" and "irrational," remained isolated. They had difficulty getting attention and fighting back. Now, thanks to widespread developments in communication networks, the "irrational" can get their message out. They can find and connect with those myriad others also dismissed by science. They can network and offer alternatives to official deployments or reason. They can reclaim their rationality on their own terms.

What happens when there is so much suspicion of terms like "reasonable" and "rational" that one can no longer tell what an informed decision on a matter like, say, partial-birth abortion or nuclear waste storage might look like? This is where America is today. We face a situation of profound blurring, of complex interconnection, that has profoundly altered the conditions we use to establish the intelligibility of an issue or judgment. We have permanent media. Although not yet seamless, as proponents of push technologies — which, like TV, deliver messages without the user having to search for them — advocate, the experience of media in millennial America smears lines between ad and information, product and producer, ad and product, entertainment and all of the above.[23] The new communication technologies make possible connections between persons and information that were once unimaginable. These include temporal and spatial connections: I can see images from Mars now, in real time. They include conceptual and visual connections, "special effects" no longer limited to Industrial Light and Magic but available from Photoshop for the splicer on a budget. How can we tell whether a person in a photo was inserted or really there?

Access to media and technology affects the practices of democracy. More opinions, more contestations are possible than before simply because of the ease of connection. Dismissing others' opinions is more likely to provoke outrage, to get some kind of response, even if only a few thousand people on the Internet are watching. The lines of thinking, the networks of discursive authority that had remained separate, are now more likely to blur as more people know more about what happens. Yet, they still may not know what it means or even if it *really* happened. How can I know which statement on partial abortion reflects "facts" the pro-life movement wants to disseminate? How can I know whether this is an issue on which I might change my mind or compromise?

UFOs, aliens, and abduction provide ideal vehicles for accessing the effects of these changes on American society. America has a long history of contestations, fringe groups, and conspiracy theorists. Now, though, any contest, any group, any theory has more opportunity to acquire an audience, to link into a network where it won't be obscured by those parts of our culture with claims to public or political status. Because of the pervasiveness of UFO belief and the ubiquity of alien imagery, ufology is an especially revealing window into current American paranoia and distrust. We might say that it's "of the fringe" though no longer "on the fringe."

Phil Cousineau's book *UFOs: A Manual for the Millennium* helps me explain why. Cousineau provides the following "Quick UFO Facts": "For every fundamentalist Christian there are five UFO believers; UFO believers outnumber Roman Catholics by a ratio of better than two to one; UFO believers outnumber the voters who placed Reagan, Bush, and Clinton in office; There are three adult Americans who believe that UFOs are real for every two skeptics."[24] Although the meanings of "belief" and "real" aren't clear, presumably including a spectrum of views ranging from the possibility of life in outerspace to the conviction that one is oneself an alien, when considered against the scientific rationalism claimed for the dominant culture these statistics suggest that UFO belief is widespread enough to conflict with the concept of a unitary public reason. UFO belief thus challenges the presumption that there is some "public" that shares a notion of reality, a concept of reason, and a set of criteria by which claims to reason and rationality are judged.

Likewise, to focus on the ubiquity of alien imagery, I want to refer to a line that appeared in a 1994 discussion of American disillusionment in the *New York Times Magazine*: "People talk as though our political system had been taken over by alien beings."[25] What are the cultural conditions that make such a sentence not only intelligible, but also not surprising? What can it mean that reference to aliens and alien abduction pervade popular media even as these references differ in their cynicism, irony, dismissiveness, or respect toward UFO belief and believers? The interesting phenomena involve more than belief in aliens and UFOs, for Americans have believed in an astounding variety of things.[26] These phenomena include the interest in aliens on the part of those who don't believe, in aliens as fashion statement or icon of techno-globalism or globo-technocism. The interesting phenomena involve the myriad acknowledgments in networked information cultures of the extraterrestrial gaze.[27]

The Theatrics of Space

The stories Americans tell about space are stories about who we are and who we want to be. They incorporate the practices within which we live and govern ourselves and the technologies that make it all, the practices and the dreams, possible. To this extent, space stories provide a key location for interrogating the link between American technology and American identity. Central to these stories is NASA.

I would like to claim that the connection between space and technology is uniquely my own, but it isn't. Its pop-culture configuration was brought to us by NASA. Itself a product of the Cold War, the space program was part of a general theatrics of space in which the roles of hero and scientist, citizen and witness were enacted. In the sixties and seventies, outerspace and the U.S. ability to conquer it appeared as a serialized account of American power and success. Technology would win the Cold War and the ratings war as it proved the superiority of the American democratic experiment.

The celebration of technological achievement had some political drawbacks. Even as the Apollo flights announced man's arrival on the moon, the astronaut image did not deflect public attention from the economic, racial, and political warfare spreading throughout the United States. If technology could send a man to outerspace and bring him safely home, why could it not solve more basic problems of poverty and hunger? Given America's domestic problems, the space program seemed, at best, a luxury we could not afford and, at worst, the most visible expression of a powerful, invasive technocracy. The advances in rocketry necessary for space flight were accompanied by the development of the digital computer.

A tension between human and technological achievement was present in the very first days of Project Mercury. For example, the issue of *Life* announcing John Glenn, Gus Grissom, and Alan Shepard as the space program's first launch team also ran an article on computers entitled "The Machines Are Taking Over."[28] Describing "the great computer invasion," the article asks whether we are "altogether wise in . . . putting ourselves at the mercy of these electronic robots." In a section headed "Our Computerized Government," it reports the IRS's use of computers to "scrutinize" tax returns and explains that "by next year one ninth of the country will have its tax returns watched in this diabolical fashion." The computers that made space flight possible were seen as contributing to a larger system of surveillance, to a techno-political colonization of American lives in fundamental and ironic contrast to space-age freedom.

Now that personal computers have let us take matters into our own hands, cyberspace is the new frontier, the realm of possibility, creativity, outlaw hackers, and nerd billionaires. Computer companies, traditional media, and politicians such as Newt Gingrich and Al Gore transmit the message that the Internet is our future, that it frees us from the confines of home and office, connecting us to people, places, and profits throughout the world. The launch of Windows 95 is a bigger event than *Galileo*'s window to Jupiter.

In stark contrast, outerspace has been reformatted around our lack of will, our acquiescence to powers apparently beyond our comprehension, our passivity in the face of increasing complexities.[29] For the week of the twenty-fifth anniversary of Neil Armstrong's moon walk, *Time* featured a cover story on the Internet. A brief article on the future of the space program describes NASA's loss of purpose and finds the agency "trapped in a downward spiral of mediocrity."[30] *Newsweek*'s cover story on the possibility of a manned Mars landing announces that we have the necessary technology but questions whether we have the will: "Real space flight is never as easy as it looks in cyber-space."[31] Twenty-five years after Apollo, the images of anxiety have reversed themselves.

That same year — in fact, about that same time — I started thinking about alien abduction. John Mack, the Harvard psychiatrist, had just published a book on his work with alleged experiencers of abduction by extraterrestrials. Mack left out "alleged." As I read Mack's case studies, I remembered that in 1973 two men from my grandparents' hometown of Pascagoula, Mississippi, claimed to have been abducted by aliens. They were fishing out on a pier by the town's large shipyard. I had fished there, taken the skiff out with my grandparents and hoped for catfish and not just sheepheads. The men who were abducted, Charles Hickson and Calvin Parker, were taken for examination (by "officials," not aliens) to Keesler Air Force Base in Biloxi, where my father worked. Hickson and Parker didn't have any sort of radiation poisoning or damage, but they seemed credible. People took this seriously. Up and down the Gulf Coast it was a big deal.

Nineteen ninety-four held other important twenty-five-year anniversaries. I was surprised when the anniversary of Woodstock got more press than the anniversary of Neil Armstrong's 1969 "giant leap," now reduced to a small step. I was also surprised that former football player and B-movie actor O. J. Simpson got more coverage than the moon, Mack, and Woodstock combined. During the next eighteen months of attention to Simpson's trial for the murder of Nicole Brown and Ron Goldman, the tabloids went wild. And everything — serious newspapers, serious broadcast news and radio — seemed to turn into tabloids.

In this setting, I began to wonder how it was possible that alien abduction could become not only a common cultural motif but also a phenomenon that some people take seriously. This question launched me into a study of the contexts and conditions in which the discourse on UFOs and abduction was produced. It also led me to the context and conditions of American society and culture since the end of World War II in general and since the fall of communism in particular. The more I ventured into the weird world of flying saucers, the more it started to look like business as usual at the millennium — or was it the other way around? Abductees claim to be harassed by government and military agents, by shadowy operatives and MIBs (Men in Black). The Pentagon admits to funding research on "remote viewing" or psychic spying. The Clinton administration acknowledges the Tuskegee syphilis experiments on African American men. The mainstream press alleges CIA involvement in drug trafficking in America's inner cities. Members of the UFO community swear that the government is covering up evidence of crashed saucers and alien bodies. The British government faces up to "mad cow disease." Conspiracy theory is everyday politics.

An atmosphere of paranoia pervades traditional media, informing discussions of the Clinton presidency, suicidal cults such as Heaven's Gate, separatist cults like the Republic of Texas, and the Internet. Indeed, sometime between the fall of 1996 and the spring of 1997, the attitude of the mainstream press toward the Internet shifts. Although tech coverage has long included utopian and dystopian trends, during the first half of the nineties the utopian spin dominates. The Internet *means* teledemocracy and information superhighways.[32] By the second half of the nineties, darker themes of paranoia and conspiracy inflect most accounts of cyberia. Rather than featuring lofty speeches from Newt Gingrich and Al Gore, traditional media deride the ABC correspondent Pierre Salinger for flashing a photograph downloaded from the Net as proof that a missile was responsible for the crash of TWA Flight 800.[33] Instead of calling for a computer in every classroom, commentators in the traditional press now advise parents how to protect their children from UFO cultists using the Internet to "recruit" new members. This despite the fact that most of the members of Heaven's Gate had been involved with the group and preparing to move to the "level above human" for more than twenty years.[34] The shift in mood is so pronounced that even the technologically enthusiastic *New York Times* agrees that cyberia is facing an "image problem." In April 1997, the "Week in Review" section of the Sunday paper leads with an article titled "Old View of the Internet: Nerds. New View: Nuts."[35] The Net is no longer presented as the penultimate exemplar of rational democracy. Now it's a sign of millennial paranoia as well as the new frontier.[36]

This is the context, then, for my reflections on aliens, reflections that link the alien to a political context of paranoia and a technological context of complexity, uncertainty, and interconnection. After losing to IBM's chess-playing computer Deep Blue, Gary Kasparov remarked: "I'm a human being. When I confront something that's beyond my understanding, I'm afraid." If, as I suspect, this is the predominant way in which Americans confront and live their lives today, then it calls for engaged and sustained inquiry.

I make such an inquiry informed by questions about democracy. Contemporary political theory already features active debates over the links between democracy, reason, and the possibility of the public. And, again, I claim that because there is no public, because there are only spaces, discourses, networks, and fields that seek to legitimize themselves through their installation as "the public," we live in new conditions under which democracy must be rethought. Likewise, because there is no "reason" that can anchor, ground, or unite the disparate networks constitutive of the many popular practices of contemporary democracy, but only discourses that aim to establish themselves as such, democratic theory can no longer presume a reality based on consensus. It has to reposition itself within virtual reality. Consequently, I provide a way of theorizing politics that is embedded not just in popular cultures but in the broader terrain of the social often analyzed by cultural studies.[37] That is to say, I consider aliens not simply as televisual or media products, but as figures within a complex of fields that includes science, science studies, and alternative science as well as ads, tabloids, and fashion accessories. Aliens can be linked under the discourse of ufology. They can also be considered icons to be clicked from a variety of different sites. I do both.

Conspiring against the Public

In contemporary America the familiar is strange: computer manuals, programming the VCR, communication with the taxi driver, automated voice mail, the man on the corner who seems to be staring at our child. The familiar isn't reassuring. It isn't safe. It isn't something we know, understand, predict, or control. Like newsstand tabloids and trash TV, the strange is part of our everyday world; indeed, so much a part of it that we don't try to bring it in. We don't try to fit the strange into something we can handle. We coexist with dissonance.

This dissonance has been a concern of academics, commentators, and activists of all kinds. Conservatives and fundamentalists formulate the problem nostalgically, stressing the decline of the family and the loss of moral values. Their proposed solution tends to rely on shoring up boundaries, be they those that establish the nation, gender, sexuality, or ethnicity. Other conservative reactions turn to scapegoats: the feminists and relativists destroying the universities, the drug addicts and homosexuals spreading AIDS, the teen welfare mothers draining federal budgets, the aliens swarming into California, Texas, Florida, and New York. More progressive responses to the familiarity of strangeness have presented the problem as one of attitude: we need to accept the strange, the different. We need to be more open-minded and tolerant. Once we appreciate multiplicity and hybridity, we will jettison the ideal of assimilation and embrace nonassimilation. "Can't we all just get along?" Though a welcome relief from the Right's barely concealed hate, progressive efforts don't seem to recognize how acceptance of otherness turns to resignation, how political apathy masks itself as tolerance.

Underneath such approaches to strangeness, whether regressive or progressive, rests a vision of public life as loosely centered in a public sphere. In this public sphere, citizens, whether they share a specific set of cultural values and traditions or have broad commitments to mutual respect and rational deliberation, are not strangers to one another or themselves.[38] Instead, they discuss matters of common interest and concern. When they do so, they understand one another. Their languages and meanings are clear, comprehensible. Disagreements are rational results of differing preferences, themselves rational results of differing outcomes in the distribution (also rational) of goods and services, talents and opportunities.[39] Citizenship, in other words, is characterized by a familiarity that is never strange.

This familiar conception of the public sphere and its citizens has already been the subject of convincing critiques, some based in sex, race, and class.[40] Despite their persuasive force, I worry that the critiques might be too limited because they still allow — indeed, require — the possibility of a group of "us," a mainstream, a public, who speak a common language and employ a common rationality. This common rationality is the standard by which deviations, irrationalities, are judged, through which exclusions are not only effected but discerned. Differences end up deposited onto some set of others, onto unfamiliar strangers. But what about situations where this supposedly common rationality and language produce strange, contradictory, incredible, irrational results? I am interested in discourses like ufology where participants think they speak and reason like everyone else, but where everyone else finds what they are saying to be incomprehensible and irrational. This seems to be the situation of America at the millennium.

Simultaneously denaturalizing and literalizing the strange and alien, the UFO discourse provides a means for grappling with the other. No matter how familiar, clichéd, or banal, the alien remains. In abduction accounts, moreover, the closer the alien gets, the more foreign it becomes. The ufological alien, the product of the understandably self-defensive discourse of the UFO community, marks the contemporary situation of American techno-political life. It appears in popular culture as an icon we can click on to run a program of nonassimilation. We can use the alien, therefore, to open a window to narratives that cling to claims of reason and reality even as they contest them.

Once linked to the indeterminability of the rationality of the public sphere, and hence to the collapse of its very possibility, the alien highlights two important characteristics of the site of politics today. Conveniently, *The X-Files*, that exemplar of contemporary popular fascination with the alien, provides handy and appropriate catchphrases. The first is "Trust no one." The public-sphere ideal relies on a minimum of trust, on at least the ability to distinguish friends from enemies and "us" from "them." As Zygmut Bauman points out, however, there are intermediate categories, such as the stranger (and, I would add, the alien).[41] These third parties, pervasive in the contemporary American social, already disrupt the fiction that we can tell friends from enemies, that there is some discernible difference that can be used to tell the one from the other. Produced through a concentrated replication of the themes of mistrust and conspiracy running throughout U.S. history and particularly pervasive today, the ufological alien is an icon for such "undecidables" and "thirds." Its presence is an invitation to suspicion.

Accounts of space aliens and a long history of suspicions toward foreigners, immigrants, and strangers both suppose a conspiracy undermining America's experiment in freedom and democracy.[42] Voices in nativist and UFO discourses alike express anxiety about breeding, miscegenation, and hybridity, about the collapse of distinctions between the alien and ourselves. In each discourse appear concerns about governing, about whether confidence in those entrusted with the protection of democratic freedoms is warranted, or if, in fact, they too are corrupt, part of some covert plot that will bring us down. In each the fear of the hidden that is always part of any notion of publicity or publicness motivates a vigilance and paranoia in the very name of the American people —"if they only knew."[43] Today's mistrust may be more indicative of a general suspicion of experts and politicians than of an actual supposition of conspiracy.[44] Rather than pointing to the marginality of conspiracy theory, however, such a dispersion of mistrust creates a particular problem for democratic politics. Specific networks of confidence become ever more fragile and tenuous. Ufology, then, is one version of larger cultural patterns of suspicion, conspiracy, and mistrust.

The second characteristic of democracy's contemporary American environment is summed up by the idea that "the truth is out there." Accompanying the mistrust of experts and politicians is a sense that, even if one doesn't know what it is, the truth is still available. Such a situation, I argue, produces paranoia by dint of what William Corlett refers to as the force of "reassurance."[45] Paranoia responds to anxieties surrounding what can be assumed to be real or certain in today's high-tech televisual culture by reassuring us that out there somewhere, however hard to find, there is a stable, identifiable truth. Those in Heaven's Gate whose Nike-wearing bodies were found in a large house in Rancho Santa Fe, California, believed they had found this truth. They complied with its demands. In this book I think through the effects of mistrust and paranoia in an effort to theorize the conditions of contemporary democracy in a technological, globalized, corporatized, entertainment- and media-driven society. I consider the discourse on UFOs and alien abduction as a cultural space that says something about *us*.

I have two motives for using this vague and dangerously inclusive "us." The first concerns the UFO community.[46] Speakers and participants at UFO conventions and writers of books and articles about UFOs use the term "UFO community" loosely to refer to anyone with a strong interest in UFOs. Like notions of the academic community, "Hollywood," or the queer community, the term gets fuzzy around the edges and not everyone agrees who's in and who's out. Problems with the idea of a "UFO community" resemble problems of queer identity: not everyone who has seen a UFO identifies with the larger group. Usually, however, people in the UFO community have a general sense of what the term means. At any rate, what is interesting about the community is that it combines a reasonable replication of the demographics of the United States (tilted toward the white middle class) together with a self-perception of being an excluded minority.[47]

The UFO community's sense of exclusion stems from its perception that most people, especially scientists, the media, and government officials, ridicule belief in extraterrestrial contact with Earth. Many who think they have seen a UFO are reluctant to talk about it outside safe, supportive circles. I've been surprised at how many of my academic colleagues have come out to me with UFO stories of their own since I began this research.[48] Abductees in particular say they are wary of talking about their experiences for fear that people will think they are crazy — a sentiment expressed by many women in consciousness-raising sessions during the 1970s. So when I ask what the UFO community reveals about "us," I'm seeing the community as a microcosm of some broader American public. "Us" refers to anyone. It signals a white middle class while acknowledging differences in sex, class, and ethnicity. Yet "us" problematizes the notion of a "center" and the possibility of generality by focusing on a set of experiences and beliefs with marginalizing effects. It gestures simultaneously toward strangers, toward those disdained by society at large. This book's title, *Aliens in America*, is linked to Tony Kushner's Pulitzer Prize–winning play, *Angels in America*. At the same time, it connects with the only singly authored book sympathetic to ufology that has been published by a university press: the Temple University historian David Jacobs's *The UFO Controversy in America*.[49]

By destabilizing ideas of us and them, center and margin, inside and outside, I want to complicate theories of American culture and politics. Radical as well as traditional accounts of citizenship and collective identity attribute some coherence to the notion of a public sphere. Whether norms of public reason are considered oppressive and exclusionary or the pinnacle of the planet's expression of freedom, the idea that the mainstream, the general populace, the community at large shares a set of common assumptions about reality is rarely challenged. UFO belief is one of those rare challenges. *The mainstream UFO is oddly challenged.*

What makes ufology significant among these challenges (which include a variety of alternative sciences and other rejections of consensus reality) is its connection to the broader theatrics of space played out in the United States since the Cold War. Most societies have cultural traditions that establish and interpret relationships between Earth, its people, and the cosmos. But the United States is exceptional. Emerging out of a tradition of stories about the "frontier" experience, the American exploration of outerspace came to be linked to the achievements of technology and democracy. As Lynn Spigel writes: "Ideas like freedom need an image, and the ride into space proved to be the most vivid concretization of such abstractions, promising a newfound national allegiance through which we would not only diffuse the Soviet threat, but also shake ourselves out of the doldrums that 1950s life had come to symbolize."[50] The American space program was produced with an eye to audiences. Folks at home and abroad would view its achievements as indications of the success of the democratic project. Anyone now or in the future could look to the Americans who walked on the moon and know that communism would not triumph. Through the space program, then, America produced a narrative of freedom and progress that would structure popular understandings of truth and agency. In this context, asking what ufology says about "us" reaches for that vague sense of America as ethos, popular opinion, self-understanding, mentality.

The American articulation of outerspace together with technology and democracy incorporates an uneasy mix of colonialist, nationalist, and globalist ideals. Until the space program, the United States rarely presented itself explicitly as a colonial power, although expansionism has been integral to its self-understanding.[51] By reiterating the expansive fantasy of the wild, lawless West, the metaphor of a "frontier" tapped into earlier notions of American exceptionalism.[52] Indeed, this very exceptionalism, the success of America's democratic experiment, was to be revealed and proven by

she wishes to blur the lines btwn culture vs politics

space became linked w/ power + democ.

breaking the laws of gravity, escaping the confines of Earth, conquering space itself. As America reached out into this "new frontier," the rhetoric of outposts, settlements, colonies, and colonization became part of the public language of outerspace. This language is fitting in that "space technology and communications," as Elayne Rapping points out, "make possible new extensions of American imperialism, both cultural and military."[53] Once linked to a growing critique of the excesses of the military-industrial complex, to increased attention to the histories and situations of Native Americans, and to continued struggle in former colonies throughout Africa and Asia, such colonial rhetoric disrupts the space program's smooth presentation of democratic freedom.

The UFO discourse resists official "space frontier" rhetoric. NASA redeployed American frontier myths of a wild, open West, one vacant, empty, and ready to be settled. Ufology challenges the assumed vacancy of outerspace and thereby intervenes critically in narratives of national identity.[54] It demands that NASA, the government, the military, and the authorities who act in America's name, allow for the possibility that, in space, *we* are the aliens.

With this nationalist celebration of American achievement came an idea that transcended the nation: Earth. Neil Armstrong was not just the first American on the moon. He was the first *man* on the moon. This global reorientation met with diverse responses. In his study of American apocalypticism, Paul Boyer mentions the critical response of some prophecy popularizers to the space program: one writer warned specifically that the program was "a scheme to promote global thinking."[55] In a collection of memorabilia from "Spaceweek 1994" at Brooks Air Force Base, in San Antonio, Texas, I found a poster by Yvonne Alden that expresses a similar sentiment. Below a graphic of the earth in space is written: "I pledge allegiance to Planet Earth, Mother of All Nations; And to the Infinite Universe In which she stands; Our planet, Among millions, Expressing Truth And Unlimited Possibilities for all!"

Despite ambivalence toward the space program, outerspace remains a theater within which American self-understandings are played out, if not exactly worked out. During the eighties, being included in the crew of the space shuttle symbolized that a member of a minority group had arrived, that this group was now accepted in and was part of American society. Discussion of the future of space exploration continues to provide a vehicle for thinking about technological innovation, American lack of will, the possibility of global cooperation, or the outcome of recent policies of privatization. Initial responses to the announcement of the possibility of life on Mars and Europa further illustrate the interconnections between space and American identity. In many traditional media, speculation focused more on that discovery's impact on what it means to be human and what it says about America than on what was learned about the solar system. Some said the discovery meant life was no longer special. Others said it ended human isolation. On the Internet, folks wondered if Fox studios might be behind the attention to life in space as a promotional tie-in to the film *Independence Day*. More serious speculation linked the discovery with a governmental interest in restoring confidence after the Oklahoma City and Atlanta Olympic bombings. And a few thought this was just the tip of the iceberg. After years of denial, why would the government reveal the possibility of life in *two* places in less than a month? Surely the government is about to reveal the truth about the crashed saucers and alien bodies. As the manager of a local market said as I leafed through her tabloids, "Aliens in space? I want to know about the ones who are already here."

The idea of a theatrics of space helps me construct an analogy that clarifies NASA's and the ufologists' competing versions of outerspace. The discourse around outerspace associated with the glory years of the space program (i.e., with the Mercury, Gemini, and Apollo projects) is like the Broadway rendition of Walt Disney's animated musical *Beauty and the Beast*. Both are scripted around big splashy productions with lots of popular appeal. Both are expensive and feature safe, familiar cartoon characters. If official space is *Beauty and the Beast*, then UFO space is *The Fantasticks* put on by a community theater group. Amateurs operating on shoestring budgets spend their spare time putting their hearts and souls into old scripts and forgettable scenes. They infuse the words with significance, finding that their own lives become more meaningful. They use a familiar language, but discover truths others miss. As they improvise and make this language their own, the familiar becomes strange, suggesting something else entirely. The strange becomes familiar, inscribed on their lives as a script to be staged.

Coming Up Next

My first chapter, "Fugitive Alien Truth," demonstrates how the ufological alien works as an icon that allows us to link into embedded fears of invasion, violation, mutation. My argument relies on the alien's link to truth. Produced by an alternative science, by a discredited discourse with claims to truth, the alien deploys scientific and juridical standards as means for assessing its truth. It uses the language of reality to contest our taken-for-granted experience of reality.

As I explain, the UFO discourse and community were formed during the Cold War. Changes in political context since the fall of communism have enabled the alien to break out of the UFO subculture and become a repository for postmodern anxieties. Truth is now a problem for all of us, not just for those trying to find evidence that flying saucers are real. The confusions and hesitations of the UFO discourse are thus a concentrated version of the facts and pseudofacts of life at the millennium. The alien icon marks the disequilibrium we face at the dissipation of distinctions between fantasy and reality, original and copy. I argue that the prominence of the alien in postmodern American culture marks the widespread conviction that previously clear and just languages and logics, discourses and procedures, are now alien, now inseparable from their irrational others.

Chapter 1 approaches the alien from the standpoint of the fabrication of UFO discourse and the widespread uncertainty about the criteria for truth. My second chapter approaches it via an inquiry into the official view of outerspace and its only legitimate inhabitant, the astronaut. Entitled "Space Programs," this chapter sets out the theatrics of space as produced by NASA for a television audience. The space program produced a narrative of freedom and progress that would structure popular representations of truth and agency. It linked outerspace with the achievements of technology and democracy. As a consequence, the astronaut came to function as a symbol for the best of America, the best American, the citizen-hero. An effect of this empowering of the astronaut, however, was the constitution of watching television as a civic duty. If space spectacles signified American achievement, then they depended on their transmission to an audience, to credible witnesses who could attest to the truth of the event, the magnitude of the achievement. Not only did this result in a domesticized vision of an engaged citizenry, a vision informed by media representations of astronaut wives, but it led to the establishment of a televisual public sphere: "If it matters, it will be on TV."

Chapter 3 looks at current space programs in the televisual public sphere: namely, talk shows that feature women who claim to have been abducted by aliens. The abduction discourse occupies the very terrain produced for the official theatrics of space, and abductees occupy a cultural position similar to that of astronauts. I explain how abductees get installed in this position as a result of the *Challenger* explosion, on the one hand, and the constellation of social practices that created tabloid talk shows as a phenomenon, on the other. I then concentrate on those elements of abduction narratives that reexplore the same American visionings of certainty, technology, and freedom that were crucial to NASA's production of the astronaut.

In my view, Elaine Showalter's discussion of alien abduction overemphasizes the sexual component of the experience. Reading only the accounts of abduction experts, the men who have carried out much of the research on alien abduction, rather than firsthand accounts by abductees themselves, Showalter insists that "abduction scenarios closely resemble women's pornography, from the soft-core rape fantasies of bodice busters to the masturbation fantasies recounted by writers like Shere Hite or Nancy Friday."[56] Showalter and others fail to connect the sexual dimensions of abduction with reproduction. Anxieties around reproduction, mothering, and the capacity to protect one's children are among the most pronounced themes in these narratives.[57] By drawing out themes already part of the American theatrics of space, my readings of the writings of women who identify as abductees demonstrate how reductive the pornographic interpretation is. Thus, in my third chapter, "Virtually Credible," I explore the reworking of the experience of the astronaut/citizen to provide a more convincing analysis of the complexity of abduction. Whereas the astronaut celebrated governmental and democratic successes, the abductee brings to the fore the government's failures, its inability to protect, its schemes and conspiracies, its relationship to aliens and the otherness it denies.

I take the title of my fourth chapter from a poster in Fox Mulder's office: "I Want to Believe." Whereas Chapter 3 stresses the continuities between astronauts and abductees, Chapter 4 focuses on the new configuration of technology that explains the disjunction, the dissimilarity in the alien theatrics of space. I draw out the multiple layerings and linkages constitutive of the abduction narrative in order to highlight its ability to provide a metaphor for Internet experiences. Moreover, Chapter 4 clicks on interconnection as the element that links abduction, the Internet, and conspiracy theory. It argues that democratic politics in an age of virtuality will need to turn to conspiracy theory as a way of making links, rather than simply accepting those linkages and explanations given by corporate and governmental power. To this extent, it theorizes the paradox of the information age: that approach to political action which is most likely to enhance freedom contributes to the production of paranoia. In other words, when the truth is out there but we can trust no one, more information heightens suspicion.

Finally, in Chapter 5, "The Familiarity of Strangeness," I link the space alien to the noncitizen, arguing the impossibility of global citizenship.

Through a critical interrogation of the slogan "Think Globally, Act Locally," I draw out the problems of presuming connections, rather than making them, in the networked technocultures of the late-capitalist information age. In this context, I return to the themes of dissolution, hybridity, and paranoia as the conditions for democracy at the millennium.

The social field of contemporary America consists of competing conceptions of the real. As we face ever more decisions on complex scientific and technological problems, as we confront increased skepticism toward political and scientific elites, and as we grow accustomed to virtuality, this distance from any consensus on reality will only increase. Attacks on cultural and science studies have blamed this situation on "postmodernism's" critique of reason. What these attacks fail to grasp is the way that skepticism extends "all the way down"; it pervades mass culture and everyday worldviews. "Common" sense is lacking. There are only particular senses. The discourses on outerspace access the distrust with which we respond to senses, realities, that are different from, even when only potentially, our own. They challenge us to face head-on the impact of the dissolution of notions of truth, rationality, and credibility on democratic society.

1
Fugitive Alien Truth

"Subscribe Abducted"

The X-Files capitalizes on and contributes to pop-cultural pre-occupation with aliens. Although Special Agents Fox Mulder and Dana Scully investigate a variety of paranormal cases for the FBI, the series' underlying theme is the governmental conspiracy surrounding the alien presence.[1] With story lines compiled from cases in UFO literature, *The X-Files* hints at varying levels of explanation, complicity, disinformation, and intrigue as Mulder searches for "the truth." Scully and Mulder have discovered what appear to be alien bodies, submerged saucers, and miles of underground files on genetic experimentation. Scully has been abducted and Mulder attacked by aliens. Yet they always lack "hard evidence"; they never quite reach "the truth." A poster in Mulder's office says, "I want to believe."

In the episode "Jose Chung's from Outer Space," the writer Darin Morgan satirizes the inaccessibility of truth within the series as well as around UFO phenomena in general.[2] The episode opens with a typical abduction scenario: a car experiences electrical failure on a dark and lonely road as a bright light paralyzes its teenage passengers. The narrative within which this scene would normally occur, however, quickly folds back in on itself as the gray aliens carrying out the abduction are themselves abducted by what appears to be an even larger and scarier alien (those in the know will quickly recognize it as a Reptilian). From there any possible narrative coherence is sacrificed as the search for truth turns up a New Age cult version of a Hollow Earth enthusiast (i.e., one who believes that UFOs originate from within the earth itself, a view that preceded the extraterrestrial hypothesis), a burned-out and lonely Dungeons and Dragons player aching to make contact with a UFO, and a challenge to Scully and Mulder's gender identities: Scully is taken for a man in drag, and Mulder emits a girly and uncharacteristic scream upon discovering an alien body. As Scully performs an autopsy on the body — an autopsy videoed, cut, and remade in a parody of the alien autopsy video broadcast by Fox Network during its previous season — she discovers that what looked like an alien is actually a human in disguise.

This motif of the conspiratorial human underpinnings of alien abduction repeats itself when one of the teenagers is hypnotized. Although in her first hypnotic regression she claims to have been examined and probed by aliens, when hypnotized a second time the girl instead recalls men in military uniforms. By the end of the show, truth itself has been abducted. When Mulder interviews an Air Force pilot, the pilot cannot confirm even his own existence.

Less mainstream than *The X-Files*, Bill Barker's "SCHWA" graphically represents the paranoia of our alien age. Constructed around the small alien with the large black eyes, Barker's "Complete SCHWA Kit" includes an illustrated book, stickers, a key chain, postcards, and a "survival card."[3] All the items are printed in high-contrast black and white, with stick figures, aliens, and flying saucers, the latter signified by simple ovals. Drawings in the book range from a conspiracy theory, stick-figure interpretation of the Kennedy assassination (the bits of skull flying off Kennedy's head are shaped like saucers) to stick figures hanging themselves as the saucers come. SCHWA graphics present HIV as an alien invasion on the cellular level. The oval saucer links surveillance, religion, viruses, corporate capitalism, and alien abduction, evoking a universe where everything is connected, out to get us, and there is nothing we can do to stop it.

Invasion (Bill Barker)

We can't even figure out what SCHWA is. The book *SCHWA*, whose drawings are credited to Barker, is published by Schwa Press. It is available from the SCHWA corporation. The same corporation is featured in the drawings as its SCHWA logo infests the stick-figure society. The big-eyed alien is part of SCHWA, but not original to it. SCHWA performatively disrupts the illusion of boundaries, of clear distinctions, of ownership, and of innocence. Sentences in the book and on various items in the kit explain, "Every picture tells a lie" and "In case of abduction: 1. Remain where you

The Kennedy assassination (Bill Barker)

are. 2. Give or do whatever they ask. 3. Forget everything that happens." The stickers announce, "This home/car/person/property protected by SCHWA," but the illusion of security is disrupted by the message that there is no resisting the aliens and the suggestion that, somehow, SCHWA itself is involved with the aliens. SCHWA's site on the World Wide Web immediately informs visitors that they have been counted. It then displays options for purchasing items from the SCHWA corporation, the same corporation implicated in the screensavers, hats, T-shirts, car conversion stickers, and counter-SCHWA kits up for sale, the same corporation in the drawings.

In contrast to these commercial ventures, the SCHWA Internet discussion group, like some Usenet groups organized around alien themes, is primarily an assortment of disaffected American and Australian students, drawn to the alien image to discuss drugs and parties. By clicking on the alien icon they access and organize the very nightmares and anxieties they simultaneously mock and disclose. Tattooed clerks selling T-shirts and stickers at the mall a town or two over from mine tell me that aliens are big with thirteen- and fourteen-year-olds. "But a lot of kids believe who don't wear the stuff," one adds, warning, in a parody of Fox Mulder on *The X-Files*, that "the hype is out there."

Fugitivity

Through conspiracies, connections, and frustrated confusions, SCHWA and *The X-Files* re-create the tangled hints and fragmented evidence characteristic of the UFO discourse. Their insight into the themes and anxieties just below the surface of American society in fact presupposes a general cultural awareness of this discourse. "Getting it" requires prior knowledge of UFOs and alien abduction.

The same holds for *Independence Day*. In one of the few creative moments in this *War of the Worlds* remake, the film cites the story of the disk that crashed in Roswell, New Mexico. Preserving the integrity of the heroic, fighter pilot, president (Bill Pullman), it uses conspiracy theory to castigate the secretary of defense for covering up the truth, implying that world destruction might have been prevented had the truth been revealed. *ID4* further follows themes well established in ufology as it locates the remains of the disk at Area 51. It even redeems stories of alien abduction: not only is Russell (Randy Quaid), an abductee, proven to be sane, right all along in what were sneered at as the ravings of an alcoholic, traumatized Vietnam vet, but also his self-sacrifice helps save the world. Like SCHWA and *The X-Files*, the better moments of *ID4* don't draw from the fantastic tropes of science fiction. They rely on the more everyday reports of saucer sightings and close encounters. They presume an audience familiar with the fact that thousands of Americans say they have been abducted and sexually traumatized by aliens.

This presumption makes sense. *Abduction*, Harvard professor John Mack's account of his work with abductees, received extensive media attention when it was released in 1994.[4] Books by Whitley Strieber and Budd Hopkins have been best-sellers, with Strieber's *Communion* reaching number one on the *New York Times* best-seller list in May 1987.[5] The latter book was made into a film, and one of Hopkins's books became the basis for the 1992 television miniseries *Intruders*.[6] Like the other testimonials by abductees (or "experiencers," as some prefer to be called), and like the case studies by their hypnotists and therapists, these books present themselves as nonfiction, as reports of actual experiences. They are offered as evidence of something real. UFO sightings and abduction narratives involve claims to truth. They deploy the language of science and law in support of the truth of the alien.

Apparently, significant numbers of Americans are convinced. In June 1997, 17 percent of the respondents to a *Time*/CNN poll claimed to believe in abduction.[7] In 1996 the *Washington Post* ran a cover story that describes an abductee's eerie sense that people tend to accept his account of the experience. The story notes: "To the extent that popular culture reflects what they call 'consensus reality,' the possible now appears to encompass small gray beings with big eyes borrowing millions of ordinary Americans, harvesting their reproductive cells, then returning them to Earth to tell their stories to therapists."[8] Americans' relationship to the possible, the plausible, the truth is changing, and this change is being played out in the alien themes and images appearing in popular and mainstream cultures.

The truth of the alien underlies its powerful culture presence. Although there are multiple possible meanings that can be linked to the myriad aliens invading popular cultures today, this very multiplicity contributes to their link to contemporary problems with truth and reality. A click on the alien automatically loads a discourse constructed around the fugitivity of truth, creating pathways to ever more conspiratorial efforts to keep it from being accessed. A posting on the SCHWA list not only employs UFO rhetoric but deconstructs it by dissolving distinctions between fact and nonfact: "There are powerful forces at work to prevent you [*sic*] knowing THE TRUTH. All will be revealed within 9 terrestrial days. A series of fact-like statements or pseudo-statements or pseudo-facts will be sent to the list on or before May 14."[9]

The entertainment news show *Entertainment Tonight*'s May 5, 1996, report on the efforts of Travis Walton to set the record straight regarding his 1975 abduction in an Arizona forest further exemplifies the "givenness" of the connection between UFOs and conspiracy, the way this link is something so taken for granted that it need not be said, something so obvious that it can function as framing or connecting motif. The clips of Walton feature his pleas for people to look at the evidence, especially as he lays it out in his new book. He claims that, had he known he would be subjected to the wide-scale derision he received when his story was first publicized, he would never have come forward.

The *ET* segment features scenes from the 1993 Paramount true-life drama *Fire in the Sky* that was based on Walton's first book, *The Walton Experience*.[10] Even though the most frightening and lurid parts of the movie anchor the Walton segment, one of the announcers stresses that Walton avoided publicity.[11] This apparent contradiction might seem to disrupt the "news" the show is presenting, reminding viewers that this is, after all, *entertainment*. But the announcer doesn't try to keep truth on a separate terrain. Instead, to alleviate the tension her claim creates, she explains that Walton went without a telephone for ten years. Merely going without a telephone, in other words, is equated with avoiding publicity — and this for a person whose book became a Hollywood film. After the segment, a group of *ET* announcers chitchat about whether they believe in UFOs. For the rest of the show they use the language of "uncovering the truth" as they introduce items on films and celebrities.

The alien dares us to take a stand, to hold a position, to accept or reject it. Confrontation with a story of flying saucers or alien abduction pushes us to one side or another: Is it real? Do we believe? The alien seduces us into a critical reassessment of our criteria for truth: How do we determine what real is? Why do we believe? The claim to truth and its challenge to our practices for establishing it are what enable the alien to function as an icon of postmodern anxieties.[12] Because its appeals to evidence incorporate scientific and juridical criteria, the alien works as an icon that allows us to link into embedded fears of invasion, violation, mutation. It uses the language of reality to contest our taken-for-granted experience of reality. The alien marks the radical strangeness and unknowability increasingly part of contemporary life. It serves as the ubiquitous reminder of uncertainty, doubt, suspicion, of the fugitivity of truth. We live with the alien while never knowing it.

Intrinsic to this challenge to truth, however, is its confirmation: the truth is out there, after all. Or, as a participant at the 1992 MIT abduction conference observed about the lack of conclusive proof of UFOs, "the absence of evidence is not *evidence of absence*."[13] By reinscribing the promise of truth, the alien reassures us that *everything* is not up for grabs, although *anything* could be. Some things are certain. We just don't know what they are.

This preoccupation with the question of truth is a primary characteristic of the UFO discourse as a whole: Are UFOs real? Are they responsible for crop circles and cattle mutilations? Does the government know? Is it covering up evidence of crashed saucers? And are aliens really abducting people from their beds and cars, examining, probing, and tracking them through implants? As an ever proliferating dispersion of statements around the truth of aliens, the UFO discourse lures us into a confrontation with truth. It compulsively repeats questions of truth, whether in its eruptions into currents in mainstream cultures or within the studies, analyses, and testimonials of those working actively to capture and comprehend fugitive alien truth.[14]

Because the UFO discourse is constructed around uncertain evidence, evidence of something that may not be there at all, its reports, cases, and files are primarily about the witnesses and only secondarily about the witnessed. Even the material evidence, the photographs, soil samples, government documents, mysterious fragments, and infamous alien autopsy film always stimulate (simulate?) investigations of the people who "found" or produced them. Are the witnesses reliable? Are their motives pure? In the UFO discourse, truth is an issue of credibility. It is produced through practices designed to establish whether someone is worthy of our trust. With the rise in claims of alien abduction during the nineties, the questions have now become whether abductees are crazy, neurotic, psychotic, epileptic, fantasy-prone, hysterical, or suffering from sleep or dissociative personality disorders.[15] Consequently, abductees are subjected to batteries of psychological tests in an effort to explain their experiences. But the tests are inconclusive. Any question, any answer leads into an ever branching network of possibilities.[16]

End-time

Although UFO flaps have occurred regularly since the late 1940s, the current obsession with aliens seems intertwined with fears of the millennium. Many have associated end-of-the-century culture with boundary breakdown and transgression, especially as heretofore excluded possibilities, be they monsters, the supernatural, or previously repressed sexualities and subjectivities, make their way into the social imaginary.[17] Not only does the alien mark that intrusion of the other so typical of end-time strangeness, but its reinscription of the promise of truth iterates the certainty of knowledge characteristic of apocalyptic modes of truth.[18]

At last century's end, visitors from space appeared in many media and locales. In 1891, Thomas Blot published the story of the sudden appearance of a Martian in his rural home.[19] Throughout 1896 and 1897, thou-

[margin handwritten note: Fears of UFOs combine w/the millennium]

sands of sightings of mysterious airships and strange, cigar-shaped craft were reported in the western United States. Occasionally, witnesses claimed to have seen or spoken with the occupants. In 1900 the psychologist Théodore Flournoy published an account of the French medium Hélène Smith's 1890 visit to Mars.[20] Around the same time, Percival Lowell built an observatory in Flagstaff, Arizona, so he could study the canal system on Mars, sharing his findings in two widely popular books, *Mars and Its Canals* (1906) and *Mars as an Abode of Life* (1908).[21] As Howard Blum notes, "It became a national craze. As America entered the twentieth century, there were newspaper contests ('Tell Us Your Idea for Talking to Mars') and even songs about 'the lonely man on Mars.'"[22] MARS!

With its "one world" outlook, chosen people, and mood of eminent arrival, the UFO discourse echoes key themes in American apocalypticism.[23] Telling and retelling how in 1947 Kenneth Arnold saw "nine disks flying like a saucer skipped over the water" and how the media distorted this account by coining the fanciful and dismissing phrase "flying saucers," ufology produces its originary moment. It does so in order to overcome it in the end: when the aliens come, the ufologists' careful perseverance will triumph over the scorn of ufology's critics as the truth is revealed and the credibility of witnesses and UFO researchers is restored. Relying on this future confirmation of the truth, ufology projects end-time scenarios based on the ontological shock we will face when the aliens come. The UFO researcher Stanton Friedman argues that government confirmation of contact with aliens and their superior technology will shatter earthly economic and political structures.[24] " The truth will shatter reality.

More explicitly apocalyptic are the testimonies of contactees and abductees. In the 1950s, cults grew up around various people who claimed to have had contact with aliens, usually Venusians or Saturnians, although some turned up from Clarion, the twin of Earth that was hidden by the moon. Most of the aliens looked like white humans, some of whom were described as tall, attractive, and Aryan. Reporting the aliens' messages, whether delivered in person or telepathically channeled, some contactees predicted the end of the world.

One such account, familiar to some academics in sociology and religious studies, is *When Prophesy Fails*.[25] This book addresses the conflicts experienced by cult members after the flood they had prepared for, the one aliens had announced to their contactee leader, Mrs. Keech, didn't occur. But Mrs. Keech wasn't the only contactee whose predictions went unfulfilled. Since most contactees warned that the aliens were alarmed by Earth's development of atomic weapons, they tended to predict either nuclear destruction or some kind of alien intervention. Truman Bethurum, for example, explained that the Clarionites feared humans would destroy their own planet in a nuclear war and thereby create "considerable confusion" among the inhabitants of outerspace.[26]

Like the contactees, some abductees report that the aliens show or implant in their minds "scenes of the earth devastated by a nuclear holocaust, vast panoramas of lifeless polluted landscapes and waters, and apocalyptic images of great earthquakes, firestorms, floods, and even fractures of the planet itself."[27] Some believers have suggested that these images symbolize "the inner apocalypse related to our current change in mind," viewing the abduction experience as a transformation of human consciousness.[28] Others read these images as justifications for the human-alien breeding project. Abductions are efforts to acquire human eggs and sperm. These eggs and sperm are combined with alien DNA in order to create a new posthuman race. The hybrids will then "repopulate our planet after the prophesied environmental holocaust."[29]

Finally, while abductee narratives incorporate divine and technological visionings of apocalypse, in popular culture the alien icon operates in what Lee Quinby refers to as "ironic apocalypse." Conceiving ironic apocalypse as an "insistence on the prevailing banality of everything," she argues that it "numbs people into inaction through its paralyzing sense of futility" and "supplants agency with apathy."[30] This banality and futility is the prevailing mood of SCHWA. It makes a more subtle appearance on a sticker made by the skateboard accessory company Alien Workshop. The sticker features a cadre of Grays and the slogan "2001 Global Take-over." Youth-culture aliens, insertions of big-eyed Grays into familiar locations in consumer culture, scream ironic apocalypse. It must be the end of the world when happy faces, Janet Jackson, anorexic Calvin Klein models, and the Cat in the Hat have all morphed into aliens.

Access Denied

Although aliens were around in the fifties and sixties, they weren't much of a fashion statement. In Cold War America, in fact, sightings of aliens, or at least their craft, had connotations of resistance. This culture of containment is where the UFO discourse grew up, where it was fabricated piecemeal from alien forms. Because it linked outerspace with amateur achievement, flying saucer society made possible a sort of populist agency that contested the presumed authority of Cold War containment culture.[31]

Minnesota UFO

The key issue was "evidence." At that time, the military monopolized all information about saucer reports. Finding and analyzing evidence under these conditions turned the question of the truth of UFOs into a question of the proper extent of state authority and the proper role of military experts. Since expert knowledge conflicted directly with "the people's right to know," ufology emerged as a sort of advocacy group. On behalf of those reporting something strange in the skies, UFO researchers challenged the interpretations proffered by military scientists. On behalf of the "people," they challenged the limits to and criteria for government secrecy.

From 1947, when the term "flying saucer" was coined in the first of three widely publicized sighting waves that would occur over the next decade, just how saucer reports would be handled was a question of power. That year, charged to study and classify UFOs, the Air Force started Project Sign.[32] Like the rest of the country in 1947, the Air Force didn't link flying saucers with extraterrestrial craft — that connection wouldn't become automatic till the early fifties. The Air Force was more worried about earthly invaders. Project Sign didn't figure out what UFOs were. It couldn't explain all the sightings. But it did conclude that UFOs did not present a threat to U.S. air security. Nonetheless, because of increasing Cold War tensions it was recommended that the military retain control over ufological investigations. The legitimacy of U.S. military and political authority vis-à-vis the American citizenry rested quite literally on the disavowal of the other and unknown.

By 1949, when the project's name had been changed to Grudge, the military took the official position that UFO reports were products of mass hallucination, hallucinations that the Soviets could, in the event of a war, manipulate to block American communications and confuse the public. Security then depended on ensuring that people knew the truth; that is, the same truth that the military knew. To decrease the likelihood of mass manipulation, Project Grudge waged a propaganda campaign designed to alleviate public fears of UFOs while downplaying sighting reports in general.[33]

A primary element of this campaign involved stripping away the credibility of those who thought they saw something strange in the sky. Properly trained observers (scientists and military experts) would then provide "true" explanations of what were "really" quite ordinary occurrences. Witnesses were dismissed as drunk, hysterical, crazy, or deeply twisted and dishonest. Prosaic (and not so prosaic) explanations for phenomena substituted for on-site research. The witness or witnesses had simply "misperceived" the phenomenon, mistaking for a flying saucer what was really swamp gas, a weather invasion, Venus, ice crystals, or a reflection.

Together with poor record keeping and an obsession with secrecy that produced a steady accumulation of half-facts and hesitations, the official ridicule heaped upon witnesses had a reverse effect: suspicions that there really was something to hide. Despite military efforts to dismiss UFOs, to assimilate them into something controllable and scientifically explicable, by May 1950 sighting reports were at an all-time high.

That year two highly visible books were published alleging a UFO cover-up, Donald Keyhoe's *Flying Saucers Are Real* and Frank Scully's *Behind the Flying Saucers*.[34] These books shift the problem of credibility from UFO witnesses to the U.S. government and military. In a parallel effort, journalists, civilians, amateur scientists, and former military began investigating sighting reports on their own and in the newly forming research groups. Contesting the Air Force's hallucination explanation in particular and its authority to define the UFO phenomenon in general, "flying saucer societies" such as NICAP (National Investigative Committee on Aerial Phenomena) and APRO (Aerial Phenomena Research Organization) worked to increase public awareness of the UFO phenomenon.[35] Through their publicity efforts and several sighting flaps, interest in and awareness of UFOs grew. By 1966, 96 percent of respondents to a Gallup poll had heard of UFOs and 46 percent of them believed UFOs were real.[36]

As David Jacobs points out, the Gallup results may well have been due to the extensive publicity around some UFO sightings in Michigan in

March of that year.[37] On March 20, eighty-seven women at Hillsdale College saw a glowing, football-shaped object hover over their dorm, fly around, and dodge airport lights. They watched it for four hours. The next day, police officers and several others in a town about sixty miles away witnessed a glowing object rise up from a swampy area on a farm. Within the next few days, most major papers and television newscasts would report on the sightings.

Under the auspices of Project Blue Book, which succeeded Project Grudge, the Air Force sent Dr. J. Allen Hynek to investigate. Hynek was a consultant to the project and a professor from Northwestern University who would later be known for supporting research on UFOs. At a press conference on the Michigan sightings, however, Hynek explained that the alleged saucers might well have been lights caused by swamp gas.

Some in the press found this answer even less credible than the possibility of flying saucers. As an article in the *New Yorker* concludes: "We read the official explanations with sheer delight, marveling at their stupendous inadequacy. Marsh gas, indeed! Marsh gas is more appropriate as an image of that special tediousness one glimpses in even the best scientific minds."[38] Under pressure from NICAP, parts of the media, and Representative Gerald Ford of Michigan, the House Armed Services Committee held hearings on UFOs in April. In May, CBS News aired a special report, "UFOs: Friend, Foe, or Fantasy," hosted by Walter Cronkite, who would later play a major role in telecasts of America's own space exploration.

The result of the hearings was a recommendation for an independent scientific investigation of the Air Force's work on Project Blue Book. After several universities (including Harvard, MIT, and Cal Tech) declined the project, the Air Force contracted with the University of Colorado. Like the other universities, Colorado feared that the UFO project might damage its credibility. It had, however, just suffered some major budget cuts and the Air Force–funded study was worth about half a million dollars.

An internal memo from Assistant Dean Robert Low dated August 9, 1966, tries to deal with the credibility problem that the UFO review posed for the university. He points out that

> in order to undertake such a project one has to approach it objectively. That is, one has to admit the possibility that such things as UFOs exist. It is not respectable to give serious consideration to such a possibility. Believers, in other words, remain outcasts. . . . [O]ne would have to go so far as to consider the possibility that saucers, if some of the observa-

tions are verified, behave according to a set of physical laws unknown to us. The simple act of admitting these possibilities just as possibilities puts us beyond the pale, and we would lose more in prestige in the scientific community than we could possibly gain by undertaking the investigation.[39]

Yet, Low offers a solution:

Our study would be conducted almost exclusively by nonbelievers who, although they couldn't possibly prove a negative result, could and probably would add an impressive body of evidence that there is no reality to the observations. The trick would be, I think, to describe the project so that, to the public, it would appear a totally objective study but, to the scientific community, would present the image of a group of nonbelievers trying their best to be objective but having an almost zero expectation of finding a saucer. One way to do this would be to stress investigation, not of the physical phenomena, rather of the people who do the observing — the psychology and sociology of persons and groups who report seeing UFOs.[40]

The review, carried out under the direction of a physics professor, Dr. Edward Condon, was released in January 1969. It sought the appearance of objectivity — indeed, it followed the suggestions outlined in Low's memo — but came under heavy criticism nonetheless, and not least when the Low memo itself was leaked to the press.[41]

In July 1968, prior to the report's publication, the House Science and Astronautics Committee held a symposium on UFOs, in part because of growing concern over the biases and inadequacies of the Colorado study. Condon had been open in his disdain for UFOs, spending most of his energies on contactees rather than on the reports provided by NICAP and Project Blue Book. The Condon staff was split and factionalized, some suspecting that only a negative assessment of UFOs would be published.[42] Although participants in the July symposium urged continued scientific study of UFOs, Condon's introduction to the soon-to-be released Colorado report presents itself as the final authoritative word on the matter of UFOs: "Our general conclusion is that nothing has come from the study of UFOs in the past 21 years that has added to scientific knowledge. Careful consideration of the record as it is available to us leads us to conclude that further extensive study of UFOs probably cannot be justified in the expectation that science will be advanced thereby."[43] Of the ninety-one cases covered in the report, thirty remain unexplained.

Resistance

Two discourses, the scientific and the governmental-juridical, established the languages in which the matter of UFOs would be delimited, discerned, and debated. Consequently, the investigative work and attitude toward evidence of the groups that formed to study UFOs was produced within these discourses as well. Groups like NICAP, APRO and, later, MUFON (Mutual UFO Network) anchored themselves in science and law as they tried to persuade scientists to study the UFO phenomenon and to induce the government to release the relevant information.

Official explanations for UFO sightings focused on witnesses' unreliability, either on their moral failings (dishonest or drunk) or on their failures of judgment (lapses in sanity or perception). UFO researchers responded by working to establish the witnesses' credibility. Using scientific and juridical languages, they sought to provide reasons to trust the words of even someone who claims to have seen a flying saucer. This had the effect of shaping the UFO discourse as a whole around questions of trust and credibility as much as around empirical evidence. Ufologists resisted the view that the judgments of significant numbers of Americans are unreliable. They rejected the presumption that citizens should be reduced to "crazies" and excluded from serious discussions important to America's security. To this extent, ufology challenged official notions of what counts as true, of whose words are credible.

In his testimony at the Symposium on Unidentified Flying Objects held by the House Science and Astronautics Committee in July 1968, Dr. James McDonald, senior physicist, Institute of Atmospheric Physics, and professor in the Department of Meteorology, University of Arizona, went to great lengths to address the question of reliability. Not only did he carefully distinguish between UFO enthusiasts and UFO witnesses, but he also pointed out the reluctance of many witnesses to report anomalous phenomena and their efforts to provide alternative, prosaic explanations for what they had seen. He concludes:

> I am one of those who lean strongly towards the extraterrestrial hypothesis. I arrived at that point by a process of elimination of other alternative hypotheses, not by arguments based on what I could call "irrefutable proof." I am convinced that the recurrent observations by reliable citizens here and abroad over the past twenty years cannot be brushed aside as nonsense, but rather need to be taken extremely seriously as evidence that some phenomenon is going on which we simply

do not understand. Although there is no current basis for concluding that hostility and grave hazard lie behind the UFO phenomenology, we cannot be entirely sure of that. For all of these reasons, greatly expanded scientific and public attention to the UFO problem is urgently needed.[44]

McDonald's testimony literally reminds symposium participants that the witnesses are citizens. It reintroduces UFO witnesses into a community of those who debate and discuss, who respect one another and take one another's views seriously. McDonald tries to include those dismissed as "crazies" in a public of reasonable people.

The challenge to governmental and military authority was also an implicit part of what for some was the dark underside of ufology: namely, the contactee cults and flying saucer clubs that raged from the mid-fifties through the late sixties, numbering more than 150 at their peak with a few, such as Heaven's Gate, still hanging on into the nineties. Contactees described personal contacts with space people, people that were like humans, never alien, but better, wiser, more peaceful. The most prominent contactees were George Adamski, Truman Bethurum, Daniel Fry, Orfeo Angelucci, and Howard Menger. They publicized their messages — which rarely cohered with one another — on local television and radio programs as well as on nationally broadcast talk shows such as Steve Allen's *Tonight*.[45] They also spoke at flying saucer conventions, selling books with titles like *Flying Saucers Have Landed*, *Secret of the Saucers*, and *From Outer Space to You*. Howard Menger sold records of music taught him by the space people.

From the perspective of evidence-oriented ufologists, contactees were extremely damaging to ufology's political and scientific efforts. They destroyed what little credibility the field had, affecting the outcome of the Condon report as well as the tone of much media attention to UFOs. Contactees claimed that aliens had given them specific messages to share with the world. Less concerned with questions of evidence, they departed from the scientific and governmental-juridical language of ufology to situate the question of alien truth on a more religious, spiritual, or mystical terrain.

The contactee narrative is generally constructed around an accidental encounter with a space person, a ride in a spaceship, and later meetings in which the space people issue the pronouncements the contactee is to deliver to the public at large. Almost invariably these pronouncements are warnings about nuclear weapons. Some contactees said that atomic fallout was threatening life on other planets. Others expressed the fear that the earth was on the verge of a destruction both nuclear and spiritual. Since the spiritual destruction was the result of a decline in love, care, and family values, the contactee message not only challenged the legitimacy of American military strategy but also linked that strategy with a threat to the American way of life.

Regardless of the disdain shown by the evidence-driven ufologists, the contactee narrative participates in flying saucer society's critique of America in the fifties and sixties. They, too, provided a site in popular culture for confronting that which was so alienating in the Cold War mentality of containment and conformity. Although George Adamski toured Europe in 1959, and was even received by Holland's Queen Juliana, the contactees were a particularly American phenomenon, providing their own rather campy version of what the military found so important to deny.[46] Again, quite literally, the legitimacy and coherence of America's political and social norms were revealed as requiring the exclusion of the alien.

In the 1950s and 1960s, ufology linked outerspace to possibility. It established a space from which to resist the expert culture of containment and assert the authority of amateur and civilian opinion and research. At a time when "the military enjoyed tremendous prestige and was largely unchallenged," flying saucer society undercut military assurances of security.[47] Military legitimacy rested on a disavowal of the unknown. Truth referred to what could be established, identified, secured. That which was unidentified could not be true. It was outside the parameters of truth, dangerously threatening to a security ever dependent on a stable, predictable, containable, real. In face of the possibility of aliens, the military looked weak, unable to provide the safety it promised. In the face of charges of conspiracy, the government looked corrupt, indistinguishable from its own representation of the communist enemy. Few other positions in Cold War society provided so consistent and potentially fundamental a challenge to military competence and integrity.[48]

The disruptive effects of UFOs were recognized at the time. In a letter to the chair of the House Armed Services Committee written in 1966, Representative Gerald Ford criticizes the Air Force's dismissal of a plethora of Michigan sightings, writing: "We owe it to the people to establish credibility regarding UFO's."[49] The Condon report not only worked to restore public confidence in the military, but also concluded that, with regard to the sensational treatment of UFOs by the media, "whatever effect there has been has been bad."[50] Shortly thereafter, a critic of ufology observed that "several generations of teenagers had grown up believing in UFO, ETH [the extraterrestrial hypothesis], and the governmental conspiracy. If the government could lie about flying saucers then it could lie about anything. The UFO propagandists of the 1950s undoubtedly contributed to the growing credibility gap between the government and the people."[51]

Although this observation exaggerates the effects of the UFO discourse, it reiterates the link I'm making between outerspace and agency in the 1950s and 1960s: ufology was doing something; it wasn't just spinning an outlandish conspiracy tale. At the very least, it was publicizing an outlandish conspiracy theory that used outerspace and the possibility of extraterrestrial visitations to challenge military and scientific hegemony. Indeed, Tom Englehardt suggests that, precisely because it was "beyond the pale," flying saucer society was able to attack the government without being accused of communism.[52] From the perspective of the dominant culture, ufology was silly. Nonetheless, precisely because it was outside the constraining equation of truth with security and identifiability, ufology was free to focus on the unknown, to indicate the limits of governmental authority and validate the experiences of witnesses without necessarily claiming that it could identify or establish the object of their experiences.

Assimilation

Ufology used the official languages of containment culture to challenge containment culture. Like science and law, it appealed to evidence. In order to defend the credibility of UFO witnesses, moreover, researchers appealed to precisely that sort of evidence they assumed would be acceptable to scientists and lawyers. Thus, they tended to reinforce official assumptions about who or what can be credible. Because ufology wanted to convince political and scientific authorities of the truth of its claims, it accepted their standards and criteria even as it resisted official efforts to monopolize evidence and discredit witnesses. Since the dominant view was that seeing a UFO signaled some kind of suspect irrationality, ufologists fought on the same terrain, making the witness as normal, conventional, and upright as any true-blue American. In effect, they tried to claim a place for them within the conversations of democracy.

During the 1966 hearings on UFOs by the House Armed Services Committee, Durwald G. Hall, the representative from Missouri, linked those who claimed to have seen UFOs with drug use and moral decline, saying:

> For some time we have even had space conversations down in the Ozarks, in the last 13 years, and it would seem obvious to me in view of the report today [that] those who take trips by the use of hallucinatory

drugs are almost synonymous with the number of space sightings we have had reported today, namely, in the order of 10,000. To me it indicates a decrease in the morals and the fiber of those who would subject themselves to hallucinatory influences in the first place.[53]

For Hall, UFO reporters are as disreputable as drug users, who he also presumes are on the other side of the border separating moral citizens from degenerate noncitizens (or, from aliens). Those on the other side don't warrant attention or respect from the rest of "us."

Similarly, an appendix to the 1968 symposium hearings on UFOs provided a scientific method for assessing the reliability of the perceptions of those who claimed to have seen a UFO. Included as an example of the method's efficacy was the detailed evaluation of a thirty-seven-year-old unmarried white man who reported a large luminous disk hovering over Tucson at 3:00 A.M., November 17, 1967.[54] "The Applied Assessment of Central Nervous System Integrity: A Method for Establishing the Creditability of Eye Witness and Other Observers" provides a thorough medical history and the results of a physical examination, laboratory studies of the man's urine and blood, a neurologic evaluation, a qualitative ophthalmologic examination, and a quantitative neuro-ophthalmologic investigation. It concludes that heavy smoking and the early stages of alcoholism damaged the witness's eyes so as to make his sighting "highly unlikely."

Results from the physical examination alone were said to indicate the probability of misperception. Nonetheless, the witness was subjected to a psychiatric evaluation, too. Although the report acknowledges the man's college education, exemplary record as a bank employee, and sense of responsibility, it finds more significance in the fact that "he was breast fed for nearly two years because his mother couldn't afford to buy store milk"; that he was "more than once called a 'mamma's boy' by his peers"; and that his sexual activity was limited to masturbating once a week to the fantasy of removing the "round, plastic, chartreuse nipple covers" from a belly dancer who performed at a local bar.[55] On the basis of these tests, the probability of the man's credibility was estimated at 5 percent, putting him in the "extremely impaired category."

Dr. Sydney Walker, the author of the assessment method, observes that without these tests, the witness might have seemed highly credible because of his respectable bank position, general demeanor, and claim to good health. Thanks to the medical evaluation, however, the witness is discredited as a sexually dysfunctional alcoholic and the sighting is explained as "an acute illusory phenomenon in which his regressed oral yearning for his mother was symbolically represented in the 'light.' That the object took the color and shape it did (like the nipple covers) further demonstrates [the witness's] all-pervasive oral fixation." [56]

This kind of assessment method — and there was at least one resignation from the Colorado research team over the legitimacy of a similar psychologically based witness questionnaire — constructs the UFO witness as an object of medical research. Instead of a participant in discussion with other scientists and citizens, the witness is something to be examined and studied, a lab rat rather than someone to be heard. The discourse of science is a site where the witness is fabricated into a test subject, not a language that the witness can use to describe what he or she has seen. Consequently, the lines in the battle over credibility are drawn. The question is whether witnesses, and UFO researchers, have the right to use these same scientific and legal languages or whether the very rules of their use turn witnesses into objects and researchers into crazies.

Hynek, the Northwestern professor who had worked with the Air Force on Project Blue Book, responded to the House symposium attacks on the character of saucer witnesses. Stressing that fear of ridicule caused most sightings to go unreported, he defended the credibility of witnesses in the same languages that were deployed in the attempt to discredit them. People risked mockery and dismissal for two reasons, Hynek said: "One, is out of a sense of civic duty. Time and again I will get a letter saying, I haven't said this to anybody, but I feel it is my civic duty as a citizen to report this. . . . The second reason is that their curiosity finally bugs them, They have been thinking about it and they want to know what it was they saw." [57] Like McDonald's testimony in the same symposium, Hynek's tries to reinsert witnesses into a public of credible citizens, into a discussion carried out among Americans who respect one another, who take one another seriously.

What this meant, though, was that McDonald's and Hynek's efforts to support witnesses actually served to consolidate the terms in which this respect could be given. Ufology so affirmed the standards and practices of science and government that it simultaneously challenged and reinscribed their authority. Those who counted as "reliable" occupied a legitimate subject position as citizens or scientists, those whose moral standing could go without question or whose professional credentials made perceptual errors unlikely.

Other ufologists contributed to this consolidation of the conditions of credibility. Many called attention to sightings from pilots, astronauts, professors, and military men. In one chapter alone of *Flying Saucers: Top Secret*, Donald Keyhoe identifies as UFO witnesses (whose *signed* reports are in

NICAP files) the following: three pilots; "a well-known Baltimore astronomer, Dr. James C. Bartlett, Jr., author of numerous scientific articles in astronautical journals"; and a Lutheran minister, the Rev. Kenneth R. Hoffman, and his wife (who remains unnamed). Similarly, Gerald Ford's letter refers to sightings by a retired Air Force colonel, a scientist from MIT, an aeronautical engineer, and twelve policemen, asking: "Are we to assume that everyone who says he has seen a UFO's an unreliable witness?"[58]

Furthermore, in contrast to the medicalized/psychologized approach to witness reliability offered by Sydney Walker, another participant in the 1968 symposium suggests that "it might be fruitful to set up formally an adversary proceeding modeled after our system of jurisprudence."[59] Dr. Robert L. Hall, chair of sociology at the University of Illinois, describes several UFO reports that met the criteria for witness credibility before a court of law. He argues that reliability should be judged in accordance with the witness's reputation, consistency, motive for prevarication, reaction to the event, and other conventional criteria.

The early struggles of the ufologists can be read in terms of their reinscription of conventional ideas as to who counts, who is trustworthy, who is actually and above all a citizen. Such an interpretation, however, needs to be supplemented by attention to the battle around the very nature of truth out of which modern saucer stories emerge. The early ufologists fought against essentialist understandings of truth that would inscribe truth in objects (and relations between objects) in the world. Rejecting this idea, they relied on an understanding of truth as consensual. If our living in the world is an outcome of a consensus on reality, they would explain, then stop and notice that not everyone is consenting to the view of reality espoused by science and government. For this so-called consensus reality is exclusionary; it is based on the silencing and discrediting of real, everyday people, people who want to be heard. If truth is truly consensual, then other voices — those of the UFO witnesses — have to be included. As long as they are dismissed and objectified, as long as they don't count as citizens whose voices and opinions are worth taking seriously, then truth will be only a play of power.

Emerging at the intersection of scientific and legal discourse, ufology was constituted through the redoubled effects of its exclusion. In the first instance, talk of flying saucers was discredited as nonsense unworthy of serious scientific or governmental consideration. UFOs were outside the domain of the dominant rationality. In the second instance, because of the outsider status of UFOs and UFO reports, establishing the intelligibility of witnesses required UFO researchers to appropriate the discourses that had originally excluded them. To be comprehensible to governmental and scientific authorities, UFO talk relied on their languages and logics, even as it remained alien to, incomprehensible in terms of, these languages and logics. Unable to equate the true with the predictable, identifiable, and containable, ufology redeployed truth itself. Thus, the resistance embodied in the UFO discourse was produced as an effect of ufology's exclusion, an effect that resulted in its adoption of the languages of science and law.

Contact

By the late eighties and early nineties, ufology appears less a critical site than a symptomatic one. During the Cold War, the need for credibility kept those who considered themselves serious ufologists at a distance from the contactees; in fact, from nearly all discussions of crashed disks, landings, or close encounters of more than strictly visual kinds. By the eighties, serious ufologists are talking about abduction. Instead of using radar and looking at the skies, they rely on practices of hypnosis and readings of the body to track fugitive alien truth. Over the past decade, the advocatory conventions of the UFO discourse have expanded to defend the veracity of people claiming to be not just witnesses but abductees. Taking them seriously, trusting the words of everyday people, now means allowing for the truth of alien abduction.

Constructed around a lack covered over and filled in by words, the UFO discourse today doesn't even need UFOs: absence itself marks an alien encounter. Budd Hopkins's *Missing Time* argues that temporal gaps and holes, an inability to account for a period of time, are potential indicators of an alien abduction. Outerspace has become the original location of aliens who are now here, next to us. We can't do anything about these aliens. We can't stop their movement into our lives.

Whether they ultimately come to acquiesce in or even benefit from their alien encounters, abductees generally recount their initial experiences in a language of fear, dread, mistrust, and confusion. Their narratives involve themes of victimization, colonization, surveillance, and the "technologizing" of reproduction and the body. Abductees describe the forced extraction of their eggs or sperm, anal probes, mind scans, and the implantation of tracking devices. Abduction is said to run in families and to occur repeatedly throughout experiencers' lives. Children as young as two and three are reported to have been abducted by aliens.[60] Some researchers conclude that the alien project is the creation of a hybrid human-alien race.

*"On the Table." Jeffrey Westover bases his art on his personal abduction experiences:
"This is a subconsciously remembered alien experience that I later found out involved the
taking of sperm from me." (Jeffrey S. Westover ©1997)*

Advocating these alien experiences as worthy of serious attention is effected by appropriating the discourse of therapy. Whereas credibility in the fifties and sixties was constructed through medical-psychiatric and juridical practices of investigation, current techniques are linked to therapy and self-help. Located at the primary site of ufological inquiry, the witness, such techniques provide more than insight into an individual's feelings and experiences. They access the production of those feelings and experiences, pointing to a truth beyond the witness.

The therapeutic site of the witness is a result of introducing hypnosis into UFO research. In the first abduction accounts to get attention in mainstream media, therapy was incidental. Barney Hill, the subject of John Fuller's 1966 book *The Interrupted Journey*, sought psychological help for anxiety and emotional problems.[61] He and his wife, Betty, had been advised, however, to consider using regression hypnosis to uncover some of the gaps in their memory of an odd experience they had while driving through New Hampshire one night in September 1961.

On an isolated road in the White Mountains, the Hills had stopped their car several times to get a better look at a recurring moving light. The last time, Barney took their binoculars and crossed into a field. Through the binoculars, he saw a number of uniformed figures looking through the window of what appeared to be a large craft. The eyes of one of the crew members frightened Barney, and he ran back to the car afraid that he would be captured.[62] As they drove away, both heard some strange beeps. They became oddly drowsy, their awareness returning to normal only after they heard a second set of beeps. The Hills arrived home later than they had expected.

Upon their return, they called a nearby Air Force base and gave an abbreviated report of their sighting. Barney, who made the call, didn't want to mention the uniformed figures. Over the next few weeks, Betty checked a book on UFOs out of a local library and wrote to the author, Donald Keyhoe of NICAP, about their experience. She had vivid dreams about UFOs and described them to Barney. In late November, two NICAP investigators, Walter Webb and C. D. Jackson, visited the Hills. Also present during the visit was a friend of the couple's, a retired Air Force intelligence officer named James MacDonald.

During their interview with the Hills, the NICAP investigators attempted to reconstruct the events of the evening of September 19. The Hills discovered that they couldn't. Two hours were missing out of their trip.[63] They also discovered that they could not account for a thirty-five-mile stretch of their drive, the stretch they had traveled between the two sets of beeps. In this context, Major MacDonald suggested that Betty and Barney consider using medical hypnosis to retrieve their memories.

Fuller explains that the major had become familiar with hypnosis during his career in the Air Force. He credits MacDonald for being aware of the potential for hypnosis to be abused, "in the hands of stage hypnotists or other inexperienced people." Yet the author disconnects MacDonald's suggestion from such "fraudulent" practices by elaborating the medical uses of hypnosis. Fuller explains that MacDonald knew of the successful results hypnosis had achieved "in the rehabilitation of servicemen suffering from war neuroses (sometimes described as 'battle fatigue' or 'shell shock')."[64] Everyone present agreed that medical hypnosis — and they stressed the term "medical"—was a good idea, especially because it seemed that the Hills had "experienced a violent trauma much like shell shock, a condition that often produced temporary amnesia — which had frequently been treated successfully by medical hypnosis."[65] Two years later the Hills were hypnotized by Dr. Benjamin Simon. Simon had served as chief of neuropsychiatry and executive officer for the Army's primary psychiatric center during World War II. He was also a consultant to John Huston when the director filmed a documentary on shell shock, *Let There Be Light*, at the hospital, Mason General.[66] Under hypnosis, each described being taken aboard an alien craft and subjected to a medical examination.

The Hill case played a seminal role in ufology. The credibility of the Hills set them apart from the contactees, thereby challenging the line ufologists had drawn between "sighting" cases and "occupant" cases. Their case thus came to establish the contours of the abduction narrative as it would appear during the seventies. A person would typically be driving in a car, at night, and would see a strange light. Upon returning home, the person would realize that he (or, rarely, she) suffered some kind of amnesia. At this point, the person would undergo hypnosis and describe being examined by alien entities aboard a space craft.[67]

The Hill case also installed into ufology a major new research tool, hypnosis. As Coral and Jim Lorenzen (founders of APRO) write in 1977: "An added step forward in the Hill case was the utilization of hypnosis in retrieving information from the abductees. Initially, the Hills procured the services of a psychiatrist because Mrs. Hill was having recurring nightmares and Mr. Hill was experiencing a recurrence of ulcers. Their decision to go to a psychiatrist to learn the reason for their traumas became a guideline for researchers gathering information about other abductions."[68] In the Lorenzens' version, Betty Hill, whom Fuller does not present as needing therapy or suffering from her nightmares, is inserted into the story of the decision to go to a psychologist. This strengthens the link between a UFO experience and therapy. Furthermore, hypnosis is positioned as a tool for UFO research rather than a medical practice for use in amnesia. This effects a change of emphasis: within the discourse, hypnosis takes on the double function of helping cure the traumatic loss of memory as well as providing *scientific* evidence (because of its medical role) of the *truth* of what is recalled.

Although Dr. Simon had been cautious in his assessment of the truth of the Hills's experience, and although a number of UFO investigators advised against the presumption that memories recalled under hypnosis were necessarily true or authentic, hypnosis quickly became linked with truth because of the prominence at the time of another technology of truth, the lie detector test.[69] Charles Hickson presumed himself to be fully aware of what happened during his abduction while fishing on the Pascagoula River in October 1973. His companion, Calvin Parker, had fainted and remained unconscious. Nonetheless, both were hypnotized. The hypnotist, Dr. James Harder, a civil engineer and director of research for APRO, confirmed to the press after two sessions with the men that it was "practically impossible" for Hickson and Parker to have simulated "their feelings of terror while under hypnosis."[70] They later passed lie detector tests. Harder also hypnotized Travis Walton after his abduction in 1975. Walton, and the six men who witnessed his abduction, also took and passed lie detector tests.

In a similar effort to establish the reliability of the memories recalled under hypnosis, Raymond E. Fowler writes that abductee Betty Andreasson passed a PSE (Psychological Stress Evaluator) test, which is like a lie detector test.[71] As he explains, "There is a standard investigative procedure applicable to CE-III cases [close encounters of the third kind] like the Andreasson Affair. It includes: establishing witness credibility, extracting the forgotten experience through hypnosis, and, finally, thoroughly analyzing all collected data pertaining to the case at hand."[72]

Although Whitley Strieber still reports on his successful passing of lie detector tests in *Transformation*, the sequel to *Communion*, by the time Budd Hopkins published *Missing Time* in 1981 the links between hypnosis, truth, abduction, and therapy were firmly in place.[73] Not only does Hopkins include a postscript by psychotherapist Aphrodite Clamar, who had hypnotized several of the abductees whose cases Hopkins compiled, but he writes: "UFO investigators have come to rely upon regressive hypnosis as the most efficient method of unlocking the forgotten period of time — usually an hour or two — and recovering the often harrowing account of what actually happened; psychiatrists and psychologists who practice hypnosis have thus become our most helpful allies."[74]

Furthermore, Hopkins retrieves the juridical link, connecting it to hypnosis as well as to therapy. In an appendix, he cites articles from the *New York Times* discussing the use of hypnosis in criminal cases. The articles, one about a rape trial, report how hypnosis enabled witnesses to call up memories they had repressed owing to the trauma of the crime. Hopkins concludes: "Hypnosis, then, is accepted as a valid tool by both courts and police departments. Properly used, the technique can be an avenue to truth, particularly so when traumatic events have buried specific details beyond immediate recall."[75]

Because of hypnosis, Hopkins is able to disconnect abduction from any accompanying UFO sighting. His work begins with the "feelings" someone has that "something" might have happened "sometime" or "somewhere." Under hypnosis, some of these feelings turn out to involve abduction by aliens. He writes: "An inescapable conclusion to be drawn from these cases is that *anyone* could have been abducted, with no memory of it, no conscious recall even of a preliminary event like the sighting of a UFO."[76]

Within the abduction strand of the UFO discourse, the UFO sighting has been replaced by the emotional response a person has to reading a book about UFOs or alien abduction. In the concluding chapter of *Encounters: A Psychologist Reveals Case Studies of Abductions by Extraterrestrials*, Dr. Edith Fiore writes: "Any anxiety reactions experienced while reading this or any other book on UFOs and CEIVs [close encounters of the fourth kind; i.e., actual contact with aliens] is a strong indicator. What is happening is this, as with any reactions of anxiety in relation to this topic, is that you are actually partially reliving the original traumatic experience during which you felt anxiety, maybe even terror."[77] For those who have such a reaction, or who experience other symptoms associated with abduction trauma (such as sleep disorders, waking up with unusual bodily sensations, feeling monitored or watched, unexplained marks on the body, missing time, and anxiety about aliens), specialists in abduction like Mack, Hopkins, Fiore, and others are available for help. Through hypnosis they uncover the truth repressed in memory, assessing truth according to the intensity and authenticity of the emotions a person expresses while hypnotized and the consistency of the person's memory with those of other abductees. The therapist not only helps the abductee access the truth of her experience, but also works to assure the abductee that she is not crazy, that the abductee knows what happened to her. In helping the experiencer accept the truth of the alien, the therapist effects a cure for the traumas and distress that led the experiencer to therapy in the first place.

To be sure, the rest of the UFO discourse is still around, just as contactee claims and crashed saucer stories were present in the fifties and sixties. Bill Clinton is often quoted as saying he wants to know what happened at Roswell. Most cites fail to note that the president was laughing as he said it in answer to a child's question. The Air Force still feels the need to debunk sightings and provide an authoritative truth of the matter. A group called CAUS (Citizens against UFO Secrecy) uses the Freedom of Information Act to get the government to release UFO-related documents.[78] Resited in the political context of the 1990s, however, accusations of governmental cover-ups are nothing new; conspiracy theories are in the air, whether re-configured by Oliver Stone or fabricated by the Unibomber, backwoods militiamen, or O. J. Simpson's defense team. UFO researchers continue to stress the "people's right to know," but the idea has been morphed through its inscription by a therapeutic discourse. A current goal is to support po-tential abductees, to let them know that they are not alone. As Hopkins makes clear, anyone is a potential abductee. Results from a 1992 poll con-ducted by the Roper Organization suggest that 2 percent of the American public have probably been abducted by aliens, a percentage that translates into roughly 3,700,000 adults.[79] Fortunately, approximately twenty ab-ductee support groups are now available throughout the country.[80]

The turn to abduction has reformatted the UFO discourse. Truth claims previously made in scientific and legal languages are expressed in a familiar hegemonic therapeutic discourse. The language and practice of therapy, moreover, have given UFOs and aliens a legitimacy in mainstream circles that they previously lacked. Arguments in the psychology commu-nity over abduction memories seem but a variation of the debates around false-memory syndrome. Accounts of alien abduction can now claim to fulfill established scientific criteria for truth on the basis of resemblance: they look like other accounts of improbable events defended through psy-chological evidence. Now, because of therapy language, the witness counts. The witness can enter into the scientific discourse as a participant whose words carry with them the presumption that they will be heard. The wit-ness speaks of her own experience, using this experience as itself the autho-rization to speak. Put somewhat differently, because of the link to therapy culture, ufology has been able to defend more successfully the credibility of the witness. Therapy language enables the witness to appeal to experience without having to establish in advance the reality of that experience. Perception *becomes* reality.

At the Abduction Study Conference held at MIT in 1992, researcher-therapist John Carpenter constructed a parallel with incest and sexual abuse, saying: "Way back, if you reported that was happening in your family, you were called crazy — you were disbelieved. Now it seems rampant. The truth is, it was hidden, and everyone talks about it now."[81] Similarly, relying on an analogy with battered-child syndrome, sociologist Ron Westrum argues that the abduction phenomenon is a hidden event, something widespread, significant, but highly underreported. The link Westrum makes between abduction and child abuse enables him to construct a stage sequence for the social recognition of anomalous events and to explain why most scientists reject the very possibility of alien abduction. He writes: "Again and again, during the first two stages, one will find that supposed 'experts' in academia are: a) ignorant, b) unaware of their ignorance, and c) contributing to the inhibition of reporting."[82]

The juridical-political credibility of ufology has also been reconfigured through the installation of therapy language. On the one hand, the stress on therapy brings with it "recovery movement" connotations of personal acceptance and self-transformation. Here, the abduction experience is an individual matter that might be discussed in group therapy, not a political concern. Nonetheless, some abduction therapists inscribe their treatment techniques with a rights language. Legal discourse becomes law talk, a set of useful metaphors for a legalistic culture. Talking law, the abductees reenter the political discourse that excluded UFO witnesses in the fifties and sixties. For example, drawing from her work with an attorney who had difficulty overcoming his "mental blocks regarding 'talking about aliens'" (blocks caused by the aliens' usual injunction to secrecy), Jean Byrne suggests that abductees understand "the 'Corporate Veil' analogy and realize that the same principles apply to alien information" and "the 'Clean Hands Doctrine' which is one of the eight principles of equity."[83] She explains that the "corporate veil" is used to shield officers in a corporation when the corporation is sued. If the corporation has failed to comply with its own rules, the person bringing the suit can "pierce the corporate veil" and hold the wrongdoers personally liable. She writes: "We may allege that alien visitors are breaking commonly recognized rules of ethical behavior by harming humans. Their very acts of rule-breaking, therefore, remove from around them any protective ethical veil which may have existed."[84] The "Clean Hands Doctrine" refers to the common-law idea that a person bringing legal action cannot be guilty of wrongdoing but must "come into court with 'clean hands.'" The idea is that aliens have dirtied their hands by mistreating humans; so, again, they deserve whatever response from humans that they get.

On the other hand, the merging of legal and therapeutic languages, like the convergence with ideas of scientific proof, permits the construction of imagined associations, equivalences, and unities between alien abduction and issues of harm that have been central to some feminist, antiracist, and queer politics. Stressing the widespread denial of abduction and the government's likely complicity in a cover-up, Westrum concludes: "Consider how badly we have handled the AIDS problem and you will get some idea of what is likely to happen with abductions."[85] Also concerned with "government cover-up, surveillance and conspiracy," Mack recounts the discussions from his support group and their concerns with future organization and planning. He writes: "This includes the beginning realization that the patronizing, cynical attitude of some media shows and coverage, including the participation of a hostile debunker (usually called a 'skeptic') on a program, constitutes a human rights violation of an authentic minority."[86]

The construction of alien abduction in the hegemonic discourses of science, law, and therapy has brought the alien home. Cold War security required keeping the alien out. Letting it in, as the abduction researchers recognize, means no more security, no more protection, no sense of control over our own technological achievements. Indeed, this is precisely the feeling the alien icon clicks onto. When there is no difference between "our" discourse and an alien discourse, the fugitivity of truth is just a sign of the times. We can't even know what our discourse is — and not because we don't know who "we" are, but because we can't tell when or if we are speaking the same language. Ironically, the consequences of the truth of alien abduction are effected simply through the discursive inclusion of the alien.

Alien Logics

The shift in political context has enabled the alien to break out of the UFO subculture and serve as a repository for postmodern anxieties. The fugitivity of truth is now a problem for all of us. No longer related to popular cultures' marginal discourses, or even confined to peripheral discussions in philosophy and political theory, the fugitivity of truth is a fact of life in the techno-global information age. The concerns of ufology, its worries about evidence and credibility, about whom to trust and whom to believe, are the concerns of the rest of us. They are a concentrated version of the facts and pseudofacts of life at the millennium.

For some the collapse in categories ushers in a new age of expanded possibilities. The real opens up to include virtually anything. The only question is finding the right search engines, the best techniques — hypnosis, meditation, Hot Bot, smart drugs, warp drive — for accessing it. For others the lack of certainty means insecurity, an insecurity countered primarily through trust. Finding truth depends on finding someone to trust, someone to believe. And here again, in seemingly endless recursion, appear the category wars: What are the criteria for credibility? During his live broadcast from Area 51, Nevada, Larry King asked: "How much stock do you put in the word of your fellow man? This is the central question of the UFO debate." Incredible, the alien implicates everyone in conspiracies to produce and suppress, reveal and deny an always fugitive truth.

Through its construction of the problem of truth as a question of credibility, the UFO discourse incorporates the reflexivity and skepticism lauded as signs of the rationality and rightness of science and law. Because it adopts the very practices that excluded it, the UFO discourse has always depended on the skeptic, critic, debunker. When Carl Sagan makes the effort of writing several hundred pages to discredit reports of alien abduction, he confirms the importance of the phenomenon. Moreover, because the skeptic enters into dialogue, engaging in a discussion about the truth of flying saucers and a hybrid human-alien breeding project, the discourse itself is confirmed as open and reflexive.

Admittedly, the UFO discourse is highly elastic, occupying a variety of registers and positions. But containing, binding, or policing these various registers is one of the ways the discourse replicates "real" science and establishes its own objectivity. Although UFO researchers are often derided for their infighting, the factionalism in ufology is no more dramatic than in standard academic disciplines. Mainstream science separates itself from the discourse around UFOs. Serious ufologists distance themselves from contactees, channelers, hoaxsters, and "nut cases." For them, the point is not to establish the undeniability of extraterrestrials hovering over small Midwestern towns. Rather, it is to involve scientists and the government and public in a serious investigation of anomalous phenomena and experiences. Some of the themes from MUFON's annual symposia announce ufology's relation to science: "UFOs: A Scientific Challenge" (1983); "UFOs: Beyond the Mainstream of Science" (1986); "UFOLOGY: The Emergence of a

New Science" (1993); "UFOLOGY: A Scientific Paradigm (1995); and, more hesitatingly, "UFOLOGY: A Scientific Enigma" (1996).

The reflexivity of the UFO discourse, its critical and self-critical practices, helps ufology reassure itself of its own rationality. The 1992 conference at MIT featured a variety of perspectives on alien abduction. Papers addressed topics such as the reliability of memories obtained through hypnosis, psychological and sociological explanations for abduction, children's experiences with aliens and UFOs, and cross-cultural patterns in abduction. Many participants were concerned with establishing a code of ethics that would set out the differences between therapy and investigation and thereby help therapists in their work with abductees. Throughout the conference, experts and abductees alike raised questions and criticisms.

The *Journal of UFO Studies* stresses its "ordinariness." Like other academic journals, it employs a "double-blind, double-referee system of previewing articles submitted for possible publication." Its editorial board includes academics from McGill, Temple, Eastern Michigan, and Utah State universities. The editor explains:

> We hope to publish only articles of quality, issues forums of expert opinion and professionalism, and literature reviews of intelligence and insight. We hope to be objective, disciplined, and rigorous. We welcome all viewpoints which can meet those standards, and, in fact, will attempt to actively recruit valued scholars of disparate positions for forums and research articles. We consequently hope to offend no one, either due to our willingness to pursue all legitimate views and hypotheses, or due to our rejection of manuscripts when they do not rise to academic standards. Please forgive us our objectivity and rigor for without these two characteristics nothing "scientific" is worth the name.[87]

Recent issues of the journal include a metallurgical analysis of an alleged UFO fragment found in Brazil in 1957 (inconclusive), a study of 347 drawings of imagined UFOs by Swiss children, a report of a psychological study testing the fantasy-proneness of abductees, and discussion fora on alien abductions and on the "tectonic stress theory" of UFO sightings. Many articles have accompanying graphs, charts, tables, and statistical analyses. Participants in the fora respond to and criticize one another's findings and results. Skeptics appear regularly.

Similarly, in *Science and the UFOs*, Jenny Randles and Peter Warrington try to seduce "serious" scientists into UFO research by criticizing contactees and sloppy, unscientific approaches to UFOs. Lamenting the "Dark Ages" of ufology, they blame its practioners, seeing them as "people whose motivations for involvement are not pure enough, whose methods are not ethical enough, and whose standards of performance are not good enough for their work to be taken more seriously."[88] To remedy these problems and produce serious researchers (via seduction and fabrication), they argue, ufology needs "higher standards," "a code of practice," and "self-regulation of one's work."[89] By becoming like "real" science, ufology will attract it and, in effect, merge with it. Its findings, as well as those who find them, will acquire legitimacy. Randles and Warrington displace attention from the credibility of UFO witnesses by working to establish the credibility of UFO researchers. The researchers' purity and discipline, something that can be controlled, will supplement the uncontrollability of UFO reports.

What is so unsettling about Randles and Warrington's argument is its matter-of-factness. With such an argument they employ the tools of reason to produce what mainstream science considers nonreason. They erase the difference between the two. Put somewhat differently, the language of science may be the same, but the facts and feelings, the alien information, resist assimilation into the categories of mainstream thought, exposing the very instability of those categories.

One strand of the UFO discourse refuses the criteria of hegemonic science. Perhaps because he is already credentialed through his position at Harvard, John Mack views the abduction phenomenon as striking at the heart of the Western scientific paradigm. Citing a conversation with his longtime friend Thomas Kuhn, Mack explains that Kuhn helped him understand that our current scientific worldview "had come to assume the rigidity of a theology, and that this belief system was held in place by the structures, categories, and polarities of language, such as real/unreal, exists/does not exist, objective/subjective, intrapsychic world/external world, and happened/did not happen."[90] For Mack, scientific criteria and standards delimit too narrowly the domain of the intelligible. What is required is a shift, a new Copernican revolution. He uses the idea of a "politics of ontology" to explain resistance to the shift in worldview necessary if we are to accept alien truth, stressing the disjunction between the "underground of popular knowledge about the world and the universe" and the opinions encouraged by elite, official "arbiters of reality." Mack thinks that "it is really going to be interesting to see when the official mainstream, the small percentage of elites that determine what we are supposed to think is real, wake up to the fact that the consensus view of reality is gone."[91] Nonetheless, as he defends the reality of abductees' experiences, Mack tends to employ conventional scientific criteria, challenging the skeptic to explain the entirety of the abduction phenomenon.[92]

Installed as practices for producing a knowledge that science disavows, heretofore reasonable procedures take an alien form. As the criteria for legitimacy are themselves abducted, the mainstream, the serious, the conventional, and the real become suspect. Not only does the UFO discourse cite scientific standards of objectivity, impartiality, critical debate, and consideration of alternative hypotheses, it also provides a location for the redeployment of these standards against institutionalized science. From within the UFO discourse, hegemonic science appears too preoccupied with securing government funding, maintaining authoritative reputations, and defending its own paradigm of reality. What distinguishes the publicly acceptable and formerly NASA-funded SETI (Search for Extraterrestrial Intelligence) from UFO research — a point made clear in the 1997 film *Contact*? At the MIT conference, in response to a paper on SETI by a Boston University physics professor, someone asked: "Is it true . . . that after 32 years of search, and the expenditure of over $100,000,000 already, you [SETI] have zero data? Have you got one piece of positive evidence to support your hypothesis? What I'm trying to do, sir, is to contrast your budget with ours, which is zero, your amount of data with our data. Would you be willing to share some of your $100,000,000 with our UFO researchers?"[93] Stanton Friedman, a nuclear physicist who earns his living lecturing on UFOs, regularly castigates mainstream academic writings on UFOs as "unscientific and often based on bias and prejudice rather than reason and logic."[94] Criticizing Menzel and Taves's *The UFO Enigma*, Friedman finds that "the attitude is very much holier than thou from the lofty perch of Harvard," that the book is "fiction in the guise of science, irrationality in the guise of reason and logic," and that the overall method of argument involves "misrepresentation, positive and negative name calling, omissions of fact, character assassination, guilt by association, etc."[95]

In an essay formulated through the languages of science, law, and therapy, Budd Hopkins details the misrepresentations and selective editing in a *Nova* television special, "Kidnapped by Aliens?" for which he had provided support and information.[96] Finding the title lurid, and the opening sequence sensationalist, he says that the show's tabloid style and mangling of the truth indicate that *Nova* "has abandoned its right to be thought of as either objective, balanced, or scientific." From Hopkins's perspective as an abduction researcher, the show was "a polemic having nothing to do with scientific investigation." In an extensive discussion of Carl Sagan's role in the *Nova* report, Hopkins writes:

Typically, on a show filled with hostile authority figures having little or no acquaintance with the data, astronomer Carl Sagan said that he believed all abduction accounts are delusions or hallucinations. . . . What evidence does Dr. Sagan, for example, present to buttress his sweeping — and to the abductees — damning indictment of their ability to separate fantasy from reality? None. None whatsoever. For a man regarded within popular culture as a kind of "Pope of Science" to offer such a wholesale denigration of UFO abductees with no supporting evidence is worse than irresponsible. In the psychological literature, there is only one report of an in-depth, blind study of the mental health of abductees . . . and it shows that Dr. Sagan's opinion is totally insupportable.[97]

Hopkins stresses the credibility of abductees, linking the bravery of those who agreed to appear on *Nova* with "the way a few rape victims will also come forward publicly, despite potential humiliation." He concludes that *Nova* "tampered with evidence and intimidated future witnesses."[98]

Because the UFO discourse already incorporates the languages and criteria of science, law, and therapy, Friedman and Hopkins can position themselves as supporting views capable of meeting the same criteria of validity that Carl Sagan's do. In fact, their language, and the language of the UFO discourse as a whole, are indistinguishable from his. Stressing the similarities among recovered memories of alien abduction, satanic abuse, and childhood sexual abuse, Sagan finds that in all three cases there are specialists, "networks of therapists who trade client histories and therapeutic methods," practioners who "feel the necessity of defending their practice against more skeptical colleagues."[99] He wonders whether "competition among therapists for patients, and the obvious financial interest of therapists in prolonged therapy, make them less likely to offend patients by evincing some skepticism about their stories."[100] Sagan notes also that "psychoanalysis is not a very self-critical profession," asking "how much training in scientific method and skeptical scrutiny, in statistics, or even in human fallibility have these therapists received?"[101] Throughout his book *The Demon-Haunted World*, Sagan's engagement with UFOs and alien abduction places him in the UFO discourse. Consequently, his very critique reaffirms its claim to scientific status. Indeed, Sagan reiterates the UFO discourse's legal language ("some are convinced that eyewitness testimony is reliable") and participates in linking abduction with child abuse.

What makes the UFO discourse's critical and reflexive practices especially effective is that establishment scientists and ufologists alike dismiss each other as intellectually recalcitrant. Since neither side is convinced, each denies the qualifications of the other even to participate in the conversation. Each is viewed as "not susceptible to reasoned argument" or "stubbornly resistant to it." [102] This similarity is precisely the problem. The UFO discourse uses the languages of science, law, and therapy to link itself to reflexivity, skepticism, and objectivity. Thus, these markers of intelligibility themselves become alien.

Of course, in everyday life the lines between talk of UFOs and talk of, say, dinosaurs, asteroids, or charmed quarks are not so blurred. UFOs bear a stigma. Harvard investigated John Mack more than a year after he started working on alien abduction. To my great interest, colleagues have jokingly referred to my own research as "white trash studies." A common (though mistaken, classist, and elitist) view is that people who believe in UFOs are poor, uneducated, white, and usually American. Poll data suggests otherwise.

Ironically, the very stigma makes UFOs and alien abduction seductive, transgressive. Those of us attracted to left-wing causes, to critical positions against political, governmental, and corporate authorities, or maybe just to underdogs in general may feel at home in ufology. In July 1997, Roswell, New Mexico, celebrated the fiftieth anniversary of the saucer crash. Thousands of tourists and hundreds of reporters crowded into the desert town to see a science fiction film festival, hear a host of famous speakers including Budd Hopkins, Stanton Friedman, and John Mack, tour the crash site, and enter contests for alien costumes and saucer designs. Shortly before, on June 24, apparently just in time to spoil the fun, the Air Force released yet another report on how the saucer was a balloon and how there weren't any alien bodies. As *Time* magazine explains, the Air Force explanation details experiments "that involved dropping dummies from high-altitude balloons to study the results of the impact. Witnesses' descriptions of the 'aliens,' the Air Force notes, closely match the characteristics of the dummies: $3\frac{1}{2}$ ft. to 4 ft. tall, bluish skin coloration, and no ears, hair, eyebrows or eyelashes." [103] Why would the Air Force have thrown dummies out of balloons? It sounds like the beginning of a bad — incredibly bad — joke.

Following its initial broadcast of "Kidnapped by Aliens?" *Nova* aired a special on class-action suits against makers of silicon breast implants. The experts occupied the same discursive position in each show. The women seeking redress for the suffering they had undergone because of the breast implants took the place of the abductees. An article on the potential dangers of silicon breast implants, in the magazine *New Woman*, has sections entitled "The Politics of Paranoia" and "Paranoid — or Right?" The author takes a skeptical approach to the claims of implant manufacturers and newspapers such as the *Wall Street Journal*, reminding women of a long history of commercial and pharmaceutical failures to ensure that products, such as thalidomide (which caused deformities when prescribed for morning sickness) and DES (which increased the risk of cancer to the women who took it to avoid miscarriage and caused malformations in the reproductive organs of their daughters), were safe for women.[104]

Clicking on the alien icon opens a window to contemporary confusion. The alien marks the way rational procedures produce irrational results. It marks a dissolution of the boundaries of the intelligible so complete that any exclusion seems arbitrary, repressive. As an icon of public acceptance of the fugitivity of truth, the alien has abducted the everyday to the extent that we no longer know when we speak different languages. When we see the alien, we abandon the presumption of common or public reason: some of us claim we are being taken up in spaceships and used in breeding experiments; others of us, in the Air Force, claim we have thrown four-foot-high dummies out of hot-air balloons. Linked to harm and abuse of children, racial, sexual, ethnic, and economic minorities, alien abduction renders action and politics suspect. The aliens have landed. Resistance is futile.

2

Space Programs

No Place Like Home

Although ostensibly about a 1960s mission to the moon, the recent film *Apollo 13* is really about coming home in the 1990s.[1] The command module is named the *Odyssey* and, like other road-trip epics, *Apollo 13* begins and ends at home. At first the travelers want to get away; by the end, they appreciate the importance of staying where they are.[2] Their journey is a series of obstacles to be overcome; through this overcoming, the travelers forge new understandings and relationships. They also get much better television coverage.

The "coming home" narrative is established in the first appearance in the film of Jim Lovell, played by two-time Academy Award winner Tom Hanks. Lovell is driving his red sports car and bringing champagne home for the party celebrating Neil Armstrong's televised walk on the moon.[3] Of the various ways in which an emphasis on home is built into the film, perhaps the most significant is the repeated use of television and the emphasis on NASA's fixation with it. The first voice heard in the film is Walter Cronkite as he recounts the fire that killed astronauts Gus Grissom, Ed White, and Roger Chaffee during a test of *Apollo 1*. We witness Armstrong's first steps on the moon through the eyes of the guests at Lovell's party as they watch Cronkite's telecast. Most of the updates we receive on the progress and problems facing *Apollo 13* we learn from television news reports.

Television, these images remind us, is as vital to the space program as it is to the American home. A challenge confronting the movie's writers and director was how to make a story exciting when the ending is already known. By having film viewers reenact the familiar role of television viewer — that is, by letting the audience get information in a common way, through television, a way that repeats how some audience members can be expected to have connected with the space program from the outset — the film makes the action real. It simulates the experience of witnessing the news on television. It positions the audience in its comfortable role as citizen-spectators. If the simulation is good enough, the conditioned response should occur: increased interest and apprehension cushioned by a connection with the familiar and the everyday. In other words, the connection with television could enable an ideal audience to worry about getting home and share in a longing for the safety of home at the same time.

As the film makes clear, however, television is a PR headache for NASA. Through Dick Cavett's monologue, it informs the audience that the *Apollo 13* launch was watched by 3 million fewer viewers than had witnessed *Apollo 12*. None of the major networks carries NASA's live telecast from the spacecraft. Major Nelson and Major Healy, on *I Dream of Jeanie*, were astronauts in a much funnier program that aired at the same time. Spaceflight had become too routine, too boring. Indeed, it was so routine that even the quintessential launch witness, the astronaut's wife, didn't plan to attend. A NASA official explains to Marilyn Lovell (Kathleen Quinlan) that the networks "say we make going to the moon about as exciting as a trip to Pittsburgh."

Trips to the moon aren't news. NASA's focus, like the film's, is on the audience at home as it attempts to interest them in spaceflight by connecting it with everyday life. This link, however, reinforces the sense that space is no longer special. The astronauts go on with their planned telecast, acting for the cameras; NASA doesn't tell them that they aren't really "on the air." Fred Haise (Bill Paxton) plays pop music and clowns around. Jack Swigert (Kevin Bacon) mentions his tax problems, something that makes him just like everybody else. Lovell concludes that "between Jack's back

Transmitted image of Apollo 11 moon walk (NASA)

taxes and the Fred Haise show, I'd say we had a pretty successful broadcast." He doesn't know that it didn't happen. It wasn't on television. There weren't any witnesses. It might as well not have occurred at all.

The film's interest in the problem of television contributes to the very domestication of space travel that put the Apollo program in jeopardy. It does so through an emphasis on urine.[4] Early in the film, Lovell is shown conducting a tour of the Vehicle Assembly Building at Cape Canaveral. When a curious though embarrassed woman asks how astronauts pee in space, Lovell sidesteps an answer with a joke about stopping at the nearest gas station. Soon after *Apollo 13* is on its way to the moon, however, Lovell appears fumbling with his relief tube. He notes that it's a shame this can't be shown on television; Haise admires the sparkling beauty of Lovell's "constellation urine" (pronounced to rhyme with Orion) as he dumps the urine into space. What can be shown on TV is limited. If NASA wanted to construct outerspace as a public space, one fit for the television viewing audience of the 1960s, Ron Howard seems more attuned to the possibilities of a privatized outerspace, one that allows for the more earthy concerns expressed in the nineties.

What is shown on television, of course, is what the film takes as its primary action: the disastrous situation of the astronauts. NASA jumps at the opportunity for more TV coverage as the networks clamor for information about the imperiled flight. As the film makes clear, however, the grab for media attention is accompanied by an increase in deception, by a problem of trust. Once *Apollo 13*'s troubles begin, NASA worries over what to tell the public. While watching an early television report on the explosion, Marilyn tries to get information from the agency, yelling into the phone, "Don't give me that NASA bullshit." As the situation on the craft worsens, Swigert starts to voice his paranoia about NASA's failure to give them a reentry plan. The agency, he suspects, knows that they are coming in too shallow to get back. Instead, they will skip out over the atmosphere, flying back into space, never to return. Although Haise and Lovell don't want to hear it, Swigert's suspicions that NASA won't be frank with them are confirmed near the end of the film. As reentry is under way, the flight director Gene Krantz (Ed Harris, who played John Glenn in the film version of *The Right Stuff*) is informed that the craft is indeed shallowing. He replies that if nothing can be done about it, there is no need to tell the astronauts.

Since the astronauts do return home, these paranoid moments quickly fade. After all, none of them was actually on television, so none of them really happened. They were effects of television, of NASA's televisual understanding of space and spaceflight, but effects easy to lose sight of. What is less easy to lose sight of — indeed, what the film pays explicit attention to, especially in these paranoid moments — are other locations of power and agency in the space program. Most of the action takes place behind the scenes, behind the screens. The film makes technological work, and geeks, thrilling. As one of the dashing astronauts serving as "CAPCOM" says to a bespectacled engineer, "You, sir, are a steely-eyed missile man." The action is not in outerspace, not in televisual public space, but on earth, at home. And this nontelevisual and hence private home is not the site of 1960s astronaut longing, but of 1990s techno-awareness.[5]

Revenge of the Nerds

These days, when the release of a new computer operating system elicits the media frenzy usually reserved for Hollywood openings — or imperiled spacecraft — this technological locus of action isn't surprising. America's new heroes — or those who savvy public relations folks offer up as such — are techno-geeks, computer guys, Steve Jobs, Bill Gates. At times, the technology displaces the hero or, in more cyborgian versions, the two merge. This is a common science-fiction theme.[6] Its appearance in mainstream news magazines, however, is not so common.

In a January 1997 *Time* cover article on Gates, Walter Isaacson describes his "search for evidence about the soul that underlies Bill Gates' intellectual operating system."[7] Isaacson writes:

> Part of what makes him so enigmatic is the nature of his intellect. Wander the Microsoft grounds, press the Bill button in conversation and hear it described in computer terms: he has "incredible processing power" and "unlimited bandwidth," an agility at "parallel processing" and "multitasking." Watch him at his desk, and you see what they mean. He works on two computers, one with four frames that sequence data streaming in from the Internet, the other handling the hundreds of E-mail messages and memos that extend his mind into a network. He can be so rigorous as he processes data that one can imagine his mind may indeed be digital: no sloppy emotions or analog fuzziness, just trillions of binary impulses coolly converting input into correct answers.[8]

Gates is not simply the personification of his company, Microsoft. Gates is a computer, and one without a particularly user-friendly interface. How is it that such a man can be positioned as an American hero, an ideal or goal toward which some of us, the best of us, might be compelled to strive?

The easy answer is $25 billion. In 1997 Bill Gates is by far the richest man in the world. But that answer is too easy. The unfathomably rich have never had a lock on America's heroic imaginings. Few would put Warren Buffet at the top of their hero lists. It is also too easy to dismiss Gates's status as simply an effect of corporate power, of the celebration of wealth that has barely subsided since the Reagan years, of the rise in corporate profits and stock prices amidst blue- and white-collar downsizing and "outsourcing," of a pervasive ideology of wealth that derides poverty as a moral failing. That doesn't work since there are, after all, athletes and pop stars and supermodels who move in and out of the celebrity space that substitutes for heroes, who give us our "hero lite." How did we get to a time and place where our heroes are indistinguishable from our technology, where it is bad to be a space cadet, but good to be a rocket scientists? How did we get to a point where outerspace no longer suggests action, excitement, and adventure, where the real hope is to come home?

To answer this question I look in this chapter at the televisual production of the astronaut, at NASA's construction of space and its explorers before an audience, domestic and global. A major difference between the cultural imaginings of the sixties and those of the nineties is in the language used to express hope and longing, in the images chosen for envisioning the future. Until the late sixties, encouraged by governmental efforts to generate support for space exploration, popular and news media used space imagery to symbolize progress and achievement. The 1964 World's Fair hosted in New York celebrated space with a "Lunar Fountain," the "Fountain of the Planets," and the "Unisphere."[9] At decade's end, even *Life* magazine's Loudon Wainright, the space enthusiast who had covered the Mercury and Gemini programs, found it difficult to get excited about the initial launch for the moon. Reporting from Cape Kennedy in July 1969, he writes: "The almost monotonous success of the flights before the Grissom tragedy has evolved to near perfection with the Apollo flights since. Of course, that's a fact worth anybody's deep gratitude, but precision has a way of dehumanizing adventure, even if the destination is a piece of the moon when a man will stand. Thanks to this technology, we *know* we will see a fantastic view. Anything is possible and most of its is predictable to the millisecond."[10] By 1979 ABC News could air a television special commemorating the tenth anniversary of the moon landing, "Infinite Horizons: To the Year 2000 and Above," asking what had become of the space euphoria that characterized the heyday of the program in the early sixties. Launch Pad 19 at Cape Canaveral is shown abandoned, decrepit, padlocked; "a ghost town on the frontier," suggests the narrator. The science fiction writer Ray Bradbury worries that we have lost interest in space. The show assures viewers that this is not the case, emphasizing the practical benefits of space travel: namely, better communication technologies, wrist radios and satellites, and, best of all, television itself.

Today space provides a neat interactive Web site, great movie location, a neat bunch of opportunities for aliens hoping to reinvigorate their gene pools. NASA space, the scientific space established as that which would be explored, conquered, and colonized, the object of human surveillance and control, is likely to be the butt of jokes, condescended to, affectionately remembered, but nothing serious. The *Pathfinder* mission is fun, complete with tie-in products like the *Sojourner* rover. Of course, there aren't any action figures. In its list of the best media moments of 1996, the electronic journal *Feed* commends Mars for "Best Career Rehabilitation":

Funny how all the slathering talk about cyberspace reduces the real thing to an overworked metaphor. As recently as the early '80s, outerspace unleashed billions of dollars of federal funds; wretched screen plays for space thrillers routinely got the red light; and inter-planetary blood baths turned mere actors into teen idols. . . . Now "space" looks more like faded wallpaper, background texture for cyberslackers' caffeinated dramas (or lack thereof). That is until scientists found a bit of crud on a rock which proved to be (very likely) a Martian fossil. . . . And like most it-girls Mars owes its newfound fame to television. For without Hubble photos on the evening news, Mars would have remained just another bit player in *ID4*.[11]

In the nineties, supported by prominent politicians and driven by the market, technological innovations enabling rapid, widespread communication, as well as access to information, entertainment, and virtual experiences, have opened up new possibilities for envisioning the next millennium. The Internet — even or especially in the context of the Mars *Pathfinder* mission — has come to stand for the future. In this chapter, I locate the hopes pinned on cyberspace in a context produced by NASA.

In the process, I show how space lost its connection with achievement and power, with the best and the brightest, and came to be linked with passivity and the mundane because all these elements were already there, already part of astronaut imagery and NASA's space vocabulary from the program's early days. Now, rather than excitement and adventure, the perfunctory dimension of space are ascendent. I disagree with Constance Penley's reading of the position of NASA in American popular culture. Penley claims that NASA remains "a repository for utopian meanings."[12] I argue that the positive associations with the space program prevalent in the sixties have been transferred to computers and networked communications technologies. What made the *Pathfinder* mission to Mars exciting was not space or space travel, since nobody actually went to Mars. The thrill is in the cheap interactive technology.

So although space imagery was always complex and contradictory, the dominant meanings of outerspace, the ideas associated with space and space travel, have changed since the sixties. Previously space was linked with the agency of the astronaut; it now connotes the passivity of the audience who witnessed the "conquest" of space on television or, more frighteningly, the horrors of the *Challenger* or of the aliens invading our homes and bedrooms. The cultural stress had been on escaping the confines of earth; now it's on finding ways to stay home — which is exactly what the *Pathfinder* mission accomplished. With the Internet, we bring everything to us, without ever having to go anywhere. We can act and watch at the same time. And, we can watch and see more than what the government produces for our consumption. We can see most anything we like.

Why risk an unsafe and alien environment, when you can blast off into cyberspace? Look at the poor cosmonauts trapped on *Mir*, that falling-apart symbol of old-style space travel? Why should anyone have to endure the confines of a dangerous journey when the effect of venturing onto the Net is virtually the same: break the confines of an earth(l)y body, eclipse time and space, discover what's out there, get new information. And, best of all, this time more than a handful of us get to participate. Wired: *Pathfinder*; tired: *Mir*. Some of the justifications are the same, as well. "There in space lies more knowledge, more data for pure research," announces a *Life* editorial in 1959.[13] "Information wants to be free!" scream wired, blue-ribboned, black-screened, libertarian Netizens. Mercury astronaut Gordon Cooper's description of zero gravity, "a freedom man has been striving for over the centuries — the ability to glide around with no effort," sounds like the hacker's dream of leaving the meat.[14] Traveling via mouse and modem is safer, easier, and more democratic than strapping a chosen few to the top of a rocket. We — a new "we" constituted through our techno-savvy — can all roam the net, and never go anywhere at all.

More than an analysis of languages of progress, my thinking about how techno-geeks came to occupy the heroic position of astronauts reflects on images of citizenship. From the beginning of the space program, the astronaut was presented as a hero, as the best America had to offer. Part of the fascination of the astronaut has always been this position as exemplar, as active agent, as representative of action. At the same time NASA was producing its space program, however, it was also compiling a vision of the public. The program was made to be watched. It required an audience, a credible witness. Someone had to attest to the giant leaps made for mankind. This public, then, also embodied a set of citizen-ideals, ideals of appropriate witnessing and credible spectatorship, frequently at odds with those associated with the hero-astronaut. The astronaut's dependence on this assemblage of witnesses linked him with a televisual public. My argument is that even as NASA produced a straight, white, elite, male astronaut, the astronaut icon because of this dependence became invested with a host of other, alien, meanings, contradictory and ambiguous meanings that invited questioning reflection on the very ideals NASA was attempting to inscribe on astronaut bodies, or at least space suits.

Contemporary cyber-imaginings reproduce some of these meanings, playing a similar role in representations of what is left of citizenship as an identity or ideal. Like and indeed part of the technological transformations that made spaceflight possible, those in computing and networked communications effect more than a revisioning of the active/passive, spectacle/spectator binaries of astronaut/audience citizenship. They confront what it is to be human. Precisely because the space age made possible a species-consciousness, made the idea of being a citizen of the planet a fact of everyday life for anyone with access to television, radio, or global communications media, it established the contours for the popular reflections on our experience of the human carried out in and through cyberia.

The astronaut does not simply reiterate a conception of citizenship known for its straight, white, elite masculinity. Rather, it functions as an icon for the tensions and ambivalence in contemporary notions of the citizen: independent, national, and global; pilot, projectile, and participant; explorer, alien, and cyborg. Interrogating the astronaut reveals tensions around control, technology, and agency. It makes visible the links between political spectacle and the audience installed as credible witnesses. The astronaut is a site in popular culture where ideas of American power and the power of Americans can be explored.

Under Alien Skies

The National Aeronautics and Space Administration (NASA) was created through the National Aeronautics and Space Act of 1958. This was not, however, creation *ab nihilo*. The new civilian agency was a renamed, reorganized, and refinanced version of a not too well funded child of World War I, the National Advisory Committee on Aeronautics (NACA). Although itself a civilian agency, NACA in the late fifties worked as an adjunct to the military and the Department of Defense and, up until the Soviet Union's successful launch of *Sputnik* in 1957, it devoted little time or money to spaceflight. In the media frenzy around *Sputnik*, however, this was to change. *Sputnik* signaled Soviet technological superiority, or so it seemed. The world would now go to sleep under alien communist skies.

Walter A. McDougall explains *Sputnik* panic in terms of perceived threats to the legitimacy of American leadership in the post–World War II global order. This legitimacy rested on two premises, premises that, as we have seen, were contested in the UFO discourse: "first, the evident superiority of American liberal institutions, not only in the spiritual realm of freedom, but in the material realm of prosperity; second, the overwhelming American superiority in the technology of mass destruction, shielding those under its umbrella from external aggression."[15] Launching *Sputnik* meant that the Soviets had the capacity to send long-range intercontinental ballistic missiles armed with nuclear weapons to American cities. Moreover, America had somehow fallen behind, hadn't noticed that the Soviets were catching up, thus suggesting that Americans' preoccupation with con-

Mission control (NASA)

sumption (already ethically fragile in light of the still-recent Depression) might be at fault. As McDougall observes, reliance on the market, especially as it was "corrupted by consumerism," became suspect; the private sector seemed too disorganized and unruly to meet the challenge posed by centralized state and economic planning.

The Democratic Party, and Senator Lyndon B. Johnson of Texas, capitalized on the media-enhanced *Sputnik* uproar. In need of an issue that would take some of the divisive heat away from the powder keg of segregation, Democratic strategists, already preoccupied with race, hit on the space race. Johnson, ever ready for a political opportunity, used his position as Senate majority leader and chair of the Preparedness Subcommittee of the Senate Armed Services Committee to hold hearings and investigations that put him at the forefront of efforts to increase the American presence in space.[16] At stake was nothing less than the safety and honor of Americans and the American way.

For Johnson, like many in politics and mainstream news media, America's space program had to reflect American ideals. If Soviet efforts in space were military secrets, then America's would be open and public, a civilian operation in the interests of peace. The U.S. program had to appear virtuous, pursued for the sake of "freedom in space."[17] The decision to house American space efforts in a civilian agency, then, was directly linked to

America's political goals against the Soviets: only a civilian agency could convey this open, peaceful image. Image wasn't all, however. The decision to refabricate NACA was also influenced by "its long history of close and cordial cooperation with the military departments."[18] These military connections rarely surfaced in open discussion, especially after 1961 when National Security Advisor McGeorge Bundy issued orders forbidding the Air Force from discussing or even mentioning U.S. spy satellites in mainstream newspapers and magazines.[19]

The decision to try to be the first country to land a man on the moon and return him safely to earth involved similar preoccupations with image, prestige, and audience.[20] With the Bay of Pigs fiasco, on the one hand, and the success of Yuri Gagarin's orbital flight, on the other, the new administration of John F. Kennedy needed a way to boost America's image. After Alan Shepard's successful suborbital flight on May 5, 1961, witnessed by hundreds of reporters from around the globe and met with "a wave of national relief and pride" in the United States, an all-out effort to beat the Soviets to the moon seemed just the thing.[21] As Kennedy said in his speech before Congress on May 25, 1961:

> Finally, if we are to win the battle that is going on around the world between freedom and tyranny, if we are to win the battle for men's minds, the dramatic achievements in space which occurred in recent weeks should have made clear to us all, as did the sputnik in 1957, the impact of the adventure on the minds of men everywhere who are attempting to make a determination of which road they should take. . . . For while we cannot guarantee that we shall one day be first, we can guarantee that any failure to make this effort will find us last. We take an additional risk by making it in full view of the world — but as shown by the feat of Astronaut Shepard, this very risk enhances our stature when we are successful. . . . We go into space because whatever mankind must undertake, free men must fully share.[22]

As with the founding impetus behind NASA, so too with the drive to the moon. Both linked the achievements of American technology with America's capacity to lead and to act, with the values of freedom and democracy that America positioned itself as representing.

Staged Credibility

The American astronaut is the dynamic product of this theatrics of space as it played out in the United States during the Cold War. Because the research, science, and technology around space and space exploration were fabricated into a "program," because space was figured as a site of political and governmental intervention, American efforts around space from their inception carried with them a sense of audience.[23] In the words of a *Newsweek* "Special Section on Space and the Atom": "The cold war is being waged in outer space. All mankind may ride along vicariously with the first spaceman, and science as a whole may benefit from his findings. But the nation that gets up there first will score an important political, psychological, and propaganda victory."[24] The space program was always in part a television program produced for audiences at home and abroad. Achievements would be the achievements of us all, or at least those of us who weren't communists.

Failures would be, too, which made the launch-pad explosion of America's first major space rocket, Vanguard I, especially painful and humiliating. The press derided it as "Flopnik," "Kaputnik," and "Stayputnik."[25] Though major PR setbacks, these failures heightened the drama of NASA's new program. What would happen next? Shepard survived, would the others? Would the networks report the ever greater achievements of an alien ideology or would American values triumph over the secret and brutal efforts of the communists? At stake were freedom and democracy, or at least their image.

The credibility of the space program depended on witnesses. For the American program to matter, people had to see its achievements. Its visibility would distinguish it from the Soviet effort. Could anyone really trust the claims of communists? People had to know what was happening. They had to hear the astronauts speak from space. They had to watch the rockets lift off. They had to see photos of the earth and the moon. They had to know it was real. After all, it was produced for them.

The credibility of claims about space travel is a primary concern in the book *Keeping Up with the Astronauts*, a photo-filled celebration of Americans in space that highlights John Glenn's February 20, 1962, orbital flight. Building a contrast with the Soviet space program, the book goes to great lengths to prove to readers that the Soviet cosmonaut Gherman Titov really did spend twenty-five hours in orbit around the world only weeks after the United States had prided itself on a second suborbital flight. It does so ostensibly in order to head off in advance the same unbelieving protests that some Americans raised after hearing of Yuri Gagarin's flight. As I read it, however, this proof is an attempt to foreground the credibility of the American effort via an emphasis on its being witnessable. "Because of the rivalry in space between the United States and the Soviet Union, and because the Soviet Union has been proved to have falsified important matters in the past," Don Myrus reminds his readers, "many Americans — even in spite of President Kennedy's recognition of the fact — doubted that Gagarin had made a space orbit. They said things like, 'If it really happened, why didn't the Russians release more information?' and 'Why were no newspapermen there to watch him take off and come back?'"[26]

If it wasn't public, a spaceflight didn't happen. American success depended on its audience. Reporting on the important role of the media in presenting and interpreting space to the public, *Newsweek* announced that "the ten-hour telecast of John Glenn's flight last February was seen in 39.9 million homes — except for the Kennedy-Nixon debates, the largest audience in TV history."[27] By the time Apollo was in full swing, the message would be clear: the triumph of democracy depends on watching television.

Since Soviet launches were secret, American launches would be staged events, public spectacles with thousands, nay, millions of witnesses. There would be nothing incredible, or unworthy of being credited, about America's achievements. Myrus's *Keeping Up with the Astronauts* acknowledges the centrality of staging with two photographs that, for all practical purposes (though not, perhaps, for all playful ones), have little to do with the accompanying text about Shepard, Titov, and the space race. The pictures, uncredited stills from an unnamed film by Fritz Lang, show what seems to be an enormous and dramatically illuminated launch pad and then the rocket itself in flight. The caption reads: "Scene from a movie by Fritz Lang on which Hermann Oberth, a German who later came to America, worked in 1929. Note tracks similar to those at Cape Canaveral."[28] These bits of cinematic spectacle stand in for what can't be represented — Titov's own flight. At the same time, they link American achievements to entertainment and theatricality, evoking the fantasy of flight even as the caption covers over details of history and technology that might make facts awkward or unpleasant.

It was public information, if not exactly public knowledge, that the brightest lights in American rocketry were ex-Nazis. After the United States' first successful launch of a satellite on January 31, 1958, headlines and magazine covers applauded the work of "missile man" and rocket scientist Wernher von Braun. *Time* and *Newsweek* both reported that von Braun and his team of scientists had developed missiles for Hitler during World War II, in particular the V-2 rocket that had rained down upon London.[29] Furthermore, like most press reports on von Braun, the news magazines mentioned that the von Braun team had surrendered to the Americans at the end of the war because they preferred that to the option of going with the Soviets. With hundreds of other German scientists, they were part of the top-secret "Operation Paperclip," through which former Nazis were assimilated into the United States.

Like most coverage of von Braun, *Time* and *Newsweek* endeavor to play down the scientist's military past as they situate him within an all-American present. *Newsweek* recounts how von Braun happened to go to work for the German military in 1932. The magazine does not mention that this was the year before Hitler was appointed chancellor, a year when Nazi popularity was rising rapidly. It notes that von Braun "felt no moral compunction about the possible use of his rockets for mass destruction and genocide," and refers to his explanation that the possibility of war "seemed to us absurd" because the Nazis were not in power.[30] That von Braun and a colleague attempted in 1942 to persuade Hitler "that guided missiles were Germany's best bet" becomes subsumed within a larger narrative of von Braun's scientific dedication to rocketry and Hitler's ignorant and mystical refusal to support the research (Hitler had dreamed the rockets wouldn't work). Similarly, *Time* counters a statement regarding von Braun's role in "rain[ing] V-2 ruin on London" with a parenthetical aside: "when the first V-2 smashed London Spaceman von Braun remarked to a friend that the rocket had worked perfectly except for landing on the wrong planet."[31]

By 1962, the fifth year of the space age, according to *Newsweek*, enthusiastic support for the moon program pushed von Braun's history out of the mainstream media. Not only were the German scientists now more likely to be referred to in terms of their American citizenship, but whatever Nazi beliefs they may have held had seemingly taken a 180-degree turn. Von Braun's team was disconnected from anti-Semitism and linked instead to antiracism. The "rocket people" based in Huntsville, Alabama, were said to fit in well.[32] But rather than being a potentially ironic comment on Southern racism, this was meant as praise for the positive force they contributed toward social change.

In the face of criticism of the huge expenditures on space, especially when such earthly issues as Southern segregation were becoming increasingly heated and contentious, NASA lauded the space effort as a key instrument for transforming attitudes that "lagged" behind technological advances. It linked the space program with desegregation, suggesting that the influence of the Redstone people had contributed to the opening up of lunch counters in Huntsville.[33] Whatever it touched, the space program would, it seemed, work a public good — even if, especially if, that meant subordinating available information to a public knowledge it was actively producing.

To be sure, the Nazi past doesn't get drowned out completely. In the *Newsweek* special issue, for example, it resurfaces metaphorically in an account of the strains the astronauts encountered, up against NASA norms of cheerfulness and unanimity, when they disagreed with technicians and administrators. The article explains that "as the image makers see it, none of these difficulties is to be aired; once the spotlight picks out a face in the crowd, all blemishes must be concealed at all costs. One reporter calls this phase of Mercury operations 'The Lock Step.'"[34] Additionally, it is possible that von Braun's unmentioned, unmentionable, Nazi experiences actually enhanced his reputation. Norman Mailer describes him as possessing "that variety of glamour usually described as fascinating, which is to say, the evocation of his name is attractive and repellant at once."[35] Writing at decade's end of the power and force of the Saturn V, the rocket that made Apollo and the moon landing possible, Mailer asks: "Who could begin to measure the secret appeal of the Nazis by now?"[36]

The American effort in space depended on its public image. Up until Neil Armstrong's moon walk, the Soviets seemed to have a clear lead in the race. So packaging was all important. American achievements, if not the first or the highest or the longest or the biggest, had do demonstrate something that made them distinct from those of the communists. The distinction turned on publicity. Celebrating the success of Mercury astronaut Gordon Cooper's flight, *Time* noted that the Soviets had already had, and would most likely continue to have, more spectacular space "extravaganzas." "But," the magazine stresses, "Russia has never done much more than tell the world of its space successes — via verbal reports — and last week's Cape Canaveral launching was seen by millions via Telstar television. It was a display of free world candor and confidence that undercut the *post facto* reports of Soviet achievements."[37]

Similarly, in his introduction to *We Seven*, a compilation of *Life* articles by the "Mercury Seven," John Dille points out that the Soviets had already performed "more spectacular feats" by the time Americans were celebrating John Glenn's orbital flight. But Glenn's mission, he writes, "was a much more daring and honest gamble. For Glenn was the representative of a free and open society, and he took his chances in full view of the world. Then, when he returned to earth, he was fully prepared — as the first cosmonauts were not — to share his adventure down to the last detail and to relate the complete story of how the flight had gone, what the bad moments were like, what he saw, and how he felt."[38] Taking a chance in public meant taking a chance on television, allowing cameras and the press access. Describing his feelings, letting reporters in on the worst parts of his experience, was how John Glenn represented American openness and freedom. Sharing everything, turning private thoughts into public information, symbolized American difference and superiority. It was the measure of credibility. That Glenn was willing (as if he actually had a choice in the matter) to appear on television under the dangerous and uncertain conditions of rocket flight became yet another dimension of his heroism, and that of the astronauts more generally.

To be public, the space program had to have a public. The very publicness of the program was itself an effect of the witnessing audience. As *Newsweek* observed in 1962, "For many Americans, the new age of space enters their lives only intermittently, through their TV screens or in headlines, usually when an astronaut is rocketed into the sky."[39] Sending a man into space didn't count for anything if people didn't see it, if they didn't believe it. Noting the lack of interest in *Apollo 13*'s trip to the moon, the program's third, *Life* pointed out that "even the drama of blast-off had been scantily attended: no world figures on hand and only a fraction of the world press there at Cape Kennedy to witness this latest audacious attempt by man to prove that his wits and guts could answer the taunt of space."[40]

Not counting the conspiracy-minded, of course, few in the early years asked whether American space efforts were real. As Don Myrus acknowledges, with radar and radio, spaceflights can be documented. The importance of credibility, then, was mostly an issue of "believing in," of believing in the American mission, believing that freedom and democracy were at stake, believing that the success or failure of one man's rocket trip signified the success or failure of liberty itself. Thus, some aspects of the space program were better placed offstage, behind the scenes. No matter what their contribution to the advancement of the United States' long-range missile capacity, ex-Nazi rocket scientists lacked the image necessary to maintain the link between outerspace and American visions of freedom and democracy. To pull this off, you really need good actors.

Seeing Stars

They were subjected to unbelievable tests, experiments really. Many were painful. Often they couldn't move at all. Tubes were inserted into rectums. Sperm was taken, though it wasn't clear why. Needles, longer than they could have imagined, appeared everywhere. They felt trapped like animals in a lab. Inhuman "doctors" refused to explain what the tests were for, why they were necessary. Sometimes completely weightless, sometimes in impenetrable darkness, sometimes presented with mysterious blinking lights, it didn't matter; the experience was out of this world. Who would believe them? Or so says Tom Wolfe in *The Right Stuff*.

The lab rat, experimental object, "Spam in a can" idea wasn't NASA's vision of the astronaut, but this unpleasant dimension of astronaut life did seep into spaces with a claim to public attention. The week before NASA announced the names of America's first astronauts, *Life* magazine featured a story on the tests used in the selection process. Warren R. Young, a science editor, explained that such tests were necessary because of the demands of spaceflight: "the space pilot will be menaced by a cacophony of sound capable of producing both disorientation and body damage, by a buffet of shocks and shakes, by devastating extremes of heat and cold and total vacuum, by the terrors and hallucinations of prolonged isolation and by the various crushing, dizzying and floating effects of wildly varying gravitational forces." The "space scientists," he continues, who already have "had trouble launching payloads of robot instruments, will soon catapult the most fragile and vulnerable package of all, the human body."[41] Young details his experience of weightlessness, being "lobbed like a tennis ball," the rising G's of the centrifuge, and a shaking, vibrating table on which "test animals sometimes die after ten minutes. . . . The vibration seems to make various organs hemorrhage."[42] He describes a ride in the Human Disorientation Device, a contraption like "a tremendous automatic cocktail shaker." He is sealed into a room-sized oven to test for his response to heat; and his feet are put in a bucket of ice, a seemingly innocuous experiment until "an exquisite little pain began to assert itself in the toes, as if a gentle torturer were carefully cutting off the tips with a sharp sliver of glass."[43]

With his own desire to undergo these pains and stresses safely and doubly inscribed onto his journalistic and scientific search for knowledge, Young pathologizes what it might mean in others. He notes that the rocket scientists received letters from numerous volunteers:

> Some of them see the trip as a form of escape, either a psychotic escape from humanity or a simple, old-fashioned escape from woman trouble. Some are thrill-seekers who think a ride into space would merely be an exceptionally cool hot-rod drag. Some are ridden by guilt complexes, either justified or imaginary, and think volunteering will bring atonement. Still others are sportsmen eager to accept the challenge of space "because it is there" and scientists who hope to find the answers to scientific mysteries.[44]

Establishing the position to be occupied by the astronaut or, more precisely, reiterating the position that NASA was in the process of fabricating, Young subsumes his scientists and sportsmen under a general psychological category of "bad risks." These are the men who can't handle stress, he explains

Project Mercury astronauts (NASA)

with reference to a psychiatric study of "Chinese prisoner-of-war practices" and to the words of a psychiatrist from Wright Field: "The neurotic, the immature, the embittered, the inexperienced and the meek succumb."[45] He who is to inherit the skies must be a "normal, emotionally mature man with a strong sense of his own importance and identity." Young accepts NASA's conclusion that this means an astronaut must be a military test pilot.

The following week's issue of *Life* heralded the seven new astronauts. Its feature begins with a photograph of the seated and suited astronauts that extends across the top of two pages. All are white men, with crew cuts and ties. An American flag stands in the left-hand corner. Below the text are photographs depicting the various tests the astronauts endured. Two are wired into chairs next to faintly ominous machines covered with switches and tubing. John Glenn appears shirtless, in sweatpants and sneakers, all military stiffness and formality as a man takes his blood pressure. In the last photo, Wally Schirra, seated wearing a bathrobe and sneakers, blows into a tube as a serious-looking man with glasses, a man with "scientist" written all over him, stares intently at some sort of meter or apparatus.

The little bit of text on the next two pages is framed by numerous shots of astronaut wives and astronaut children, astronaut families running at the beach, preparing for vacation or sitting together on a couch. The final two pages of the article feature significantly more text, and yet more images of machines. Chimps are shown in isolation booths. A man appears to be in a high-tech dunking chair. Another looks as if he is being inserted into a bomb. The only clear face is that of the flight surgeon in charge of the "ducklings, probings, checks that proved the fliers' fitness." Dr. W. R. Lovelace II, presented as the author of this section of the article, justifies the extensiveness of the tests performed on the astronaut candidates in terms of the potential for small defects to cause big problems under the extreme conditions of spaceflight. He does not explain why sperm counts were necessary. A gallon of urine per candidate per day, however, is said to have been required in order to get a total for each man's daily excretion of steroid hormones.[46]

This initial coverage of the astronauts set the tone for subsequent coverage of the space program from the Mercury astronauts' training through the Apollo program. With one exception, the types of images — family man in domestic space, lone hero in outerspace, cyborgian inhabitant of a technological space — continued to appear, commenting upon and unsettling the official image of the astronaut NASA sought to contain. The exception involves a fourth type of image that appeared only after the astronauts actually started to ride the rockets: images of spectators. *Life* in particular brought the audience in, producing the public as part of the space program, illustrating how people watched launches, be they live or on television.

Such images took two primary forms. The first spun off from the photos of astronauts in domestic space: their wives watch and observe, standing in for the rest of America as they served and looked out for the space travelers. *Life* published endless photographs of astronaut wives staring at the television or gazing up into the sky. Their undemanding support, humble pride, and fearful confidence in their astronaut husbands, itself an idea as contradictory as the rest, represented the combination of thoughts

*Wives of the Mercury astronauts (Don Uhrbrock, *Life* magazine ©Time Inc.)*

and feelings presumably coursing through the public at large. Photographs of the private, domestic lives of astronaut wives and their children came to be situated in the space of the public. Images of women in private came to symbolize public reception of the space program.

The second sort of observer image linked to the astronaut is the general crowd scene: numerous spectators, rarely interacting with one another, watch something that is itself outside the picture's frame. These public witnesses are engrossed in what they see, transfixed, spellbound. *Time*'s photographic coverage of Cooper's seven-and-half-hour orbital flight in May 1963 shows ten witnesses.[47] Seven are women. Two men are senior citizens, significantly older than the astronauts. The third male is a young boy. All are white and middle-class. Including the poor might call into question the costs of the space program. Including African Americans would deflect attention toward that other race. The pictorial public doesn't compete with the astronauts; they look up to them. While the astronauts are in outerspace, this public remains at home, taking care of everyday things, of basic needs. They are Americans, citizen-spectators, seeing just what they are supposed to see.

Life's coverage is notably similar. Under the heading "Everyone Was Up There with Gordo" is a photograph taking up seven-eighths of the page. The photograph features half a dozen or so white, middle-class Americans. It is the kind of image frequently used to suggest "typical Americans" or "the public" in mainstream magazines during the fifties and sixties. The

Joan Aldrin, during husband's Apollo 11 *moon walk (Lee Balterman,* Life *magazine ©Time Inc.)*

"Everyone was up there with Gordo!" (Priya Ramrakha, Life magazine ©Time Inc.)

few men, again out of competitive range with the astronauts, wear ties; the younger women have short, well-kept hair. The older woman in the center of the picture wears a hat and the sort of jewelry associated with words like "tasteful." She wears a wedding ring and her hands are clasped to suggest prayer. The caption reads: "Concern for Cooper. Reflecting personal involvement felt around the world, a woman prays for Cooper as she and the crowd around her watch the flight on a TV screen in New York's Grand Central Station."[48] In this photograph, a woman in public, unrelated to though nonetheless personally involved with the astronauts, stands in for the public as audience. Her link to the domestic sphere, her ring, indeed, her gender, represents the transfer of involvement from astronaut wives in particular, to wives in general, to the general public itself. She is part of a domesticated public, the public that stays at home and watches while others are outside exploring. She is a credible witness.

The specificity of these images of the American audience produces precisely the public NASA addressed. The image creates the public NASA needed to witness its achievements in space: a supportive, believing, accepting public. It is a public that would necessarily be at home; a public that has nothing better to do than witness the achievements of others. What is to be installed as the public is an effect of the image: the domesticized, white middle class is to represent — to be — the public. Conversely, the public is the domesticized, white middle class.

Of course, this installation of the public through a particular image of a white middle class is not new or unique to *Life* magazine or space program photographs. Nor is this the only way a particular group of people comes to stand for the public. Rather, the constitution of a particular audience as the public that the space program addressed is representative of general practices of linkage and exclusion through which larger conceptual associations are territorialized on specific bodies.[49] Such practices can usefully be understood in terms of Allucquère Rosanne Stone's notion of *warranting*, "the production and maintenance of this link between a discursive space and a physical space."[50] If to witness a particular governmental spectacle is to be the recipient of messages addressed to "the public," then representations of the witnesses "warrant" their standing as the public. By the time the space program was under way, the links warranting the white middle class as the public were already in place. By excluding other Americans, other races and classes, the photograph (like NASA's own televisuality) places them behind the scenes, not part of what happens in what is installed in public space or matters for what is claimed to be the public sphere. For some — the very rich, the very powerful, even the merely somewhat wired — this location will be a site of action. For others, it will be a place where they can be acted upon with impunity, at least until the television cameras get there and start revealing the suffering that accompanies second-class status.

What this public audience was supposed to be watching was proof — right there on television — of the superiority of the American way. The astronaut was the most visible sign of this proof. As an emblem of the best of America, the image of the astronaut was from the outset an uneasy combination of often contradictory expectations and demands. As the introduction to *We Seven* gushes, "What kind of man could manage to be part pilot, part engineer, part explorer, part scientist, part guinea pig — and part hero — and do equal justice to each of the diverse and demanding roles that was being thrust upon him?"[51] The astronaut embodied the difference between American and Soviet achievement: American technological prowess, the benefits of a market economy, as well as the less tangible ideals of openness and freedom.

The physical requirements seemed to be dictates of technology.[52] Astronauts had to weigh less than 180 pounds and be no more than five feet, eleven inches tall. They could be no older than forty; their age idealized in terms of being "young enough to be in their physical prime . . . and yet mature enough to have lost the rash impulses of youth."[53] They had to be physically and psychologically strong, with "nerves of steel." The psychological qualifications were constructed in terms of the presumed stresses of an alien environment. Because space was full of unknowns, "a hostile environment," daring and courage were necessary. Because the systems were untried, untested, unpredictable, "the men would also have to be the kind who would remain cool and resourceful under pressure"; they would have to be "masters of their own destiny."[54] Because of the stresses of potential crises, of the not-yet-known and the to-be-experienced, astronauts would have to be "devoid of emotional flaws which could rattle them or destroy their efficiency." NASA also put forth background and educational qualifications as basic to its programmatic needs. Thus, astronauts had to be test pilots because of their training with fast, complex machines, and they had to have engineering degrees because they were to be involved with designing the spacecraft and other equipment.[55] They had to be people who could deal with what others had not yet imagined.

When first introduced, these requirements were enough to produce white-male astronaut bodies, bodies with "only small variations in size, shape and coloring to distinguish them one from the other."[56] They also produced bodies that had reproduced: all the Mercury astronauts were married with children. These bodies had been through similar sorts of conditioning, nourishment, and training. Not only did all the astronauts have military and test pilot experience, but all had been raised in small towns; all had been reared under a traditional ethos of effort and success. NASA's requirements, in short, produced astronauts as America's ideal citizens: strong, ambitious, straight, white, middle-class men.[57]

That the requirements were themselves effects of this image is hinted at already in the program's early years. John Dille observes that, during and after his orbital flight, John Glenn "portrayed the perfect image of the modest, dedicated and patriotic hero. He had probably done more in this one day than dozens of other people could have done in months to sell the U.S. space effort to Congress and to the nation."[58] Yet Dille acknowledges as well that Glenn had spent a lot of time thinking about the astronaut image, that Glenn was convinced "that they are the first of a new and even heroic breed of men who have the enormous responsibility of serving as symbols of the nation's future."[59] Similarly attuned to the image of the astronaut, Clare Boothe Luce suggests why NASA required astronauts to have penises. In an attack on NASA's refusal to let women become astronauts, right after Valentina Tereshkova in 1963 became the first woman in space, Luce presents the astronaut as more than "the world's most presti-gious popular idol." She writes: "he is the symbol of the way of life of his nation."[60] So understood, it makes sense that astronauts were educated, middle-class, straight white men; for they represented how those Ameri-cans of impact and influence, those voices that carried, saw not just them-selves but their place in the service of the American public. This was the public the astronauts represented. This was the credible public that wit-nessed American spaceflight on television and not flying saucers in some unpredictable location.

The astronaut "warranted" the public as straight, white, and middle class. It connected bodies with notions of competition, achievement, and success. By reproducing military norms of service and test pilot norms of courage, the astronauts exemplified not only a particular sort of masculin-ity, but a masculinity linked to a specific family structure, a specific home, a specific femininity and sexuality. Why else the stress on sperm and sports?

All America(n)

This Beaver Cleaver public, meanwhile, was not without rifts and con-tradictions. Rather than being suppressed under NASA images of space he-roes, though, for the most part these rifts themselves became inscribed into astronaut symbology. Paradoxically, the cause of this inscription was NASA's effort to present before a viewing audience the superiority of the openness and freedom of American life and the achievements of American technology.

Although NASA was always interested in selling space to an American public, the media had their own reasons for emphasizing the astronauts' private lives. In interpreting space, print and television media faced prob-lems of knowledge and human interest. Were emphasis to be placed on the technical and scientific aspects of spaceflight, reporters and editors would need to "master a huge body of scientific knowledge."[61] And they would have to find a way to communicate this knowledge to a wide market of readers. Stressing more everyday elements of space travel such as the reac-tions of the astronauts and their families was easier. A science degree wasn't a requirement; it was barely an asset. Critical of ABC's space commentator Jules Bergman for his lack of polish (despite a science fellowship at Colum-bia University), *Newsweek* applauded CBS's Walter Cronkite, "a liberal-arts graduate of the University of Texas who has the least technical knowledge but the most dramatic approach ('Gosh! Golly!')."[62]

The stress on the everyday had two effects: First, it lent credibility to the openness of the U.S. space program even as it undercut the normative image of the astronaut. Second, it contributed to the representative claim of the astronaut even as it routinized space travel.

From the initial coverage of the Mercury astronauts, privacy was presented as that which the astronauts had agreed to sacrifice for the sake of the nation. That most of the Mercury astronauts flew with rectal thermometers inserted was not a secret. Noting the astronauts' "absolute lack of privacy," Norman Mailer stresses the contradictions they embodied. "The heart pressure, the brain waves, the bowel movements of astronauts were of national interest," he writes; "They were virile men, they were prodded, probed, tapped into, poked, flexed, tested, subjected to a pharmacology of stimulants, depressants, diuretics, laxatives, retentives, tranquilizers, motion sickness pills, antibiotics, vitamins, and food which was designed to control the character of their feces."[63] By 1969, when Mailer is writing, however, the astronauts had become less emotionally accessible than in the Mercury years. Neil Armstrong and Buzz Aldrin, unlike John Glenn, were all NASA-speak, procedural, technocratic. For the emotional component of astronaut lives so central to the criterion of openness, therefore, the media and NASA looked to astronaut wives.

Openness, especially after Glenn's emotive performance, required access to feelings. His emotions seemed, to the reporters covering his flight and the spectators turning out for the ticker-tape parade that honored him at home, the key to his realness.[64] His feelings signified his sincerity. "When he told a joint session of Congress that he still gets a lump in his throat when the American flag passes by, he meant it," explained *Newsweek*, "And the public sensed it."[65] If the Apollo astronauts wouldn't, couldn't, produce the responses of fear, anxiety, anticipation, and exhilaration expected of one leaving the planet, then the wives would. The wives could provide the required image of realness. And they didn't have to express anything NASA hadn't sanctioned. Openness didn't mean open to criticism or open to views other than NASA's. It simply meant feelings, sentiments. For straight, white, middle-class Americans in the sixties, feelings meant women.

Life's preoccupation with astronaut wives and families, a preoccupation NASA encouraged, might have been thought an ideal way of producing a space hero while still acknowledging the emotional domestic concerns presumably of interest to its readers. In a *Life* article on astronaut widows, Dora Jane Hamblin points out that "despite the high drama of their husbands' work, astronauts' wives are and were suburban housewives tied to homes, meals, chauffeuring chores for their children."[66] With wives and children snugly ensconced at home, the astronauts were free to venture where no man has gone before.

Precisely this image of the adventuresome husband, however, was a problem. Hamblin's reporting is notable in that, unlike the earlier *Life* coverage provided by male correspondents and the Mercury wives, hers strays from the "happy and proud" script, suggesting that a woman's happiness may require more than being a wife, even an astronaut's wife. She notes that "astronauts' wives spend most of their lives wishing their constantly traveling husbands could come home nights, like other husbands, and pretending not to hear in public places whispered conversations about 'Mrs. Who?'"[67] Describing the "magnificent agony" of the wives of the *Apollo* 7 astronauts, Hamblin details the excesses of everyday life facing Harriet Eisele, Jo Schirra, and Lo Cunningham during the mission. "Kids had to be back in school and they were so keyed up they forgot their books and lost their band instruments more frequently than usual," she explains. "Groceries had to be bought, visiting relatives were getting bored and refused to admit it, neighbors rushed in and out with a continuing 'togetherness' tic, and the wives had no hole to hide in."[68] In a report on astronaut widows, Hamblin quotes Betty Grissom: "After the accident people called me a lot, thinking that I would be alone. . . . They don't realize. I was always alone, the boys and I. Gus was never here."[69] By illuminating the instabilities of supposedly ideal marriages, the private lives of the astronauts exemplified the tensions and instabilities within the straight model family. Hamblin suggests that the widows may be better off, having the opportunity to figure out who they are and what they want, now that their husbands are dead: "Actually, the hardest thing the widows have had to bear is the sudden acquisition of freedom."[70]

Germaine Greer, in the classic feminist text *The Female Eunuch*, places astronaut wives at the center of her "Misery" chapter. Acknowledging the glory reflected back onto an astronaut's wife, Greer refers nonetheless to a statement by a NASA psychiatrist "that Cape Kennedy was the world's most active spawning ground for divorce."[71] She notes the high incidence of housewife alcoholism, "higher than anywhere in America except Washington." For Greer, the explanation for this misery is the astronauts' lack of emotion. "The deliberate desensitizing of astronauts has its problems; they might contain themselves brilliantly on the moon, but they contain themselves everywhere else, too, including their wives' beds, for the degree of sexual activity at the Cape is agreed to be very low."[72]

Once established, the ordinary domesticity of astronaut lives, a shaky, unhappy, and typical domesticity, had a reverse effect of distancing the astronauts and their wives from other Americans. The more they were like other Americans, the less they could stand apart from them and represent them. This was especially clear with respect to those who served in Vietnam. Their deaths rarely if ever were accorded the same status and significance as those of the astronauts. Hamblin explains: "The wives are acutely, specifically, aware of the Vietnam widows, the wives of men whose deaths make no headlines except in local papers. The astronauts were almost all of the proper age and profession to have been in Vietnam had they not been in the space program, and their widows know that society has provided more cushions for their future than it has for war widows."[73] As the death toll mounted in Vietnam, it became harder to ignore that soldiers were dying anonymously; indeed, unheroically. In death, an astronaut became an instant hero — or was he a hero just by being an astronaut? The war, like the assassinations of Martin Luther King Jr. and Bobby Kennedy, like the Soviet invasion of Czechoslovakia and the increasing unrest in U.S. and European cities, like the incident at Chappaquiddick that occurred soon after *Apollo 11* lifted off, called the link between astronaut and hero into question.

The ambiguity of celebrity status weakened the link further. The more the astronauts were perceived as advocates for NASA, as lobbying for more government funds, the less they looked like heroes. "NASA was vending space. Armstrong was working directly for his corporate mill," observes Mailer as he watches the astronaut tape an interview with NBC.[74] Feelings in an astronaut might be desirable, but not economic dependency. If too closely associated with the economic, the astronaut would invite questioning into the financing, the costs, of space. The astronaut needed to be above the money the program needed. The *Nation* piously proclaimed: "They have been glamorized; they can be unglamorized. A sense of decorum is a good thing, even for a hero. Or especially for a hero."[75]

The astronaut also needed to be above personal financial need, or greed. The press railed against the exclusive $500,000 contract between *Life* and the Mercury astronauts. *Newsweek* observed that the contract violated an "ethical standards" policy established by President Kennedy, whereby presidential appointees were barred from receiving payment for public appearances or published writings.[76] Although the contract was allowed, *Newsweek* hinted that John Glenn and President Kennedy had reached an agreement while waterskiing. When the Mercury Seven were offered houses by a Houston real-estate developer, however, NASA balked. Free houses, nicely furnished, would have put too much stress on the already thinning link between astronaut and hero. *Business Week* urged "Heroes Must Be Pure," pointing out that the astronauts initial acceptance of the offer, which they rejected only after criticism in the press had put pressure on NASA, "drove home to NASA the fact that the public image of the astronauts is an integral part of the national space program and largely accounts for the whole-hearted public support of the program."[77]

In their concern with the position of the astronaut before the witnessing public, NASA and the press reveal more than a preoccupation with image; they expose a more fundamental sense of what "the public" *should* want, should expect, should in fact see. The public produced for the space program isn't supposed to see anything messy or dirty, anything "impure." It isn't supposed to witness economic need or the faults and instabilities of idealized heterosexual marriages. The public, in other words, is put on a pedestal not unlike the one that has supported idealizations of white, middle-class femininity in the nineteenth and twentieth centuries. Let the men, the active ones, take care of the problems. If they are doing their duty, playing their role, then those left at home won't even think to worry about problems facing them on the domestic front. They can watch space heroes instead.

Consequently, television was crucial. After *Apollo 1*, all the Apollo flights were equipped for live television transmission. *Life* explains: "The telecasts are in keeping with NASA's stated policy: to conduct its missions, from launch to splashdown, in the public eye."[78] Moreover, reading the moon landing as "almost" enough to compensate for the turmoil of the sixties, the magazine opined that "putting two men on the moon and getting them safely back was marvelous enough, but nearly as breathtaking was the fact that anyone on earth with a TV set could witness the mission unfolding step by step.[79] But as the film *Apollo 13* establishes so clearly, not all television audiences are ideal citizen-spectators. Some folks may well prefer to watch something else. The more geared to television the space program became, the more it had to contend with the expectations of these fickle, not so ideal, not so dutiful audiences. Describing the telecast from *Apollo 10*, "for the first time in living color," Albert Rosenfeld notes that "the TV viewer, conditioned by Rowan & Martin, may be a bit disappointed by the humor. He may also expect that the circumstances of the flight demand comments more exciting and imaginative than 'fantastic' or 'mighty fine.'"[80] Neil Armstrong worried about the quality of the telecast from the moon, fearing that the viewers at home might be disappointed in the moon walk because of the quality of the picture.[81]

Jut as it sought to project an image of openness, so did NASA use the space program to present a particular image of freedom. Free houses could have threatened the image of freedom NASA wanted to project: Soviet cosmonauts received free houses, not American astronauts. In the Soviet Union, benefits were free; in America they were freely earned. America's heroes weren't cosmonauts, tainted by an alliterative slide toward communism. They were straight-A, all-American astronauts who would do their jobs not because they were forced to, not even because they were paid to; they would do them because they were free to. Freedom, in other words, depended on a contrast with the Soviets, even as it connected with other threads of meaning.

This preoccupation with being not-Soviet was installed early on in the form of the opposition between passengers and pilots. In the early days of the space program, astronauts and cosmonauts had basically no control over their capsules. They were passengers. They rode the rockets. Tom Wolfe puts it still more strongly: the astronauts were "test subjects," "redundant components" of a superior technological system; they simply needed to be conditioned to "do nothing." [82] Lauding the astronauts for their experience as test pilots, however, NASA and the press stressed the difference between the astronauts and cosmonauts. Astronauts had freedom in space, unlike communist cosmonauts.

Although Alan Shepard was the second man in space (and made a suborbital rather than an orbital flight), NASA depicted his televised flight as the first instance of a man piloting a space vehicle. [83] Describing Yuri Gagarin's initial orbital flight in a Vostok craft named the *Swallow*, Alan Shepard and Deke Slayton write: "He'd gone higher and faster and had raced all the way around the planet, but the Russians had played it very tight against the vest with a supercautious approach, and Gagarin had been a fascinated passenger. The *Swallow* had flown its entire mission on autopilot. Gagarin had gone along for the ride. Not that the Vostok hadn't had a manual backup system in case the automatics failed. The Russians didn't want to risk using the system and having it fail on them." [84] In a similar vein, Myrus stresses the "27 major tasks" and "about 70 communications" Shepard performed during his flight, concluding: "One thing is certain — he didn't just go along for the ride." [85] By the end of Project Mercury, Slayton, who had become the head of the newly created Astronaut Office, could say that the biggest change in the program since its inception was that "the Astronaut has become a full-fledged pilot both in theory and practice. The Mercury capsule was built for completely automatic flight, which relegated the Astronaut to little more than passenger status. But time and again, crises would come up on Mercury flights that forced the pilots to take over in order to complete the mission." [86]

The American program, therefore, stood for freedom. America trusted its astronauts to make their own decisions, to take initiative, to think for themselves. They were not programmed communist automatons, cogs in a vast machinery. Astronauts were active, as anyone sitting back and watching their accomplishments on television could see.

To be sure, this emphasis on freedom had effects that subverted the image NASA sought to create. As *Apollo 13* shows, NASA was not always honest with the astronauts. The astronauts were sometimes confronted with situations where they could not think for themselves, where they could not take the initiative, where they were just as programmed as any cosmonaut. During John Glenn's orbital flight, Mercury Control received indications that his heat shield may have come loose. If so, the capsule could have burned up during reentry. The control center decided "not to burden" Glenn "with such a tremendous cause for worry."[87] Reflecting on the event, Glenn expressed his thought that the pilot should not be kept "in the dark, especially if you believe he might be in real trouble. It is the pilot's job to be as ready for emergencies as anyone else, if not more so. And he can hardly be fully prepared if he is not being kept fully informed."[88]

The most obvious connection made between space and freedom drew from America's frontier tradition. In an October 1962 *Newsweek* editorial, Kenneth Crawford explains: "Space is quite literally the new frontier and the American people are the true heirs of a frontier tradition. Now that space has been opened up, they take it for granted that we shall be the pioneers who take advantage of the opening."[89] The frontier tradition appeared as part of the justification for space exploration. Frequently, NASA officials, politicians, and astronauts, when called to defend the program, would invoke America's history of conquest and adventure. "Because it's there," "because of Americans' natural spirit and curiosity" were answers that hit on the country's sense of destiny. In the words of *Apollo 10* astronaut John Young, "The moon fascinates me personally the way Africa once fascinated people, the way any unexplored territory is still fascinating . . . one of these days the world must colonize the moon just so our grandchildren (or maybe our children) will have a place to live."[90]

Remarks like this may explain the whiteness of the Mercury, Gemini, and Apollo programs. In America, the colonizing image, celebrated or condemned, is white. For African Americans, Africa would not appear as some empty, unexplored territory. Space had to be vacant and ready for conquering and occupation, just as America had been before.[91] Freedom required a terrain that was itself unconstraining. Put somewhat differently, if they were to explore freely, astronauts, like other American explorers, could not be limited by obligations to already existing peoples, environments, or species. The emptiness of space thus reiterated a prominent motif of the frontier tradition. In doing so, however, it added to the critical tensions already building up against this tradition as Native Americans asserted their rights and histories and as struggles in Vietnam and throughout Africa drew attention to colonialism's legacy.

The emphasis on freedom as choice, agency, and initiative had further negative repercussions as the space program became more spectacular and televisual. Just as the astronauts' image was threatened by links to money and greed, so was NASA's. With such extensive financial and economic investment in the program, the agency (even during the glory years of Apollo) was an easy target for allegations of partisanship and insinuations that exploring space was less important than keeping the new bureaucracy and space industry employed. Indeed, the more that was invested in the program, the less credible it became. Given limited resources, choosing to explore space rather than confront domestic problems of poverty, racism, and urban violence seemed even harder to justify. By the time of the moon walk, many in the United States were more concerned with the effects of the Pill, women's liberation, the new "Gay Pride," and the sexual revolution; others were preoccupied with the student movement, Woodstock, and the breakup of the Beatles; even more were preoccupied with "Black Power" and ending the war in Vietnam. When active involvement was increasingly demanded and *possible*, choosing either to provide, support, or witness space spectacles was a passive response.

The freedom and agency of the astronauts were also subverted by precisely that which made the astronauts possible: technology. Since the initial response to *Sputnik*, the space program highlighted the importance of technological expertise, superiority, and achievement. Technology would determine the victor in the competition with the Soviets. Interpreting the technology, explaining what made it so necessary, so great — indeed, celebrating the technology — tended to devalue the position of the astronaut as human and to present a vision of the astronaut as cyborg.[92]

From the early days of the program the astronauts' fragility and vulnerability were stressed. To survive in space, they had to supplement their bodies. "Naturally," in the sense of that mythic naturalness supposedly inherent in citizen-heroes, astronaut bodies would be left exposed to the harsh vacuums, radiations, and stresses of space. Only cyborgs could survive. *Newsweek* explained that "despite his frailty, man has decided to leave the protective confines of earth and travel through space to the airless, lifeless, waterless surface of the moon. To overcome his physical weakness, he is relying on his wondrous intellect, and on the collective technical capacity of an entire nation."[93] Qua cyborg, the astronaut was not some "natural" hero, facing and solving problems through his own strength and initiative.

Qua cyborg, the astronaut was part of an interdependent collective, part of a group effort. Technicians, citizens, "the collective technical capacity of an entire nation," supplemented the astronaut's weakness, enabling his achievement and protecting his life.

To be sure, the technological supplement wasn't easy or conflict-free. As Tom Wolfe makes clear, given that the astronaut was primarily a test subject, a passenger, a redundant component, his heroic status could not rest primarily on his talent or accomplishments, especially during Project Mercury. Consequently, heroism was construed in terms of bravery. And the reason bravery played such a significant part is that "our rockets always blew up."[94] Because of the string of highly publicized failures preceding manned spaceflight, that some men would be willing to ride a rocket struck many in the press as uniquely courageous. The technology seemed unreliable; consequently, the bravery of the astronaut was remarkable. Once the technology stabilized, though, the astronaut didn't seem significantly braver than many other Americans, no braver, say, than those fighting in Vietnam.

For some, the technological advances, especially as linked to computers and television, were so incredible that they cast doubt on the reality of NASA's achievements. Norman Mailer finds the moon landing "so unreal" that

> no objective correlative existed to prove it had not been an event staged in a television studio — the greatest con of the century — and indeed a good mind, product of the iniquities, treacheries, gold, passion, invention, ruse, deception and rich worldly stink of the Renaissance could hardly deny that the event if bogus was as great a creation in mass hoodwinking, deception, and legerdemain as the true ascent was in technology, engineering, and physics. Indeed, conceive of the genius of such a conspiracy. It would take men mightier, more trustworthy and more resourceful than anything in this century or the ones before.[95]

This idea is still around. The 1970s B-movie *Capricorn One* (featuring O. J. Simpson) depicts a faked Mars landing. Some conspiracy theorists, the 3,700 members of the Flat Earth Society, and about 20 million other Americans seriously question whether the Apollo program ever landed someone on the moon.[96] Most support their position by referring to the fact that the only evidence they've seen has been on television. Why believe something just because it's on television? For this audience, the televisuality of space establishes not the credibility of NASA but the likelihood of deception.

The televisual unreality of NASA space, the virtual reality of space on screens, impacted and impacts upon more than the conspiracy-minded, however. Indeed, it contributes to the cyborgian character of the astronaut. Astronaut training relied on simulation. To root out fear, to eliminate contingency, the astronauts repeated each move of a spaceflight countless times. "The idea was to decondition the beast completely, so that there would not be a single novel sensation on the day of the flight itself," explains Wolfe.[97] He describes Alan Shepard's experience that, even though he was the first American in space, "the real thing didn't measure up. It was *not realistic*."[98] Because of the repeated simulations, Shepard could only compare his launch to the centrifuge, his view to photographs, the sounds to recordings. "For he was introducing the era of pre-created experience," Wolfe writes; "His launching was an utterly novel event in American history, and yet he could feel none of its novelty. He could not feel the 'awesome power' of the rocket beneath him, as the broadcasters kept referring to it."[99] For Bruno Latour, "what is admirable is not how one can get into space, but how the complete space flight can be simulated in advance."[100]

The extraterrestrial environment was thought to be so alien that the astronauts had to become "normalized" to it; space had to become familiar. Yet as they became cyborgs, the sense of the difference of space from their human environment, the possibility of wonder, dissipated.[101] In this respect, Neil Armstrong was "a shining knight of technology."[102] He wasn't the first man on the moon; he was the first *cyborg* on the moon. Armstrong, Mailer observes, preferred to speak in computerese, especially under pressure. English was too vague, too imprecise. "The message had to be locked into a form which could be transmitted by pulse or by lack of pulse, one binary digit at a time, one bit, one bug installed in each box."[103] Indeed, Armstrong was so integrated into space technology, so conjoined with machinery, that "after twenty hours in a simulators" he had "dreams of computers."[104]

Neil Armstrong is the link to Bill Gates.

The Final Frontier

The co-optation and supplanting of space imagery by computer and Net advocates is deliberate and direct. Responding to the increase in on-line commerce, the database software vendor Oracle developed a merchant-server based on the Java Internet programming language. The server was code-named Project Apollo.[105] Microsoft sent out a mailing that advertised new Net software to developers; the dominant image was not of a computer, but of a Saturn V rocket. A commercial for U.S. Robotics features astronaut Sally Ride explaining: "You need stamina — that's true in space and it's true in cyberspace."[106]

But the link between computers and space has been in place for a long time. Images of consoles and monitors appeared with those of launches, orbits, and moon walks. As Shepard and Slayton write: "In the twentieth century, two distinctly different technologies emerged: the digital computer and the liquid-fueled rocket."[107] Net guru Howard Rheingold credits NASA with a founding role in the development of virtual-reality technologies. In his words, "NASA, appropriately, was the institution that launched the first real public exploration of cyberspace. . . . NASA was the opening of the era of the reality-industrial complex — the network of academic and commercial research and development and entrepreneurial ventures that might grow into a new technology-based industry."[108] And, of course, much science fiction relies on the link between computers and space. Stanley Kubrick's film of Isaac Asimov's *2001: A Space Odyssey* is but one vivid example. "Hello, Dave."

Now, as the film *Apollo 13* and *Feed* signal, computers do more than support the explorations of a few good men. Today outerspace is just one content among many; and NASA-space pales before colorful, exciting, ufological space. It isn't surprising that folks on the World Wide Web would try to jazz up the photos transmitted from Mars, adding aliens and making them their own. The reasons for exploring space remain the same: because it's there; because we can; because of the increase in information. In light of some versions of the practicalities of global, consumer, entertainment culture at the millennium, however, cyberspace easily wins out. More people can cruise the Net than can experience a launch. Cyberspace isn't so dangerous, despite the specter of pedophiles and pornographers and UFO cultists looking for suicidal volunteers that haunts apocalyptic cyber-skeptics.

The failure of space exploration to inspire, to symbolize the future, is not, I have argued, simply the result of cyberian achievement or even marketing. Rather, it is an effect of the contradictions arising out of NASA's preoccupation with openness, freedom, and democracy; it was inscribed into the very televisuality of outerspace. By Apollo's end, it was more than clear that the astronaut could not represent America or Americans. The raced, sexed, gendered, and classed specificities of the astronauts excluded too many Americans. Not only could few Americans see themselves as astronauts, but many wanted to see more than astronaut achievements. Some wanted to "do their own thing."

NASA's use of television to produce witnesses for its achievements installed heroic astronauts and citizen-spectators at the interface between political and popular cultures. Ideally, the active heroes would have been supported by a passive, feminized audience who through this support would realize their own hopes and dreams. But the technologies of space and television, of computers and communication, displaced this ideal. Television brought public space inside. In so doing, it subjected political spectacles to the demands of the medium and made possible similar sorts of criticisms, resistances, and fantasies.[109] Watching television was linked to the activity of citizenship. Furthermore, the computerization of spaceflight detracted from the agency of astronauts. Automatic pilots transported dependent, passive, cyborgian passengers. Technicians called the shots. Today, armed by Bill Gates, they run the show, sending computers to Mars.

Astronaut space suits now appear as uniforms for the Centers for Disease Control in films and reports on Ebola (which often stands in for AIDS). They now function as containment suits for the fabrication of silicon wafers and computer chips. The cyborgian astronaut has given way to the cyberian citizen, the Netizen. In computerized entertainment culture, cruising cyberspace, expanding cyberspace, is much more exciting than watching a rocket launch on television (though not, perhaps, for some, as exciting as watching a live rocket explosion). We can watch more than what the government or a select few produce for our passive consumption, more than what is fed to nourish a particular public within the pregiven limits of a healthy society. Networked computers provide a better combination of domesticity, spectatorship, and action than the televisual public space offered by NASA. Networked space, moreover, has forfeited claims to some "public" sphere, space, or status. Netizens are astronauts *and* audience. Millions visited NASA sites during the *Pathfinder* mission.

NASA tried to increase its audience share, and produce a new audience, by turning the space shuttle into a marker of inclusion. By that time, some folks had cable, remotes; others had better things to do. Interest picked up with the Reagan administration's "Teacher in Space" program. This program took the domestication of space to an extreme: it brought on board someone from the audience. But Christa McAuliffe wouldn't really become an astronaut, not in any ideal sense. She would remain a passenger. She would reenact the role of spectator by recording her experiences in space. The blatancy of the appeal to the everyday contributed to the decline of trust that would culminate the next year, the year after the *Challenger* explosion.

3
Virtually Credible

More Good Reasons to Stay Home

Things have changed since the sixties. Today, in the so very progressive nineties, women can be astronauts. In 1996 Shannon Lucid spent a record-breaking 188 days in space. Admittedly, she didn't get the TV coverage or adulation of a John Glenn or Neil Armstrong, but she made the evening news, and more than once. Despite her achievement, Lucid is not cast as a hero. In *Newsweek*'s cover article on Lucid's spacetime, reporter Sharon Begley refers to the astronaut as one of the "flying Ph.D's." She presents Lucid's experiments with candles and quail eggs as part of NASA's effort to change its "macho image."[1] Scott Carpenter, one of the Mercury Seven, is quoted saying, "Test pilots are members of a more heroic society than Ph.D physicists, and heroes give the enterprise a certain mystique and glory it needs for funding. But in a well-rounded space program you can have both.") He acknowledges, generously, that it is better to be a rocket scientist than a space cadet, and better still to be a test pilot; in Carpenter's world, still the only real hero.

Carpenter's simultaneous feminization of physics and bracketing of Lucid's time in space from the domain of the heroic reminds us that astronauts don't get parades anymore. The excitement is no longer there. For Begley, current astronauts are not even real astronaut; they're just "gloried teamsters who drive the space shuttle into orbit to deliver satellites."[3] Outerspace is now earthly, mundane. As predictable as the shuttle's launch schedule, outerspace has lost its mystery. And even when a launch is canceled, it's only for scientific reasons, certainly. Certain, scientific, predictable, mundane astronauts fail to capture the popular imagination. They are as everyday as housework and bills. As is usually the case when women enter a profession, so it is with astronauts that their prestige has declined.

As I have argued, however, the decline in prestige associated with the "everydayness" of astronaut achievements was an effect of NASA's effort to make the astronauts approachable and predictable, to make them representative Americans, to make their successes our own. NASA's goals, and the use of televisual spectacle to achieve those goals, came into conflict with themselves. The celebration of technology clashed with the representations of freedom. The spectacle of openness exposed many places in American life that were shut out of the theatrics of space.

What remains of NASA's equation is the link between space and the everyday. If the debacle of the "Teacher in Space" program and the explosion of the *Challenger* demonstrate anything, it's that this connection continues to be powerfully seductive in American popular culture. It is particularly powerful in those images of straight white men and women used to represent ideal citizens in an idealized televisual public. Within these fields and thematics the men's activities are heroic; the women are left to signify the everyday. This was Christa McAuliffe's role as the first "teacher in space."

In her study of the ill-fated decision to launch the *Challenger* on the cold morning of January 28, 1986, Diane Vaughan explains: "The successful launch of a mission including an 'average citizen'—a teacher—was a major statement about the reliability of space travel."[4] Constance Penley develops this idea, pointing out the myriad problems NASA faced at the time. She describes the Teacher in Space program as "the largest public-relations bandwagon ever mobilized by the space agency." Thus:

The hook was precisely McAuliffe's representative mediocrity, which was immediately given the more appealing spin of her "ordinariness." NASA hoped the public would reidentify with the agency and its costly projects through identification with McAuliffe in her role as ordinary wife, mother, teacher, and private citizen in space. McAuliffe had to bear a huge representational load: all the hopes for future U.S. space exploration at a time when that future looked precarious.[5]

Whereas the astronaut's representational status was grounded in his very extraordinariness, his courage, his strength, his best-of-the-brightestness, McAuliffe's was all the humbler, oriented toward that domesticized, feminized white public which had long witnessed America's achievements in space. Now, after their years of patient support, their dutiful television watching, this audience would get a chance to participate, to be part of spaceflight, to experience the adventure.

If any of us in the "public" identified with McAuliffe, what might we have lost as we witnessed the *Challenger's* explosion over and over again, and as we failed to acknowledge that McAuliffe and the other astronauts died not in the explosion but in the crash more than two minutes later?[6] If we didn't identify with McAuliffe, what opportunities might we have missed, opportunities to contest yet again the warranting of some bodies as representative, to resist the production of some actions and events as the best grounds for calling others of us together as public witnesses? As we learned more about the pointlessness of the *Challenger's* loss, of the Reagan administration's self-serving manipulation of the launch time, some of us turned our back on politics. Trust in government seemed misplaced. Judgment seemed a matter of media, ratings, and approval. The disaster gave us another good reason to stay home, to turn from outerspace and toward the new opportunities available in cyberspace, in personal computers, VCRs, and camcorders. The *Challenger* explosion, in other words, made us more willing to think about outerspace coming to us.

The death of Christa McAuliffe in 1986 can be linked to the popularity of abduction in 1987. Underlying both is a crisis in judgment, in credibility. Science and technology are not reliable. Public reasons are strictly televisual. How can we know what to believe and whom to trust? Although abduction stories had been part of ufology for more than twenty years, although a couple had even received attention in the mainstream press, it was in 1987 that two abduction books, Whitley Strieber's *Communion* and Budd Hopkins's *Intruders*, made the best-seller lists. These two books, moreover, changed the tone of the abduction story circulating in popular culture. Rather than an outside event, happening mostly to men on the road, as hinted at in *Close Encounters of the Third Kind* and described in the widely publicized cases of Betty and Barney Hill in the early sixties and Travis Walton in the seventies, abduction in the late eighties happens inside, in bedrooms.

Moreover, as Strieber and Hopkins describe it, the aliens are much more interested in sex, genitals, and reproduction than earlier reports let on. Strieber occupies in his texts a traditionally feminine position. Not only is he a parent, heavily identified with his home and his child, but he is also repeatedly violated and abused. His home, his bedroom, is a site for his vulnerability. He is raped and afraid either to remember or to speak his experience. Hopkins makes women featured figures in narratives of alien abduction. He describes in detail the intrusions of aliens into the reproductive dimensions of women's lives, giving voice to women's fears and anxieties as their bodies are colonized to produce a hybrid race.

The *Challenger* explosion marks the end of public fascination with and interest in the American space program (though interest seems to be returning with reports of Martian life and the use of the Internet to bring the Pathfinder mission into the homes of everyday people). NASA was already facing problems with declining public willingness to support further ventures in space. McAuliffe's death hastened this but, even more, the *Challenger* disaster created a strong link in popular culture between ordinary women and the horrors of outerspace. Outerspace was now alien space. The link between alien space and women, available in science fiction, had not yet been part of science fact, although the media focus on the domestic lives of the astronauts was a move in this direction. Constance Penley evokes the "horror of women in space" as a cultural disavowal both of women who "forget their place" and of the death of the *Challenger* crew at the moment of splashdown. I want to link this horror of women in space with abduction, with the horrors experienced and evoked by abductees. Prior to the *Challenger* disaster, outerspace remained for the most part a terrain for the heroic achievements of men. Christa McAuliffe's death opened cultural imaginings of space to the sacrifice and victimization of women.

The *Challenger* disaster, moreover, crashed through the barriers crucial to political spectacle's capacity to call into being a believing public. Televisual political spectacles are produced to be witnessed. Their credibility, their power as demonstrations of political will, achievement, triumph, is an effect of their being witnessed. With the *Challenger* explosion, however, the witnessing becomes detached from credibility because what was witnessed was incredible, unimaginable, horrible. Viewers saw what they were not supposed to see even as they fulfilled their duty to watch. Under these conditions, witnessing the disaster was witnessing the corruption and political venality of NASA and the Reagan administration, the baseness of the motives for the Teacher in Space program, the sham that was the space program. It was witnessing the very dullness of space travel: the crew hadn't been figured as heroes; their deaths lacked that dimension of meaning and purpose. And it was witnessing anew the alien qualities of space and technology: that which was supposed to protect us, that which was supposed to let us claim space beyond earth, was revealed as contingent and unreliable and deadly as space itself.

The field of intelligibility, the terrain in which witnessing was situated, changed. It shifted from the object or event to the contexts and complexities in and through which the event was constituted. The ever repeating horror thus called into being, interpellated, not a civic public united in mourning, but myriad networks for questioning, searching, and criticizing.[7] Indeed, the *Pathfinder* mission acknowledges these networks, recognizing the importance of multiple points of access to space, science, and technology. But this was not the case with the *Challenger* disaster; or, rather, it was the *Challenger* disaster that contributed to the possibility of and need for a new way of connecting with outerspace. To witness the explosion was not simply to follow the script written for the audience in the theatrics of space. To witness now meant to interrogate the conditions that produced the disaster — or to ask how many times duty required watching the *Challenger* explode.

No abductee has ever been given a parade. Compared with astronauts they are victims, not heroes. Many are taken into space, chosen in accordance with some unknown criteria rather than through competitive tests with clear, objective standards. Some stay at home, and space and its alien inhabitants come to them. Again, though, they are chosen, a select group. The criteria for their selection are no doubt unfathomably demanding. Why else would the aliens be able to find American women fit for the rigors of space when NASA had such trouble locating women qualified enough to be astronauts? Penley notes that during the late 1950s twenty-five experienced women pilots went through the battery of tests for the Mercury training program. Thirteen passed, but the program was shut down and NASA refused to approve women for space travel. "The women pilots had been found to be more resistant to radiation," Penley writes, "less subject to heart attacks, and better able to endure extremes of heat, cold, pain, noise, and loneliness."[8] Some abductees feel honored to have been chosen, especially to participate in an intergalactic breeding project.

If not a new breed of men, as John Glenn predicted of the astronauts, the abductees may at least be new breeders, taking on, in their own special way, the familiar role of mothers of future citizens so often inscribed on women's bodies. Nonetheless it remains the case that NASA picks astronauts; aliens pick abductees, and that just isn't enough for a parade.

America doesn't celebrate its victims, although their return may be cause for commendation, especially if complicated negotiations and arms deals aren't necessary to secure it. Instead, America ogles its victims. Contemporary political and economic policies and practices enable most urbans to dwell upon the homeless, to note the details of their bodily habits and smells almost daily. Poor children with enormous black eyes gaze out from all manner of appeals for donations — if not completely charitable, then at least tax-deductible. Contemporary corporate culture and trash media provide a variety of spaces within which one can make a spectacle of oneself.

Abductees may not get parades, but they do get on television. Their televisual presence, moreover, links them with the real, with that which happens. Alan Nadel notes that the public space in which history is enacted is televisual.[9] If a tree falls in a forest or a nanny beats a child in an empty apartment and it's all on video, then, yes, it happened. If a man walks on the moon and a woman describes being taken into an alien craft for a vaginal scraping and television is there to catch it, then, yes, it happened. Or at least it makes sense to think so, especially in a culture where folks watching television can be hailed as the public, where witnessing a televised spectacle is supposed to be a civic act. Under these conditions, seeing is believing — except when what is witnessed is incredible, except when you have two thousand channels.

Like the astronaut, the abductee is a televisual identity. It is an identity sustained by its relationship to a television-viewing audience, to a mediatized society that can transmit information about its available meanings and contours globally, rapidly, electronically. The abductee is an identity possible in part because it is produced in a location that is itself a media product. It occupies that point where space, government, and technology intersect, a point fabricated as the domicile of the astronaut. Astronauts figured prominently in the news media of the 1960s. Abductees are regular fixtures on the 1990s news alternatives: daytime talk shows, Larry King, unsolved and true-life mysteries, tabloid TV. This is not to say that all abductees appear or even want to appear on television. Many abductees refuse to go public. Nonetheless, most report that reading or watching *Communion* or *Intruders*, seeing something about abduction on television, or talking with someone who had was their first step toward naming and understanding their abduction experience. And those outside the abductee community, those with little to no interest in such alien matters, still pick up on the references to abduction pasted into sitcoms like *Seinfeld* and *Ellen*.

Entertaining Abduction

Skeptics often dismiss abductees as publicity hungry. The assumption behind this dismissal is that the desire to appear on television is strong enough to override any thought about what might occur on the air. Televisual space is supposedly so alluring that it can seduce anyone into doing or saying most anything in front of the camera, or at least anyone who is not on a moral or intellectual ground as high as the skeptic's. Perhaps some people crave this sort of publicity. Perhaps their sense of what is public or what it is to participate in public life or in the life of a public is strictly televisual. Perhaps the only actions that count for them as public actions are those that are conferred legitimacy through the televising of their performance. Or maybe some of the people who appear on *Geraldo* and *Sally Jesse Raphael* and *Marcel Williams* are masochists or exhibitionists who get off on the cycle of confession, ridicule, and occasional redemption in the ritual of tabloid talk shows.

Not surprisingly, abductees present their public appearances rather differently. "Going public" is an act of bravery, a sacrifice made on behalf of public safety and knowledge. An ad announcing the availability of abductee Leah Haley for speeches and engagements mentions that she "has been featured in *Omni* magazine and has been a guest on *The Joan Rivers Show*, *Encounters*, *Stein Online* and many others, and has delivered speeches from coast to coast. Her courage has been an inspiration to tens of thousands of others who have had to cope with extraordinary situations." To speak in public is, for abductees, heroic because what they have to say is not suitable for public discourse. Talk of aliens and flying saucers is outside the terms of American public debate; it is beyond the parameters of legitimate discussion. Abductees acknowledge that, from the perspective of the dominant culture, their words are illogical, unreasonable, unscientific. Yet they insist, as a matter of right, truth, and survival, that these words be spoken. They speak, braving the incredulity they know they will encounter, because they experience it themselves.

Abductee, Anna Jamerson, writes: "I'm not sure I will ever really accept my involvement with the aliens; it's just too bizarre, too far from the reality I have known for all of my life." Like those of other abductees, Jamerson's words overflow with doubt, ours and her own. Despite or perhaps because of this lack of certainty, Jamerson insists that she will continue to fight against the aliens. "I'll fight for my sanity, for my right to choose to live my life without interference from them, for your right to know what is happening to me and thousands of your friends and neighbors, and for abductees' rights to be taken seriously in their quest for physical, emotional and mental support in dealing with their personal alien invasion."[10]

We in the public, the privileged "we" connoted by the very notion of "the public," might want to ogle abductees, even buy their books, but we certainly would not choose to entertain their ideas. Better to let them entertain us. In his essay "The Celebrity Freak: Michael Jackson's 'Grotesque Glory,'" David D. Yuan links alien abductions with contemporary reenactments of the freak show. In the tabloid hierarchy of the weird, Yuan suggests, competition for the top rung is between extraterrestrials and celebrity freaks like Michael Jackson.[11] Like many of those who are unwillingly "enfreaked," abductees are afraid that people will laugh at them. They fear, as abductee Beth Collings puts it, being "unceremoniously categorized as *crazy as a rabid hound*, a person to be *shunned*, a person in dire need of *professional counseling*, even a person who is possibly a victim of childhood abuse."[12] Even as they feel their duty to tell — to warn — the rest of us, they know we have no duty to watch or listen to them. They know that their appearances are less likely to hail us as citizens than they are to call us into being as armchair therapists, proud rationalists, or stone-throwing sadists.

Given the limits and presuppositions of so-called public speech, UFO investigators and abduction researchers commend abductees for overcoming their fears and telling the truth, especially the sexual and reproductive details, about their experiences. In his introduction to *Abducted! The Story of the Intruders Continues . . .* Budd Hopkins praises Debbie Jordan's "pioneering decision" to reveal information about a disappearing pregnancy and hybrid child. For his best-selling book *Intruders*, she had been willing to tell her story about a pregnancy that, though seemingly normal, mysteriously stopped, ending without a trace until she recalled an abduction experience in which she was shown an alien child that she realized was her daughter. Hopkins finds that Jordan's "uncommon courage has made it easier for hundreds of men and women since then to unburden themselves, thereby immeasurably aiding UFO research and facilitating the work of therapists and investigators."[13] Similarly, in his introduction to

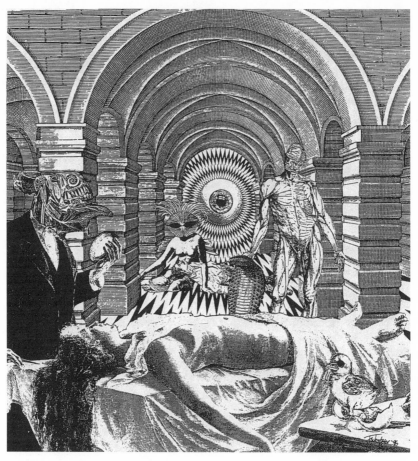

"Missing Fetus Syndrome." Jeffrey Westover writes, "This is the female version of 'On the Table.' A fetus, egg, is extracted from the female body and a hybrid offspring, the chick with black eyes, results." (Jeffrey S. Westover ©1997)

Katharina Wilson's *The Alien Jigsaw*, Hopkins lauds the "extraordinary bravery, intelligence, and strength possessed by very many abductees."[14] His language evokes the remarkable courage and talent usually admired in astronauts.

Although they inhabit a similar space, abductees lack the kind of support NASA put behind the Mercury and Apollo astronauts. Outside the protective gravity of MUFON and their various abductee groups, they enter alien televisual space untethered. In the cultural mainstream, in the televisual public sphere, these subcultural heroines play the sacrificial role of victims. When Ricki Lake featured abductees, their parents, and a blond, blue-eyed woman in silver shirt who claimed to be an alien, the audience was vociferous in its ridicule and condemnation. The abductees were repeatedly accused of lying, foolishness, and an inability to face reality. Making themselves vulnerable, publicly violating the boundaries of the real, they were roundly condemned. The heroism of the astronauts always involved their vulnerability in alien space, their willingness to venture beyond the already known.

Those few in Ricki Lake's audience who voiced support for the abductees tended to adopt a relativist "everyone is entitled to her own opinion" sort of language. From the position that only arrogance would lead one to deny the possibility of life on other planets, these defenders moved quickly to claim that, although they didn't really believe in abduction, they could understand if someone else did. Momentarily detouring into the protective field of personal uninvolvement, they nonetheless sought an epistemological compromise, one based on two quite reasonable suppositions. First, a supporter would posit that Earth is surely not the only planet that supports intelligent life. Second, she or he would claim that each person offers a unique perspective that should be respected. For the *Ricki* audience, as well as for many within the UFO community, and in fact most folks with whom I've gotten into casual discussions about aliens, the conviction that underlies and connects these two suppositions is one of humility. It's as if supportive members of the audience are asking themselves, "Who am I to judge?" They remind me of my Southern Baptist upbringing and folks' efforts to avoid backsliding into the sin of pride.

Controversial metaphysics aside, that the call to give abductees a hearing is constructed through an appeal to the unique value of each individual person gives abductees' public appearances a rather democratic and protestant character. Against a scientific priesthood, the individual is held up as an independent source of knowledge. Supporting abductees, or at least respecting their right to their opinions, appears to be radical, a way to resist (for a time) the dominance of scientific and governmental elites invested not simply in a particular determination of the real, but in set hierarchies for the production and validation of legitimate knowledge. Entertaining abduction becomes a momentary popular enactment of what it might mean actually to respect uniqueness and individuality. It is a performative rejection of the circumscription of permissible, public, reality. It's a rejection that ironically reiterates and claims as its own the terms of ideal discourse in a public sphere.

Rejecting reality has become possible because of the culturally widespread move toward inscribing knowledge onto that which is known primarily through experience. Various Marxists, feminists, and multiculturalists have stressed the importance of knowledge gained at the margins; the importance of the standpoint of the oppressed as epistemologically superior to the falsely disembodied, disconnected view from nowhere. There are myriad perspectives on the world, each with its own legitimate claim to truth. Critics of moral theories that rely on ideal role-taking or taking the position of another argue quite reasonably that doing so is impossible. One can never completely take the perspective of another person. At least once a week, sometimes twice, I hear someone say, "You can't understand if you don't know what I've been through." If I haven't been where they've been, seen what they've seen, dreamed what they've dreamed, I can't know what they know. And the claim goes further: neither can I *judge* what they know.

Some have viewed this tendency to refrain from judgment or to condemn the judges as irresponsible, depoliticizing, and morally lax. I agree that it quite probably is depoliticizing, but for different reasons. The issue isn't one of moral laxity but of epistemic confusion. Judgment, in the world of alien abduction and Ricki Lake, is wrong because it can't be defended; it is groundless. There isn't enough common reality to justify judgment. The differences in social and economic position, in historical privilege, in sex, ability, desire, in race, ethnicity, and language, in religion, belief, and philosophy, in ability, intelligence, and inclination, in information, knowledge, and access to technology that are called upon to be acknowledged, expressed, or respected point not only to differences in goals and values but to different experiences of the world, of the real. Possible standards, possible ways to choose among alternative accounts of reality are not readily available to the majority of contemporary dwellers in American society. We lack, in the compelling word/image offered by Thomas Dumm, "united states."[15]

The uncommonality of reality is not simply the result of global immigration and migration. It is more than an effect of the beginning of the end of some practices of repression and discrimination. For accompanying the shift to a stress on experience as a primary source of knowledge has been a technological reconfiguration of experience. Many Americans, especially but not only in the white middle class, see the contemporary world, the world of plane crashes, semiautomatic urban assault rifles, Chernobyl, and AIDS, as profoundly dangerous. Many think that we in America need safety and security; we need things to be under control. Of course, what counts as dangerous depends on the "we" one occupies. Some want gang-free neighborhoods; others want violence-free television. In New York State, children must wear helmets when riding bicycles. I know Texans who are still irate over seat-belt laws. Virtual reality, like Walt Disney World before it, appeals to the need for safe stimulation. Certain activities, like surfing or skiing, as the film director Iara Lee illustrates in her beautiful and provocative 1996 screen work *Synthetic Pleasures*, can come inside, into low-risk environments. If worried still about the dangers even of indoor surfing, I can continue inward and don the glove and goggles of a VR machine. Or I can cruise the Net. Again, the problem of judgment, one that seems profoundly depoliticizing, is that if the knowledge we need to make a judgment stems from shared experiences, what do we do when experiences are reconstituted so radically that we can't tell if we, or anyone else, actually has them or not? [16]

Most of us encounter this problem of judgment in various degrees in all sorts of different ways in our everyday life. Strangeness is familiar. If we see a video of a crime, do we see a crime? Does a photograph of an unspoiled rain forest signify that it is really spoiled? [17] If we suspect that our child was molested and then, after five hours of work with a therapist, the child says it happened, do we believe it? [18] How do we know whether oatmeal reduces cholesterol, whether aspirin helps prevent heart attacks, or exactly which tampons are connected with toxic-shock syndrome? In an essay on the need for critical investigations of televisual truth, Andrew Barry reminds us that "knowledge provides the means by which individuals should seek to govern their own activities — to act as informed liberal citizens." [19] My argument is that we in late-capitalist societies lack neither information — we're inundated with that — nor knowledge — that we also have. What we lack is the capacity to discern and distinguish, to use and deploy, to judge and evaluate the knowledges we need for ethical decisions and responsible political action. We don't know what's real. Repeatedly, as consumers, as citizens, as friends, as parents, we are put in a position of having to make choices based on technological assessments, health benefits, and interpretations of statistical data not only about which we know very little but which are also accompanied by opposing expert opinions.

Abductee TV ritualistically enacts the transgression and reinscription of reality, at least virtually. In an uncertain and technologically complicated world, a world of governmental cover-ups and political lies, of corporate-sponsored science and general policies of plausible deniability, the public sacrifice of those who testify to experiencing the alien helps to secure a bounded sense of order. At least something can be certain. Simultaneously, supporting abduction provides a critique of precisely this world where protectors harm and security is a threat. Voiced as a belief in the words of someone brave enough to speak in public, to violate the boundaries of permissible speech, the act of supporting abductees protests the official denial of precisely those lies, lapses, and limitations that are already constitutive of the everyday experience of social, political, and technocultural life in America at the millennium. And, in the very act of support, you get to be on TV.

Remote Control

Abductee TV reruns the space program NASA presented in the sixties and seventies. Its familiar chords are made up of the selfsame notes of space, technology, and politics that shaped official public imaginings of a space-age future. Of course (since I can't resist playing out the metaphor), the abductees sing a different tune. Unlike a space that could be explored, colonized, and conquered, a technology that, efficient, quantifiable, and perfectible, would provide the means, and a politics of freedom and democracy that would justify the ends, the space, technology, and politics of abduction are alien. The difference, filtered through the perspectives of abductees and astronauts, is about confidence, certainty, and control.

The space of abduction might seem to be the same space that astronauts started to explore in the 1960s. In fact, it is much more alien than the coordinated space NASA tried to conquer. Herself explored and colonized, the abductee isn't launched onto a certain trajectory to precise coordinates she can locate and identify. Betty Hill, one of the first public abductees, claimed to have been shown a map. Although it didn't tell her where she was, it seemed at least to give an origin to her abductors. A schoolteacher, Marjorie Fish, attempted to re-create this star-map with beads and string. After four years of work, she concluded that the aliens' home base was a planet circling the star Zeta Reticuli. Skeptical of these findings, Carl Sagan argued that any apparent pattern was the result of chance.[20] He used computers. She used string and styrofoam balls.

Most abductees don't get maps. Their ventures, when they remember them, are unlocatable, unguided. They don't know where they are or where they might be going. They don't know who or what is taking them. They don't even know if anything is actually happening to them at all. In an unknown place in an unknown space, the abductee's view only occasionally coincides with the clear and certain perspectives of astronauts, although some astronauts, Gordon Cooper and Deke Slayton, have seen UFOs.[21] More often than not, the abductee can only guess that what she sees is inside something, even though she may not be completely sure of what. Usually it's the inside of a laboratory, where, like an astronaut, she is an object for alien experiments.

This linking of outerspace, laboratory, and the domestic sphere occurred during the Mercury, Gemini, and Apollo space programs. As we have seen, readers of *Life* magazine were treated to detailed accounts and full-page photographs documenting the experiments and tests performed on the astronauts at various stages in the training and preparation. Readers knew about the sperm counts and rectal thermometers. At the same time, the magazine made a special effort to connect the space program with the more earthly concerns of its readers, especially of women.[22] To give a further example, in each of three articles devoted to Gordon Cooper's May 1963 flight of twenty-two orbits around the earth, *Life* includes photographs of Cooper's wife and information about the astronaut's life on Earth. The issue for May 24 features not only a large picture of a bare-chested Cooper with a thermometer in his mouth, but also pictures of his thirteen-year-old daughter Jan feeding her cat, his wife Trudy on the bed with Jan and a second daughter, Cam, and the headline "He Didn't Sound as if He'd Been Anywhere."[23] American technology is so good, *Life*'s headline implies, that going into space isn't like going anywhere at all. With the right technology, space is just like home.

Like the combination of outerspace and domestic space, the link to technology that abduction follows is already familiar from the early years of the space program. For astronauts, technology guarantees and reassures. It enables them to escape the confines of Earth; to adopt a view from above, a God's-eye view; to transcend the mundane. Technology is a vehicle that transports them into the future. For abductees, that future is here. Abductees realize that, like so many other promises, the promises of technology remain unfulfilled. Where are the flying cars? Not only is alien technology invasive and incomprehensible, but virtually all technology is alien. As the inverse of the helpful robotic gadgetry that sparkled in exhibitions lauding "households of the future," the technology that abductees experience is notable for the way it renders the familiar strange. When the server at the colleges where I teach crashes, or when my answering machine intersperses month-old messages with today's calls, I feel abducted by technology. Helping a friend retrieve lost data when her text file is suddenly five pages shorter than it should be, I suspect that others have this experience as well.

As she comes to an awareness of the alien presence in her life, Leah Haley hears "odd noises on the telephone." Describing the noises as "sometimes clicking sounds, sometimes other phones ringing in the background, sometimes music," she also perceives "a faint sound like a cassette tape winding slowly around a reel."[24] Her computer disks somehow end up re-arranged and out of order. Part of a file with a letter to her therapist, the abduction researcher John Carpenter, is erased. She reports: "I was frustrated over my inability to exercise control over these strange incidents that left me baffled as to their purpose."[25] In her new house, the security system fails to work properly. "The security company could find no explanation for the malfunction."[26] Like the doctors whose expertise nonetheless fails to account for her experiences of pain, so too the security company can't live up to its name. That which remains beyond the expert, that which is inexplicable, is alien. At one point Haley writes: "I could not understand how I had acquired this flu-like illness. To my knowledge, I had not been near anyone who was ill. . . . As I thought about my condition, I realized how easy it would be to eliminate someone merely by injecting germs or drugs."[27] Haley can't endure the gap left at knowledge's limits. She refuses, turning instead to alien possibilities or, just as likely, governmental violations, if history is to be believed. There must be an explanation for the lack of control, the insecurity, the helplessness she feels. After all, she is part of a society and has grown up in an America that promised us freedom, security, and opportunities, especially to hardworking, middle-class, Southern white women like Haley.

Limited explanations and technological failures disrupt the lives of Beth Collings and Anna Jamerson as well. Both in their early fifties, Collings is divorced, Jamerson single. Jamerson works for the U.S. Forest Service. She owns the horse-breeding farm where Collings works as a trainer and riding instructor. The "magic" of technology, its unpredictability, its failure to live up to their expectations, its inability to protect them, marks the alien reality in which they live.

Under incidents of electrical interference, Jamerson lists "street lights, copying machines and computers; power failures in our bedrooms (always between 3–4 A.M.); and light and televisions turning themselves on and off—even when unplugged."[28] In June 1992, during the Abduction Study Conference at MIT, they meet C. D. B. Bryan. A reporter from the *New Yorker*, Bryan writes about the conference and his interviews with Collings and Jamerson in *Close Encounters of the Fourth Kind*. In one section of her co-authored book, *Connections: Solving Our Alien Abduction Mystery*, Collings describes a series of problems with Bryan's tape recorder. His voice would be clear; her voice, and Jamerson's, faint, absent, or unintelligible, like "foreign language spoken backwards at high speed."[29] As long as she and Jamerson are in the room, the tape remains jammed in the machine. Once they leave, it pops free. While Bryan is out of the room, the two women chat with a reporter from the *Atlantic* who jumps in fright as the machine's cord snakes back and forth, entwining itself around a chair leg. Although convinced by the "intelligence, dedication, and sanity of most of the presenters" that abduction is not a joke, that "something very mysterious is going on," Bryan does not mention any of the problems with the tape recorder in his account of the interview.[30]

With the help of local UFO researchers, in the spring and summer of 1992 Collings and Jamerson install numerous surveillance devices in Collings's bedroom in an attempt to protect Collings from abduction or, that failing, at least to come up with actual evidence of the alien intrusions into their lives. One such device was a motion sensor that triggered an alarm and a desk lamp. Collings describes an evening when, reading in bed, she becomes suddenly alert. Although she had not yet connected the alarm, the light comes on, remains lit the requisite fifteen seconds, then goes out. Collings writes: "I had shrugged off that unsettling event, figuring that electronics, like magic, could not really be explained or fully understood; it was only as reliable as the electricity that sustained it. And the electrical circuitry in the house had already proved somewhat unreliable."[31]

Collings recounts events from previous months that she still could not explain. One night in March her television comes on, seemingly by itself. Collings unplugs the set. For good measure, she also unplugs a nearby lamp and moves it to a chair. She details her experience:

> I hadn't bothered understanding why the TV had turned itself on; it was just magic after all. But sometime during the early morning hours another magical manifestation disrupted my sleep. I awoke to find the room flooded with light from an unlikely source. Struggling to focus, I squinted into the glare. The light seemed to be emanating from the desk chair. . . . Then I remembered: I had put the lamp there earlier that evening after the TV incident — but I had unplugged it, hadn't I? I crawled out of bed in slow motion . . . reached down, and snapped off the light. . . . I don't recall groping my way back to bed. It's as if time just stopped with that singular, defiant action of switching off the light. Had these mysterious events been preludes to an abduction? Had I been switched off along with the light? Or was it just more electronic magic?[32]

Describing the night's events to Jamerson and "Bob," the UFO researcher, she moves from complaining about the electrical malfunctions to self-doubt; perhaps she had imagined the whole thing, or dreamt it. Regardless, the malfunctions continue, sometimes affecting Jamerson's room as well.

They step up the surveillance, installing an ever increasing battery of sensors and alarms. Of the Illuma Storm, a programmable lamp suggesting bottled lightning, Collings finds that she "questioned the device's reliability." The machine seems "faithful to its own obscure urges, no matter what stimuli might have otherwise activated it." Nonetheless, she is, at least initially, reassured by all the sophisticated equipment. "But," she writes, "one by one, toy by toy, I began to feel invaded by the very devices intended to provide me with comfort and peace of mind. My bedroom had begun to look like a Radio Shack warehouse — or an FBI experimental gadget lab."[33]

The gizmos never quite work (though Collings thinks they detect activity that might have gone unnoticed). They act up. She is abducted and they fail to go off. They end up unplugged. Collings wonders if she unplugs them in her sleep. Bob installs a video camera, but the Illuma Storm doesn't provide enough light and Beth has enough trouble sleeping as it is. Finally, feeling more invaded than comforted, and tired of the lack of privacy, Collings dismantles the sensors and alarms.

Describing events from the same period, Jamerson focuses on their "strange telephone service." She lists the following "anomalies": "We frequently have single rings on the line (I thought everyone got those), callers that refuse to identify themselves, calls where people refuse to talk, strange voices or humming on the line, and calls from purported government officials."[34] Jamerson first notices the problems with the telephone when she suspects that their phone is tapped. She begins keeping a log. They get a call "in an unintelligible language (tonal patterns interspersed with clicks)" and a caller who says only one thing — "*Don't*" — before hanging up. Someone will call on the business line, ask for a "nonexistent person," and then call the home line and ask for the same person. They are frightened by these "double calls," not least because the callers sometimes identify themselves as FBI or Secret Service. It's not that they believe the callers. Jamerson thinks that part of the purpose of the calls could be to make them paranoid: "Make people that say they have been abducted by aliens also tell of government interference, which of course would be denied, and thereby discredit everything they say as a product of a paranoid personality."[35] She admits that it was working.

Bob (supplier of the Illuma Storm and other gadgets) provides them with a Caller ID box, which Jamerson immediately finds frustrating since it identifies local numbers only and most calls to their farm have to be long-distance. Nonetheless, on July 17, 1992, she calls the phone company to have the Caller ID service connected. The operator who assists Jamerson informs her that, owing to a "special handling code," he can't change her service. He doesn't explain what a "special handling code" is. He does, however, tell her that because of this code her account can be accessed only with a password. Immediately thereafter, the operator reverses himself. This time he says that the special handling code is not on her account, but on one with the same phone number in a different area code. He then suggests that instead of having Caller ID installed, Jamerson should use *69 (a return-call feature). By pushing *69 on her phone, she could automatically call back the last person who rang her. When she explains that *69 doesn't work in her area, she is assured to the contrary. Jamerson is, not surprisingly, puzzled: "Why did he suggest I use *69 if 'special handling' really was only on the other number that matched mine in another area code? Caller ID did not work on my phone."[36]

The complexities tangled up with codes and Caller ID become still more intricate when Collings calls the phone company about the problem on July 20. A supervisor tells her that the "special handling codes" on the business and residence lines have been removed, so that Caller ID could be added, suggesting they would be reinstated after the change in service. When Collings asks to speak to the man who helped Jamerson the previous Friday, she is told that he is no longer with the phone company. On July 24 Jamerson calls again and is told that Caller ID had been hooked up on July 21. A supervisor informs her that there were no "special handling codes" on her account and never had been. Caller ID works, eventually.

Jamerson asks a friend who had worked at the phone company about the "special handling codes." She learns that it is a secret service, one that phone company employees aren't supposed to mention. Put on tapped telephone lines, these codes were available only to account holders or to "a government agency, with court approval." Jamerson tries to get help from staff members in the offices of her senator and representative, but "neither office felt it was something that they wanted to deal with."[37] And they still get harassing calls, such as one for Jamerson's dead grandfather and another for a Bob Luca, the name of the husband of abductee Betty Andreasson, someone they have heard of but don't know.

Like the technology that monitored the achievement of the astronauts, that which pervades the lives of abductees may be an extension of the eye, or ear, of the government. But unlike NASA's celebrated gadgetry — more precisely, *like* the widely reported faulty O-rings of the *Challenger*— most of the surveillance systems that abductees encounter don't work very well.

Not only is the practice of surveillance confusing, entangled in bureaucracies of contradiction, but the technology is strangely autonomous, having a mind and desire of its own. No one seems to understand it, really. No one, however confident, can completely control it. When it will work is unpredictable; although, eventually, it will—somewhat like abductions themselves.

Or could it be that the very inadequacies in the surrounding technology, in the practices of surveillance, are deliberate? After all, for decades, Americans have been promised that the power of the atom is at their disposal (although those reassured by such promises may well be a small, demographically select group). Perhaps, then, technology does work, if not for us. Jamerson concludes her account of the telephone problems:

> What I don't understand about all of this is why these guys are so inept. If they wanted to monitor our phone calls, why did they make it so obvious? Our technology is advanced enough that I need never have suspected the phones were being monitored. Why did they bungle it so? They wanted us to know. Why? *Big Brother* is watching? My message to them is, "Why don't you come by and protect Beth from being abducted? Don't just sit on the sidelines and watch and listen. Help us!"[38]

Collings and Jamerson suggest a relationship to technology that is always antagonistic, alien. Despite their best efforts, it will not work in their favor; something will malfunction, come unplugged, short-circuit. It won't help them. Technology, connected to the government and the phone company (or are they connected through it?), intervenes in abducted lives on behalf of interests alien to their own. Errors are only seeming. Closer scrutiny reveals a control underneath a carefully fabricated mistake. But it is a control rarely exercised in the ways we've been promised. Unable (perhaps unwilling) to help, it remains a remote control enabling the watchers to stay informed even when, especially when, they don't get involved.

Get the Message

Abductee politics and the perspective abduction provides on American government and politics at the millennium seems to have little to do with freedom and democracy. Unlike the space programs produced by NASA, this phenomenon makes no attempt to embody a particularly American ideal of freedom. Yet, precisely because some of the abductees were credible witnesses, precisely because they were part of the audience for the televisual demonstration of the greatness of American freedom and technology, precisely because they believed the promises made in the image of Apollo, their incredible stories bear their own kind of witness to some of the meanings freedom has in America today. Leah Haley writes: "I had always been proud to be an American — to live in a place where I was free and to feel protected by our armed forces. Yet, the very people I thought were supposed to protect and defend me had treated me like a prisoner of war."[39]

Although the government stands behind technology, its interventions subvert rather than attest to the ideals it voices, or at least so it seems in abductee politics. If it watched the astronauts in order to protect them, the government watches abductees while doing nothing to secure their safety. Just as the government, or at least its agents and agencies, knew the astronauts by name, so does it know the abductees. It monitors them, singly, in their everyday lives and activities. Someone, perhaps funded through black budgets and traveling in black helicopters, is there, watching. Abductees always feel a personal connection to the government because it *knows*; they have a sense of immediate and tangible involvement in the political affairs, in the politics that matter in today's America. If the government's complex systems of surveillance helped bring news of space travel to the general public, similarly complex systems cover up the truth of abduction, forcing it into secret crevices accessible only through conspiracy theory.

Karla Turner, a Ph.D. in English who, before her death from cancer, wrote several books about her abduction experiences, those of her family, and those of other women — considers the possibility that the government has actively consented to alien abduction.[40] In *Into the Fringe* she repeats a widely circulated rumor of an alliance between the United States and the aliens, an alliance that has since crumbled, bringing on the imminent possibility of a mass confrontation. To prepare, the government is pursuing a two-pronged strategy. The first relies on the development of super-weaponry "capable of defending us against alien technology."[41] (Some in the UFO community thought that the "Star Wars" defense plan [Strategic Defense Initiative] was a response to the alien, not the Soviet, threat.) The second prong involves public education about the aliens' approach, pursued through the media. Turner reports the rumor as saying that "the aliens who are here now are just the forerunners for a much larger group, and that group's arrival is expected within the next four years. The government hopes to avoid worldwide panic by preparing us through advertising and entertainment media for our encounter with alien beings."[42]

Turner and her family carry out investigations designed to establish whether there is any truth to the rumor. They find that, just as predicted, *E.T.* and other alien-friendly movies appeared during the period of alliance, part of an effort to get Americans to feel affection for aliens. After relations between the aliens and the U.S. government soured, so did the media treatment of aliens. Turner reports:

> When the rift took place — a shoot out of sorts at an underground base, in which the humans got the worst of it all — the government attitude changed, and we were presented with malevolent reptilian aliens in the miniseries "V." And now we had a new series, "War of the Worlds," which we watched anxiously each week. In every episode, we saw some fact or detail which we recognized from actual cases, mixed in with the more creative aspects of the show, and as we watched we did feel as if a deliberate effort were being made to acquaint the public with at least part of the truth.[43]

For Turner and her family, the truth television reveals is encrypted. Hidden in images, under advertisements, through tales of fantasy and horror, are political truths that the government wants us to know. The government is trying to tell us something. It sends messages to us through television.

During the space program, the government sent open messages via its vast, staged spectacles. Now television tells us about our world in ways that have to be discerned, interpreted. Presumed fictions may be facts. Uncontested facts are actually fictions. Not everyone will get the message, not everyone will receive the address. NASA produced the space scenes that appeared on television sets throughout the country and around the world. Now the government stands behind the production of space images popularized in movies and miniseries. These televisual hailings, however, don't call a public of citizens into being. Rather, they interpellate a variety of smaller networks, networks of those who know, of those who may suspect, even of those whose docility is necessary for the new world order.

Of course, Turner does not think that everything she sees on television is true. She just doesn't know what is true, what is rumor, what rumors are true, and what truths are rumors. Not knowing, she allows for possibilities that previously she would have ridiculed; "the government's deal with aliens, the underground installations with vats of human body parts and prenatal nurseries of stolen fetuses."[44] As she researches the stories for herself, she becomes ever more confused, discovering that the various truths and rumors conflict, contradicting one another and themselves. She tries to fight off "feelings of anger and fear and disorientation," telling herself that "humans can lie, and so can aliens." But this doesn't really help, since she still doesn't know whom to believe, whom to trust, and when. At the conference at MIT, researcher Richard Boylan asked the audience if they trusted the aliens more than the military. A chorus of yeses answered him.[45]

In *The Alien Jigsaw*, abductee Katharina Wilson dismisses the possibility that the aliens are simply spreading disinformation, trying to deceive abductees and undermine support for the American government. Sensibly pointing out that public trust in the government is already at an all-time low, she reminds those who might attribute this sort of tactic to the aliens that "one major lesson we learned during the Reagan and Bush administrations was that white-collar crime pays, and extremely well. Do we really need the aliens telling us something we already know? I do not believe so."[46] Wilson extends Turner's suspicions, concluding that, if her own experiences are any evidence, the government and the military, or at least covert groups within the government and military, are deeply involved with the aliens. The American government works with aliens. It helps them. It stands behind the secret experimentation on citizens against their will.

Wilson urges ufologists and other researchers to take up the matter or risk "inviting the possibility of another holocaust upon those they consider to be different." Elaborating on the link between abduction and the Holocaust, she writes:

> Even though the German citizens were told what was happening to the Jews, Poles, Gypsies, the mentally ill, and whoever else the Nazi regime found inferior, they could not believe the information. Their minds simply would not allow them to accept the idea that their government could be responsible for such atrocities. Do not discount what I and other abductees are reporting simply because your mind will not allow you to believe there is a connection between some members of our government and some of the aliens. Do not discount what I am reporting because you automatically lump all such information into your government conspiracy category. I am not a government agent disseminating disinformation. . . . I have to remain open to the idea, although it is *extremely* difficult for me, that our government may in fact be trading alien technology for genetic material, or at least is aware of what is being done to us and has chosen to look the other way.[47]

In Wilson's abduction experience, UFOs and the U.S. government are linked together. They are linked together as tightly as NASA and astronauts and the success of American political vision and American technological know-how. The price of technology is the essence of American citizens, what makes them human, different, their DNA. For Wilson, it makes sense to think that the U.S. government values technology more than it values the bodies of its citizens. Distinguishing her beliefs from conspiracy theory, Wilson turns to history as a warning, as an example. We have already lived the unimaginable, the alien. We have already seen the government experiment on its citizens. We have already heard it lie. For Wilson, the alien and unimaginable and the historical reality of holocaust are not so very different from government itself. She can't tell which memories are alien and which are political, governmental: "Who is to say these were alien-related experiences? Who is to say someone from a secret government agency did not come into my home, drug me, abduct me, hypnotize me, and then fill in the gaps with their own screen memory?"[48]

Wilson provides warnings. She doesn't offer any answers, solutions, or predictions. Predictions have failed to come true. Solutions have failed. Answers have been misleading, have led to more questions. Perhaps because she equates and elides Holocaust, government, and aliens, she doesn't present her writing as an attempt to persuade people to think differently about abduction and UFOs. Argument, thought by some to be an important part of the process of democracy, is futile, perhaps because democracy can bring about Holocaust, perhaps because democracy doesn't mean anything when government is alien. Wilson feels herself to be profoundly outside and other, the product of experiences few share and most ridicule. She writes: "People have to reach their own conclusions about the UFO phenomenon. All I can do is report what I remember."[49] One can heed her report, take note of her warnings, but not much else. It isn't exactly that she is hopeless; rather, it's that it isn't clear what hope can mean when understanding is closely linked to the unthinkable. It isn't clear what hope is when any memory may be a screen, when few experiences can be known at all.

Unlike the space programs brought to us by NASA, those depicted by abductees produce a different constellation of space, technology, and government. When women go to outerspace in the 1990s, they are taken, not launched. Consequently, their stories are much more attuned to the alien possibilities of technology, watching, and political authority. Technology doesn't work in the ways they expect. Governmental practices of surveillance are less principled and more covert. Authority is rarely exercised to enhance the rights and freedoms of those who lack it. But like Burger King commercials featuring theme music from *I Dream of Jeanie* or ads for America OnLine that use music from the space-age cartoon *The Jetsons*, there is something familiar about the background assumptions in abductees' accounts of their connection to outerspace. Both employ the link between space, laboratories, and the domestic. Both presume a governmental interest in space; that is, a construction of space as a field for political contestation and even for potential cooperation. Both presume that the government watches what happens in space. In fact, very much like *I Dream of Jeanie* and *The Jetsons*, the familiarity of the motifs played out in abduction has a lot to do with television and with the ways technology makes watching at a distance possible. The government uses television to broadcast its version of the theatrics of space; this fact of life in the space program is articulated in a potentially paranoid register in abduction. Anything and everything we see on television might mean something else, might contain or release alien information. Since we can't know for sure, we better stay tuned.

Real Virtuality

Abductees and astronauts are linked but, as with any links, there are gaps between them. The analogy isn't perfect. Abductees' experiences exceed ordered astronaut missions. Leah Haley, for example, receives mental flashes. One evening while praying and meditating, she was told to read "page 29." She didn't know what book was meant or who gave her the instructions. Nonetheless, she concentrated and began to make out a few words, words she confirmed by writing down a message as it was transmitted to her telepathically.[50] The message was apocalyptic: Earth will be destroyed, and chosen members of the family of God will be transported from Earth to another universe. Haley also learned that the aliens are storing information in people. Anna Jamerson discovered that what she thought was a memory of being raped by her father was actually a screen memory hiding an abduction. She knows that most people would assume that abduction is the screen, but she still blames the aliens for ruining her relationship with her family. In *Connections* she includes transcriptions from a hypnosis session in which an entity named Sonna seems to speak through her. Jamerson doesn't know whether she is channeling the information or whether it is part of her subconscious.

Beth Collings saw a naked man in an enormous white cowboy hat. This (as well as an experience with a giant bee) she interpreted as most likely of an alien nature. Karla Turner's husband has a prebirth memory of being made by aliens. Turner herself mentions two people she knows who have seen aliens disguised as hillbillies. Katharina Wilson had an experience with an alien masquerading as Al Gore. She feels that abduction has helped her become more in tune with the suffering of animals, and she welcomes the expansion in consciousness. Not all of her experiences have been negative.

These are just a few examples from the lives of abductees that unsettle the analogy with astronauts, the abduction narrative itself, and the lives of the very women who recall them. Knowing that these memories don't fit, that they seem ridiculous, the abductees still claim them. They hold on to their experiences, resisting the efforts of interpreters to compile them into coherence.

Given the investment the abductees have in their experiences, the cost of hypnosis and the time of writing, ownership of what makes their specific experiences unique might be empowering. It might attest to the abductees' creativity or to their contribution to UFO research. Many are stimulated to write poetry, paint, or sculpt. Abductees have contributed to the recently organized Abductees Art Project. On the World Wide Web you can listen to music composed following an abduction. Beth Collings told me, however, that there was nothing creative about abduction, that she had been writing long before the phenomenon intruded into her daily life. Simultaneous with an empowering experience of contact, then, may be the sense of loss: whatever happens is always under alien control. Put somewhat differently, it is the fact of unintelligibility, the fact that aspects of the experience cannot be incorporated into a coherent narrative, that proves how really alien it all is. These excessive details testify to abduction.

Abduction researchers Budd Hopkins and David Jacobs generally leave out the more bizarre and idiosyncratic dimensions. They focus on the breeding project, on the theft of egg and sperm and the production of a hybrid species. Usually this is the story that gets picked up by mainstream media, that scripts a "movie of the week." In contrast, Harvard psychiatrist John Mack stresses the transcendent dimensions of abduction. He invests a narrative of ecological redemption in abductees' stories. I read abduction as the dark underside of official space, as a return of the repressed dimensions of astronaut heroics. Abductees express a lack of agency, a lack of control that doesn't hide behind the illusion that one might steer a Saturn V rocket. The confusion and fear throughout their accounts evoke a nostalgic longing for a future we seem to have abandoned. We don't explore space anymore. Some of us never did. We aren't on any star trek. We just stay where we are, consuming fantasies and virtual realities. That women in their homes, sometimes wives, give voice to the pain of loss even of a myth of adventure doesn't surprise me. But of course their stories give voice to more. They bear witness to a lack of control, insecurity, and violation, to a lack of response from those who are supposed to protect and care.

Stories of abduction attest to the sense that we aren't going anywhere. Things are coming and happening to us. This interpretation of abduction doesn't diagnose or psychologize the abductees; it reads them, but it doesn't engage them. Abductees want to know what is happening to them. They want control over their lives, control they connect in part with the retrieval of memories. In this respect, their orientation to the trauma in their lives and their sense that remembering is necessary for healing connects them with the survivor movement.[51] In an essay on sexual abuse of children, Helen Daniels observes that "survivor narratives can potentially change what constitutes truth in our culture."[52] I agree. But what might that hold for our close encounters with one another? For occasions when we need collective decisions? What might it mean for us when conflicting conceptions of the true and the real come into contact with one another, when we cross the streams and when worlds collide?

The notion that abduction provides a cultural expression of the confused passivity accompanying the collapse of the real is not the interpretation offered by abduction researchers, but it doesn't contradict their claims. It doesn't contradict them because it doesn't debate them; it doesn't take a position on the truth of the claims to abduction. Abduction researchers want to establish the legitimacy of their findings. Indeed, their efforts are one location in contemporary culture where truth *is* contested. They try to describe the phenomena scientifically. The researchers look for patterns, commonalities, systematicity. They want a comprehensible narrative.[53] Often they supplement their interpretations with larger explanations for why aliens would abduct people. The "breeding project" and "ecological awareness" are the two most prominent alternatives.

My reading asks why abduction is a familiar theme in popular culture. The answer, as I've been arguing, involves the theatrics of space produced by NASA, the shift from outerspace to cyberspace, and the widespread crisis of truth as we begin dealing with the real virtualities of the information age. These three lines intersect to create a site capable of being occupied by reports of abduction. They establish an environment where stories of abduction can flourish, can get attention and become noticed as making claims to truth. What they don't do is explain abduction reports per se.

Another reason why my interpretation of alien abduction shouldn't be read as conflicting with those from inside the community concerns ufology and the abduction discourse in general. The researchers disagree with one another. Even here there is not one view, one interpretation, one answer, one bounded whole. Hopkins's and Jacobs's assessments of the aliens' intentions are more negative than Mack's. But although these researchers highlight different aspects of the experience, they all agree that it is complex, unbelievable, varied and, at least at present, undecidable. They agree

that the intricacies of alien theatrics, memories recovered through hypnosis, and governmental conspiracy can contribute to a situation in which reality itself, as Karla Turney says, *isn't*. They agree that heretofore conven-
tionally and scientifically accepted assumptions for reality cannot account
for the experiences claimed and remembered by abductees. Unlike the abduction researchers, I stress these ambiguities and tensions. My reading of
abduction, then, is a metareading.

Judgment is not certainty. It always involves elements of risk, of ambiguity. Yet the presumption has been that citizens and voters and viewers
and witnesses can make defensible judgments, that there are criteria according to which people can make reasonable decisions about the practices
that affect them in the world. The criteria to which we've become accustomed, however, are no longer convincing. What we see on television isn't
news, it's entertainment. What is news is produced to serve particular political or economic interests, interests we may not share. Technological devices might help, but I'm not sure how to work them, how reliable they are,
which ones are better, and what exactly they can discover. Should I trust
my doctor? My insurance company? Pharmaceutical manufacturers? In his
compelling analysis of the effects of epidemiology on contemporary American medicine, Jonathan B. Imber writes: "'Informed consent' is the professional safeguard designed to protect everyone but the patient from what
cannot be known until the risk is taken."[54] I'm more than a demographic
moment, and I don't want to reduce my life, my experience, or my body
parts to actuarial tabulations or Vegas odds.

Abduction, especially through the ubiquity of the alien icon, provides a
window through which we grasp sharply the incredibility of the criteria for
judgment. It iterates out questioning and curious relationship to the experience of our bodies. It reminds us that feelings, even symptoms, aren't de-
terminate but can point in multiple possible directions: What can it mean
for women to claim that they have felt and seen on their bodies evidence of
alien experiments? Abduction replicates our suspicious acceptance and,
indeed, enjoyment of technology and our allegedly scientific ways of interpreting the world: What is evidence? Why are there no sensible explanations for abduction? What does sensible mean? It reinscribes our critical
attitude toward experts: Do we trust someone from Harvard? Do we trust
experts who are funded by large corporations or by the government? Abduction pushes these questions into our awareness — but usually safely,
given the stigma attached to UFOs and UFO belief. Regardless of our individual beliefs, though, the questions are already there. They appear in
myriad forms and places throughout the networked interactions of con-

temporary global technoculture. Since the sixties the relationship of everyday folks to knowledge and information has changed. This is the new condition of democracy.

Unlike the astronauts, then, whose cultural position was predicated on the privilege of an uncontested claim to reality, a claim buttressed by science, government, and media willing to follow the scripts NASA provided, abductees experience fundamental uncertainty. Because this is the uncertainty of contemporary America, they have come to occupy an important site in cultural space. Abduction narratives, memories, and experiences are fragmented and undecidable. Like others in America, abductees try to find havens of credibility. Some abductees look to the conventions of the existing narratives. I spoke with an abductee from El Paso who described her experiences as "like what the rest of them say" and "Just like all the rest." Yet her written memories involve being eaten by dinosaurs and given a new body by aliens. Some abductees rely on the words of the researchers. Testimonial writings are almost always prefaced — authorized — by big names like Mack, Hopkins, Carpenter, or other ufological insiders who, whatever their intentions, preinterpret the writings that follow. Only Karla Turner was authorized by a woman, the researcher Linda Moulton Howe.[55]

Abductees struggle for credibility as they appeal to readers' open-mindedness, sympathy, or presumed assumptions. Without a countdown to announce when they are launched into out-of-this-world encounters, abductees try to find bases for their claims. But because their experiences conflict with the very heart of consensus reality, any grounds they find dissolve into false assumptions, into something that a skeptic will dismiss as a naive understanding of science or a misunderstanding of the nature of memory. Their efforts to defend or protect themselves become further manifestations of the virtuality of contemporary reality. We repeat this experience daily.

4
I Want to Believe

Leather Certainties

In March 1991 Leah Haley had her first hypnosis sessions with John Carpenter. A licensed clinical social worker from Springfield, Missouri, Carpenter has hypnotized or counseled more than a hundred people who think they may have been abducted by aliens. He participates actively in MUFON symposia and regularly shares his findings with the UFO community. At the 1992 Abduction Study Conference at MIT, Carpenter presented some of the evidence for multiply witnessed abductions, the interventions of some non-Gray types of aliens, the "Nordics" and the "Reptilians," and the reliability of hypnosis as a means of recovering lost memory.[1] Carpenter's videos are available for $29.95.

By the summer of 1996, Haley was at the MUFON annual meeting in Greensboro, North Carolina, autographing copies of her full-color children's book, *Ceto's New Friends*. During most of the conference she worked at the book exhibit, at the table for Greenleaf Publications. The Greenleaf catalog announces that Haley, "the most credible of all abductees," is available for speeches. While browsing through the alien mouse pads and crop circle art, I overheard some conference participants whispering about Haley's being in a saucer when the government shot it down.

Haley sets down her memories of alien and governmental interventions in her life in *Lost Was the Key*.[2] She fixes July 7, 1990, as the date when her world "started to crumble." That weekend, her brother tells her about a book he read by Budd Hopkins. Haley tells him about a dream of being in a spaceship on a platform surrounded by little creatures with large black eyes. Her brother mentions that the subject of Hopkins's book, *Intruders*, had a place in her yard where the grass wouldn't grow. Haley says that the yard of her previous home had a similar spot. Drawing from Hopkins, Haley's brother asks her if she'd ever had any strange illnesses. She answers that around the time of the spaceship dream she went to the hospital for tests because of pain and burning in her kidneys, bladder, and urinary tract. Haley explains: "The doctor couldn't find anything wrong, so he told me my problem must be caused by stress. Several months later, I concluded by trial and error that spicy food was causing the problem."[3] She also mentions pain in her ear. She attributes it to an allergy to copy-machine ink. When her brother asks whether the doctor agreed, Haley replies that he didn't, adding: "The doctor couldn't find anything at all wrong with me, so he said it must be stress. Doctors are such jerks. Why can't they admit they don't know what the problem is instead of telling people it's just stress."[4] Haley and her brother talk about seeing a UFO as children.

After that weekend, Haley considers writing to Budd Hopkins in New York, but puts it off for a little over a month. Her explanation for waiting contributes to the impression that she finds, or wants to find, the whole thing "nonsense." She insists her dream was just a dream. But she isn't completely sure. She covers over her doubt, at the same time inviting the knowing nod from readers who have heard this story before, who already recognize denial as a symptom, as proof: "It had to have been [a dream]."[5]

Accepting abduction, acknowledging alien interference in their lives is, for most abductees, a painful and time-consuming process. Their books, offered as testimonies to their experience, frequently begin like Haley's with an apocalyptic evocation of the day when the world, or reality, stopped. In painstaking detail, they document not just the evidence of abduction but the process of becoming abductees, of coming to think about their lives, experiences, and memories in ways most of them would have dismissed or

"Incubation." Jeffrey Westover writes, "A prime component of the abduction experience from a female perspective is the impregnation and the removal of a hybrid child. The child is then put in a boxlike incubation chamber." (Jeffrey S. Westover ©1997)

laughed at had it not happened to them. Anna Jamerson writes: "I accept and reject their existence daily. I can believe in them when I know I have been abducted the night before, but that only lasts for a few weeks. When they become inactive for a month or so, I'm sure I made all this stuff up. I go back to denying that they are really abducting me. . . . Beth calls it my denial phase. I go through it continuously it seems."[6] For many abductees the struggle over the real never ceases.

The preoccupations of everyday life themselves become signs of evasion, indicating to those who know (who suspect) that one is refusing to acknowledge and to deal with abduction. That Haley teaches accounting full-time, is working on a master's degree, has a husband who works out of town "most of the time," is raising two daughters virtually alone, and is getting ready to begin construction on a new home, that all this takes priority is symptomatic of abduction. Haley is displacing her anxieties over the truth onto the everyday parts of her life. Her absorption in these very mundane, time-consuming activities seems — again, to those who know, who have been there — part of an effort to avoid facing the possibility that, in the words of abductee Karla Turner, "reality isn't."[7]

After writing two letters to Hopkins, Haley receives an information kit from his abductee research and support organization, the Intruders Foundation. A note refers her to John Carpenter, who, in Missouri, is closer than Hopkins to Haley, who lives in northern Alabama.[8] Her brother accompanies her on the ten-hour drive to Springfield.

When they see a man with a lounge chair and sleeping bag heading into the office where they've been told to wait, Haley doesn't want to believe that it's Carpenter. "A person undergoing hypnosis is supposed to have a leather couch!"[9] She's disappointed after her brother confirms that the sleeping bag man had, in fact, gone into Carpenter's office. "Oh great," she winces, "Here I've come over four hundred miles to be hypnotized by a man who doesn't even have a couch."[10]

Later, Haley tries to see the therapist's and his assistant's evident concern as compensation. "While I was gone to the rest room, I thought how nice it was to have someone considerate of my needs for a change," she writes. "At home I was always the one who had to take care of everyone else's needs. I decided I liked John and Grace. They were professional, friendly, and easy to talk to. Maybe it wasn't so important to have a couch to lie on after all."[11]

Maybe the comfort of a lounge chair, a sleeping bag, and of caring, responsive people responding can assuage a variety of doubts. And if they can't, if the legitimacy of leather and the authority of an analyst's couch sustain a truth and an experience of truth not available to everyone, perhaps it's better then to work through the doubts, to give sleeping bags a chance. Perhaps it is better to let the doubts in rather than blanket them under "stress." Perhaps it is better to forfeit the privilege of leather, especially if one suspects it of signifying more privilege than knowledge, more the presumption of owning than the hunger for truth. Unlike the doctors who present her with answers, Carpenter works with Haley to ask new questions. Haley recognizes the comfortable security doctors provide: she looked to them first. But what she discovers is that leather is more a status symbol than a sign of understanding. Leather suggests the confidence and certainty that accompanies the truths some use to explain, diagnose, and dismiss the lives of others. Maybe the leather couch is there to catch those exhausted by the effort of fighting for the truth of their experiences.

At first, Haley talks and Carpenter listens, attentive and respectful. Haley describes the time she and her brother saw the UFO. She relates the dream about being in a spaceship and the allergy to copy-machine ink. She mentions problems with the security system in her home, anxieties stemming from headlights reflected in her rearview mirror, and noises seemingly coming from her game room. Haley documents the extent of the inexplicable in her everyday life. She recalls a time when she saw two men in a restaurant, men she thought were watching her. She tells of a strange young man in her office who she feared would rape her.

In the first hypnosis session, Haley recovers the details of her childhood sighting. Searching in the woods for the UFO, which appeared to have landed, she comes across a hairless, chalky-colored creature with large black eyes. A beam of bright light approaches her. She sees a round, silver object hovering in the clearing. Lying on a platform aboard the craft, she discovers that she is naked, that additional creatures surround her, that they are poking her arms and legs with a needlelike instrument.

During her second session, Haley remembers a night when her teenage daughters were toddlers. Having felt an urge to go outside, she finds herself standing in the middle of the yard, looking at a spaceship and a beam of light. Aboard the spaceship, creatures perform "gynecological procedures" on her and "lab tests." She feels a piercing sensation as if something were being inserted behind and inside her right ear.

Later she watches videotapes of two women who retrieve abduction experiences through hypnosis. Haley explains: "I sensed that John wanted me to see the videotapes so I would accept the reality of the abduction experiences and admit that I had indeed been hypnotized." [12] As the video hails her, she is struck by the similarities between her hypnosis experience and what she sees on tape. She wonders if the sameness is a sign of reality, if it means that she remembered something real. She's troubled by the possibility. "I usually slept in nothing but panties and socks," Haley writes. "Maybe, while practically naked, I had been seen by someone as I was being beamed aboard a spaceship. The thought embarrassed me."[13]

Back at home, she tries to let it all go, at least for a while. Indeed, as she describes the preoccupations of her daily life, the very commonality, typicality, familiarity of her depiction of domestic life starts quickly to fill in the ruptures, the cracks in reality, effected by abduction. How can someone so normal have been through something so strange? Oddly, though, when Haley's writing links these preoccupations to aliens and spaceships, the everyday familiarities themselves change. What is it, then, that lies beneath the seemingly normal? Haley's accounts of going to work or talking to friends become subroutines of normality stuck in an alien program. Her efforts to get a bit of control over the data recovered in hypnosis, to explain them, integrate them, especially if one reads these data as fundamentally inassimilable, add to the overall sense of strangeness and fragmentation. Her efforts to explain, like the effort to use the languages of science and law so long a part of ufology's production of credible witnesses, link the alien with that which disavows it. After the trip to Springfield, Haley's husband buys her two new nightgowns.

High Strangeness

In the preceding chapter, I point out the ways abductees are like astronauts, how they occupy a similar cultural location and represent a return of some of the repressed dimensions of the 1960s, NASA-constructed astronaut. Installed at the domestic intersection of technology, televisuality, and space, abductees not only tell the stories of space coming home, but in that telling they bring out the paradoxes of credibility in the techno-global infotainment age. In this chapter, I'm interested in the shift from astronauts to abduction and the change that shift represents. For even though abductees occupy a site that developed in the sixties, abduction is a story of the nineties. Its twists and turns and wild connections evoke the new space of exploration — cyberia.

Like the astronaut, the abductee cannot be reduced to one side of a simple binary opposition along the lines of, say, pilot and passenger, male and female, hero and victim. Abductees, especially those whose testimonies I've been describing, are not passive victims. They are the authors of their stories, the writers of their own scripts in the theatrics of space. In *Lost Was the Key*, Haley recounts her experiences in a narrative of discovery, not just of her self and her past, but of her place in a governmental conspiracy of national significance. She casts herself in a heroic, active role. NASA scripted the astronaut identity. Even those abductees who have yet to write books are often likely to write their lives, to testify to what they've experienced, to produce and share the knowledge of abduction. Many turn to the Internet to provide audiences, information, and sites for self-presentation. Like those who have appeared on *Ricki* and other talk shows, many feel called to come forward, perhaps to challenge the government or to wake up the rest of us to what is happening in this country, and in this world.

Wild daytime talk shows like *Ricki* became possible in 1987, the year *Geraldo* got started, the year television became less regulated.[14] The proliferation of such shows, the unconventionality of their themes, and their morph into spectacle are linked to more, however, than the rise of the "public abductee." The rise of the talk show also parallels the growth of the Internet, both in time and in the paranoid reactions each evokes in its critics. Each has become a space for a newly marketed and marketable mass fringe rather than for an officially sanctioned and sanctified culture.[15] This is simultaneously their primary attraction and major threat. Each features sex, lots of sex, in a variety of shapes and forms. Each provides a major forum for alien talk. It's as if the alien-human hybrids are the offspring of all the virtual sex pulsing through trash TV, the Internet, and one-nine-hundred numbers.

Abductee televisuality is thus not strictly analogous to that of astronauts. Rather, it links up with and depends on the very technological transformations it thematizes. If astronauts can be linked with mainframes, rocket scientists, and big-budget, big-government programs, abductees are part of a more populist technoculture of globally networked PCs. Their reports, their experiences — the contradictory, paranoid, fantastic, fragmented, overlapping, interconnecting, alien content they provide — enact modes of being human on a technological, televisual, virtual Earth. On the Web, one site, one link, is as plausible as any other. "News" is as likely to be found at disinformation.com as it is at CNN.org. In abduction, a scratch is as likely to connote an alien encounter as it is a not-yet-removed staple from a dry-cleaning tag. The "truth" depends on the network within which the information is situated or produced. We in America are interested in abduction because we make the same sorts of links, just within different networks. The fact that abduction accesses the stresses and excesses of millennial technoculture doesn't get to the truth of abduction (as if getting to truth were still a possibility), but it does suggest why American popular culture over the past ten years has become an increasingly alien space. Fabricated in the context of a postwar American articulation of space, technology, and government, abduction reports express contemporary tensions around truth and trust. The seeming incoherence of abduction reports (or, in the UFO community's artful term, the "high strangeness" of their cases) is an iconic display of the dilemma of truth in the information age.

The presentation of this incoherence, this strangeness, in abductees' writings reiterates the problem of reality that we all face. Movie stills reappear as illustrations in magazine articles that purport to be factual. A graphic produced for a Web site becomes evidence in print media for the reality of that which it depicts. Resemblance to a scene from the movie *Communion* is offered to support a claim to truth. A prop for a film becomes an exhibit in a museum and subject to autopsy. That a person has appeared on television is evidence of sincerity and importance. Information circulates through and interconnects nearly all commercially available media — books, magazines, television, video, movies, newspapers, tabloids, tapes, and the Internet — and each cross-references and legitimizes the other, the alien. Am I describing the UFO community or a technocultural, media-driven, networked America at the millennium?

Like the space program, the Internet has Cold War origins. Like the CIA, ufology considers 1947 an originary date. As the aliens came home — became personal — so did computers. Initially products of military and defense interest in a rapid and decentralized information flow, networked computers had spread by the early seventies to major universities like Harvard and MIT.[16] The creation of message networks like Usenet in 1979 and FidoNet in 1983 enabled home computers to send and receive messages virtually anywhere in the world. The latter let users set up bulletin board systems (BBSs). For the first time, people from outside government, academia, and the computer industry could gather together without having to be physically present. They could congregate and not be charged with loitering.

By the early nineties, commercial on-line services achieved a visible market presence. "Surfing" the Net became less an activity of hackers, nerds, and cybergeeks; "going on-line" became part of everyday life. But not everyone who's wired "surfs," not anymore. Surfing, a cool sport inaccessible to most, might have represented an earlier cyberculture. Today the metaphor doesn't match with the experience: the download time of complex graphics quickly dispels the illusion of speed and air. Ads for Lotus remind us that we can "work" the Net.

In 1996 the number of World Wide Web users reached 35 million, doubling the estimate from 1995.[17] Although middle-class white men between the ages of eighteen and fifty-four continue to exert a dominant presence on the Net, this is changing as corporations and consumers move in. It's difficult to escape the Internet: movies and television shows flash their URLs; Disney relies on the Net to promote *Hercules*; network news invites viewers to visit their home pages; the supermarket near my house announces that specials are advertised on its Web site. Even those without a computer must confront the technological invasion. Even those without computers experience their effects. Meanwhile, aliens from UFOs invade popular culture, and daytime talk shows reproduce like mad.

Because of the Internet, abductee televisuality is not simply a down-to-earth low-budget, 1990s substitute for the astronaut spectacle of the 1960s. It is more participatory and accessible. It is less coherent. Indeed, the discourse can easily adapt to and represent the protean character of the Net because it is itself structured as the product of an ever changing variety of voices in conversation. Abductees read Hopkins, Jacobs, and Mack. Hopkins, Jacobs, and Mack get the material for their books by working with and hypnotizing abductees. Each individual case, each experience, contributes to the knowledge that constitutes the abduction phenomenon.

Through her work with John Carpenter, Leah Haley contributes the story of the crashed disk to the general account of the connection between the aliens and the government. Similarly, Budd Hopkins draws on the writings of Anna Jamerson and Beth Collings to support his argument for the depth of the alien presence in our lives. Jamerson and Collings believe that they are deeply attached to and involved with each other because the aliens brought them together as small children. Hopkins has found other abductees who claim similarly alien-induced relationships.[18] A new thematic strand on the Abductees Anonymous home page on the World Wide Web involves the problem of spontaneous involuntary visibility suffered by some abductees. To my knowledge this has not yet appeared in print or become part of the narrative accepted in ufological circles.

Abduction is interactive, like an oral history or group testimonial continually updated through new postings. Some postings are of course more successful, steering the discourse in more pronounced or direct ways. Some have more commercial backing, more impact on the market, more input from it. Nonetheless, abduction can't be captured or encapsulated. A miniseries, even a good one, can't sum it up or confine it. Attempts to define or set the narrative, though important for researching and understanding what is going on, are themselves abductions. This was one of the primary tensions at work in the 1992 Abduction Study Conference at MIT. It is also a major impetus behind the independent writing of abductees as they try to prevent further loss of their already tenuous hold on their experiences. Similarly, it is now impossible to contain the Net. Sites multiply, reproduce, morph, and fail daily. You can never see it all. Simply accessing a site can cause it to produce new pages, new links. The best thing about the World Wide Web: no reruns. And that's a major move from the sixties.

The similarity between the abduction discourse and the Internet is in part a result of this new technology. The multiple voices and fragments disrupting the coherence of the abduction narrative are generally those that benefit from on-line support groups and that learn from and contribute to abductee Web sites. But abduction's resemblance to the Internet can't be reduced to such a simple causal explanation. Individual cases and stories as well as the data collected by researchers all exhibit the "kaleidoscopic jumbling together of partial and fragmented visions of reality" that is characteristic of cyberspace.[19] Katharina Wilson begins her book by noting that she is relying on a dream notebook she has kept since childhood, a notebook in which she includes not only dreams but also reflections, memories, and the abduction experiences that are similar to, but not the same as, dreams. Her writing (again, like that in the other testimonials to which I've referred) repeatedly shifts among various levels of experience. These shifts are like surfing through television channels, like the rare blocks of time when MTV actually shows videos, or like the links we can create on the Internet.[20] My point, then, is that the instability of reality in abduction — the fantastic jumbling of dreams, confabulations, and memories; the shifts from feeling to science, to paranoia, to government — in fact describes experience in cyberia. Cyberia, cyberspace, is the space of abduction.

When traveling in cyberia, we don't go anywhere. We stay at home. Things come and happen to us. We point and click, the real motions behind interactivity. If we can send E-mail or buy a book at amazon.com, then we're definitely more active than the Mercury astronauts. Their simulators may have been better, but there are more of us. We can write our own simulations (or buy, rent, borrow, pirate, and download them) and avoid, if lucky, invasive medical experiments on our bodies. Our memories are screen memories, not much different from abductees' recollections of the gray dogs, cats, and owls, of the scary children and the hillbillies in hats that hide their experiences with invasive alien technology.

This is not to say that screen memories aren't real memories. We remember them, after all. Our fragmented impressions elicit strong emotions; we shift among links and strands, producing and produced by new associations. In cyberspace we shift from academic journals to abductee home pages to cancer or AIDS information sites to virtual malls to celebrations of Elvis and *The X-Files*. We can easily make links from porn sites to live sex on-line to the hybrid offspring of abductions. In cyberspace, hybrid alien fetuses appear as the potential consequence of virtual intercourse. There is no such thing as safe sex. What can be counted on as reality becomes ever more unstable.

This influx/reflux of leveled information is not a product of the Internet alone. It has to be understood as a fact of global, corporate, consumer, entertainment culture at the millennium. Now that infomercials merge with commercials and documentaries, now that Elizabeth Taylor can appear on consecutive sitcoms advertising her new perfume, now that movies and cartoons come with toys and accessories available at Burger King and virtually every store at the mall, now that the *New York Times* and the *Wall Street Journal* include cover stories on UFOs, and political figures can talk about abduction and flying saucers, American political culture is cyberia. This is our life, no matter where we are. It is the environment for rich as well as poor, for all the various races and ethnicities clamoring for voice and space in America. It is the environment, moreover, in which such claims have to be heard, have to get attention, if they are to be recognized. Ninety-eight percent of all Americans own a television.

Seeming Digital

Some folks have responded to the rise of the virtual with irresponsible paranoia. That is to say, they fail to deal with contemporary indeterminacies and instead repetitively, compulsively, reassert their particular "truth." Thus, some — not all of whom are neo-Luddites or technophobes — think that they can solve the "problem" of virtuality with a strong appeal to a strong reality. Mark Slouka locates this reality in the physical world and in face-to-face interactions.[21] I wonder if he mistrusts books. Kurt Andersen thinks that the traditional press and their fact-checking rules can protect reality from cyberian incursions.[22] I guess he is reassured by the vagueness of categories such as "facts" and "reality" and the nostalgia they invoke. Others reassert the authority of experts, education, and evidence. And I think about Leah Haley, Budd Hopkins, and John Mack.

Appraisals of the Internet that fixate on the truth of the content of Web sites, discussion groups, bulletin boards, or chat rooms resemble UFO and abduction "debunkers." For all their appeals to facts and credibility, debunkers are less skeptical than many believers, less skeptical than those in the UFO community who are willing to question consensus reality. Similarly, some Net critics attempt to install in cyberia notions of accuracy and the commonality of truth that have deep connections to the liberal ideal of a rational public sphere. This resembles alien debunking because it doesn't allow for other ways of thinking about what happens on the Net. They assume cyberia is a public sphere. Or attempt to make it one.

The idea of the public sphere brings with it presumptions about truth, discussion, and consensus. Debate in such a sphere, for example, requires that everyone accept the same conception of reality. Everyone has to agree about what facts look like. Not only would most liberal political theorists discount the claims of abductees, if they ever considered them, but they would argue that religious beliefs don't "count" as compelling reasons in public discussion. For them, to say that a view is religious, traditional, particular, magical, paranoid, or irrational is to provide acceptable grounds for not taking such a view, or those who may hold it, seriously in political debate. Matters like these are considered too divisively private to matter in public. Similarly, to say that a position is violent is sufficient to exclude from the realm of the public those who take such a position. Millennial America has witnessed the effects of such exclusionary conceptions of what is claimed to be public in Waco and Ruby Ridge. It seems more accurate to say that the exclusion is prior to the violence. Thus, the liberal public is preserved and protected by the bracketing of certain ways of thinking or points of view. This bracketing, in fact, creates the public.

Like the abduction narrative, then, the Internet is a vehicle for the return of issues and concerns that liberalism has sought to repress.[23] Each involves competing conceptions of the real as sites produced by ufologists, CNN, Nicholas Negroponte, and teenagers from New Jersey vie for hits even as they are linked together. Each involves, like so many other sites increasingly visible in millennial America, contests over whose words count and how this issue might be decided or fought out. Each involves the unceasing disruption of official narratives of truth, authority, and reality.

Few discussions of the cultural and political meanings of the Internet acknowledge the basic conflict in the shaping of the information age. Even enthusiastic supporters of Internet technologies don't recognize that reality is at issue. They assume that the surplus of data, the masses of information surging through the Net, can be assimilated into the ever more general production of knowledge.[24] These supporters refuse to consider the variety of networks through which information is produced, accessed, deployed, and integrated. Net detractors have glimpsed the problem but presume that a solution requires, at some level, the shoring up of the real, the limiting of the technologies and techniques that draw attention to the conventional and political arrangements at stake in some conceptions of reality.[25] Detractors and supporters both miss the point: what happens in cyberia is an unending disruption of settled beliefs and ideas, be they about TWA Flight 800, the best mulch for azaleas, or the meaning of abduction. Focusing on any one site or network of links is thus a mistake. The disruptions are produced by the possibility of available alternatives, by the endless buttons to click and windows to open, by the amassing of information to which we have fragmented and unclear relations. Our information is not interpreted for or given to us in advance, although it is as packaged and glam as ever.

The Internet doesn't interpellate a public. Rather, it forces its availability onto those who can and will respond to various contradictory hailings, onto those who will link up with others to form networks of association around ideas, desires, and fears that previously may have floated alone outside the "public sphere." In this respect, the Internet contributes to the production of a perspective, a way of being, a subjectivity, as extraterrestrial as a new hybrid species. This extraterrestrial subjectivity linked to the Internet is about the technological alien, about the noncitizen produced as an effect of actions and interactions, connections and communities that cannot be imagined within our nationally established terms of community.

If networked interactions contribute to the transmission of information and the formation of alliances that transgress national boundaries, then they involve virtual migrations that bring aliens into ever more domestic spaces. At the policy level, the production of Internet aliens subverts jurisdiction and responsibility. Peter Ludlow makes this point when he discusses the potential legalities of encryption technologies on the Internet. "It is one thing to allow the United States government to be free to intercept all communications between its citizens," he observes, "but what happens when those citizens work for corporations based in other countries, or when U.S. corporations communicate with corporations in other countries?"[26] At the level of representation, the production of aliens calls into question visions of ethnicity, language, history, community, and space that presume the coherence of notions of citizenship and nationality.[27] Global fashion, or at least Calvin Klein's corporate entertainment vision of it, connects disparate localities as it produces the image of cultural similarities. Photos that make us look alike link us to one another by saying that we *are* alike. English, with a cyberian inflection, is the language of the Web. Anything more than six degrees of separation from Bill Gates seems too quaint even to be real, a "preserve" already artificial.

Of course, after Heaven's Gate, it comes as no surprise that the Internet produces aliens. Those who were drawn to this apocalyptic UFO group, like many whose actions on the Net are important aspects of their lives, relied on a network of associations that resist conceptualization within the spacialized discourses of public spheres, states, and communities predicated on the virtual reality of original, face-to-face interactions. What to believe and whom to trust are questions not connected with the central(izing) authority of truth in its scientific, patriarchal, or sovereign guises. Instead, they are part of a broader dispersion of questions regarding the credibility of particular persons about particular matters at particular points in time.

Traditional media have good reasons to be paranoid about the Internet. But they hit on the wrong reasons. Those criticisms that focus on truth try mistakenly to provide reassurance about the possibility of a public sphere of free and democratic discussion. This reassuring discussion relies on an ideal of original, natural, face-to-face interactions about important matters by people who agree on what counts as important, respect one another, and don't watch too much television. Television is crucial to this idealized public, first, as an embodiment of the passivity, triviality, and desire it has repressed and, second, as precisely that technology through which the public is called into being in contemporary America.[28] "That's one giant step for man . . ." Thinking about the Internet as the public sphere works reassuringly to alleviate some of the strain of this paradox.

More than a new or even a final frontier, cyberia refers to the dispersion of battles in the information age along numerous fronts and fault lines. The questions of trust and credibility on the Net are particularly vexing to those who have been disconnected (or those who have never been connected) from life on the screens, from the games and role playing already deeply inscribed in contemporary technoculture. If we don't believe what we see on television, why would we believe what we access on the Net? Testimonies, the claims of expert witnesses, and the findings of investigative committees are as reliable as the networks within which they have meaning; installed elsewhere, as the Simpson jury made clear, they're as implausible as mad cow disease or Gulf War syndrome. Anxieties over truth on the Net function primarily to reassure our trust in other sorts of mediated interactions; indeed, to pathologize our justifiable paranoia. Like the hysteria around pedophiles abusing children who happen upon modems and user-friendly software, like the sacrifice of abductees on televisual altars, anxieties over truth on the Net channel our suspicions about our everyday world into the safely foreign realm of the technical, as if we were not embedded in technoculture already.

"Just the Facts, Ma'am"

How can claims to truth be defended when reality is virtual? What can count as evidence when collective and individual memories are as staged as an Apollo launch or a saucer abducting a woman in the middle of Manhattan?[29] The writings of some abductees suggest that the answer can be found in detail, unceasing waves of minute detail. Katharina Wilson provides a "researcher's supplement" to her book, *The Alien Jigsaw*. In this supplement she correlates her abductions with specific points in her menstrual cycle. She concludes that her abductions most often took place in the week immediately following ovulation. She analyzes the memories and dreams recorded in her journal, and published in *The Alien Jigsaw*, in order to provide quantifiable data on the physiological and emotional effects of her abduction. During or after 3 percent of her abduction experiences (she recalls or has reason to believe that she was abducted 119 times), Wilson felt full or bloated; during or after 2 percent of her experiences, she felt pain in her nostril.[30] She details the presence of military personnel in abductions, the various locales visited during an abduction, and the different sorts of aliens involved. I should add that Wilson does not conclude that her evidence actually proves anything. Rather, she provides it as a supplement to the evidence offered by other researchers and abductees.

Karla Turner, Beth Collings, and Anna Jamerson all describe daily rituals of combing their bodies for evidence. They discover small cuts, scars, and bruises. They find needlelike puncture marks, bumps, and sometimes blood. Jamerson says that even when new marks turn up, she isn't convinced they are necessarily new.[31] Turner observes: "As evidence of alien contact, they are useless if there is no memory of an event to go with them."[32] Still, as they search for truth, these abductees become ever more preoccupied with the minutiae of the everyday, observing and recording details that would have remained unnoticed. What cannot be explained, understood, or remembered points toward the alien even if it doesn't prove it.

For more than a week, Turner records the sounds of her house at night. The tape from the third night played back a series of eighty-five sounds not unlike "the noise a six-foot-tall can of hair spray might make: short, breathy aspirations that were more mechanical-sounding than organic."[33] Her efforts to document abductions are ultimately as unsuccessful as Collings and Jamerson's. At the Abduction Study Conference at MIT, Richard Boylan, a psychologist who is also an experiencer, dismissed attempts to "capture an event on electromagnetic recording equipment, or to use stealth technology." Boylan argued: "You're dealing with people who can read your minds, what do you mean stealth technology? If they don't want to be captured, they'll catch it while you're forming the plot. They can also sense you coming through technologies better than we'll evolve for awhile." [34]

The vast compilation of data, of information, are confounded by an inability to determine not just what the data might mean or where they might fit, but whether they are real or staged data. Many studying and experiencing abduction think that the telepathic and technological superiority of aliens enables them to produce experiences and memories. What is not clear is whether these productions can be thought of as real and what "real" means in this case. All abductees report screen memories. Haley mentions a light show seemingly put on just for her to photograph. The pictures don't turn out. Wilson views theatrics as a central part of the aliens' study of human behavior. She considers whether some of the variety of alien forms might be explained by masks or disguises, "since the only thing we *are* sure of is that the aliens are extremely good at deceiving us." [35] Budd Hopkins explains the multiply witnessed abduction of Linda Cortile in New York City in 1989 as an event deliberately staged for an important political leader. [36] Hopkins includes the text of a letter sent to him by this "third man," a witness Hopkins suggests is a highly placed official in the United Nations although he refers to him as "Poppy." NASA isn't the only space agency oriented toward an audience.

Obsessively gathering information is not the only response to the virtuality of abduction. There are more transcendent reactions, reactions that seek to escape what is felt as the limits of accepted reality by summoning the spiritual, the religious. By their second and third books, Betty Andreasson and Whitley Strieber are connecting aliens with angels and stressing the transformation in consciousness effected by abduction. John Mack, too, stresses the possibility of higher meanings in abduction, what the phenomenon might "teach us about the redemptive and transformative role of emotion in human life." [37] Finding that abduction violates the separation between the spiritual and the physical fundamental to Western thought at least since the seventeenth century, he suggests that such a transgression may reflect the very purpose of abduction. Mack writes: "We seek power to dominate, control, or influence a sphere of action. But the abduction phenomenon by its demonstration that control is impossible, even absurd, and its capacity to reveal our wider identity in the universe invites us to discover the meaning of our 'power' in a deeper, spiritual sense." [38]

The Grassy Knoll

Many in the UFO and abduction communities are convinced that the government is covering up the evidence of aliens. Not only that, but they think the government systematically lies about the aliens, sending out disinformation to confuse researchers and make those in the community look stupid. They think, in other words, that the American government is not accountable to voters in a democratic process, that secret groups and forces within the government act in ways that are antithetical to the principles of democracy, and that, for all its promises of safety and security, the government fails, sometimes deliberately, to protect some Americans from violence.

Some African Americans believe that the government, particularly the CIA, introduced crack cocaine into urban areas with large African American populations.[39] The drug trade may have been linked with munitions deals and support for the Contras in Central America. Some believe that the Los Angeles Police Department tampered with evidence and framed O. J. Simpson for murder. Some believe that AIDS was specifically introduced in black bodies.[40] A few believe that the deaths of 913 people in Jonestown, Guyana, were part of a "black genocide operation intended to be one of many such programs to entrap, enslave, and eventually kill off black people."[41] Some believe that the U.S. government carried out syphilis experiments on African American men in Tuskegee, Alabama. Some African Americans believe, in other words, that America has systematically oppressed black people, denied them jobs and opportunities, established separate and unequal procedures and criteria for justice, beaten, imprisoned, and killed black men, subverted African American leaders, devalued black bodies, and denied basic necessities of humane physical and medical care to African American citizens.

Some women think that pharmaceutical companies have either inadequately tested silicon breast implants, covered up problems with the implants, or used large grants to influence scientific experts to discredit claims about the implants' dangers. They think, in other words, that there is something harmful to women about having plastic surgery to enlarge their breast size and that there are powerful and influential people in this country in whose interest it is to underplay this harm.

Some people believe that the moon landing was faked. Others think Pathfinder landed in New Mexico. They believe that the U.S. government is more likely to use television and technology to deceive and manipulate than to carry out something wonderful and admirable.

Throughout American history people have believed that the pope was plotting to take over the country, that the Freemasons designed Washington, D.C. ("Almost every one of the signers of the Declaration of Independence was a Mason. The U.S. Constitution was also framed to fit Mason precepts of liberty, equality, and fraternity"), that the ACLU was out to undermine family values, that communists were taking over the State Department, that the Trilateral Commission was the real power in this country.[42] Americans have feared and organized against what they saw as alien peoples (Irish, Germans, Italians), alien religions (Catholicism, Mormonism, Judaism), alien ideas (communism, Freemasonry), illegal aliens (Mexicans), alien technology (electricity, television, computers, genetic engineering), and aliens (extraterrestrials). This attitude has been part of the history of America's understanding of its own identity, part of establishing the meaning of "American," the content and boundaries of the nation.[43] Throughout American history some people have sought to defend what they understood as democracy against what seemed to them to be the hidden machinations of a secret society. Often this defense has been inscribed on the bodies of those who could least bear it. At other times it has been targeted at elites, intellectuals, and (the) government itself.

Like the Internet and abduction, conspiracy theory is a way of processing information, a way of making links in the combined sense of discovering as well as creating. If abduction is about content and the Internet is about media, then conspiracy theory is about interpretation and analysis. Through its links and associations, conspiracy theory codes critical reflections on democratic society as a particularized set of threats. Like abduction and the Internet, conspiracy theory challenges secrecy with information. And, of course, to ask about the "truth" of this information is to miss the point. As Paige Baty writes, "On the one hand, the conspiracy theory searches for the truth. On the other, many truths are repeatedly shown to be the products of fictions, plots, and lies."[44]

In an influential essay from the mid-sixties, Richard Hofstadter tries to capture the essence of conspiracy and the "paranoid style" as they have appeared in American politics. I want to stress two of the characteristics he attributes to this "paranoid style": the element of distortion and the element of evidence. First, although Hofstadter doesn't claim that the style in which a political idea is expressed determines the worth of that idea, he nonetheless finds it more likely that bad, false, and deeply right-wing views will be articulated with paranoid rhetoric. "A distorted style," he reasons, "is a possible signal that may alert us to a distorted judgment, just as in art an ugly style is a cue to fundamental defects of taste."[45] Second, Hofstadter notes that paranoid scholarship usually begins with defensible assumptions and a set of facts that are used to prove the truth of conspiracy. He writes: "It is nothing if not coherent — in fact, the paranoid mentality is far more coherent than the real world, since it leaves no room for mistakes, failures, or ambiguities." For Hofstadter, then, "what distinguishes the paranoid style is not . . . the absence of verifiable facts . . . but rather the curious leap in imagination that is always made at some critical point in the recital of events." [46]

Hofstadter isn't wrong. But because he has decided in advance what can be categorized as having a paranoid style, a decision he makes based on his assumptions that social conflict is "something to be mediated and compromised," he doesn't consider what makes conspiracy theories useful for those who deploy them. [47] For him, they can only be signs of pathology, deviations from the right and reasonable procedures of consensus politics. For him, there are only two kinds of politics, normal and distorted, and the possibility that the normal is itself already a myth, illusion, or simplification deployed in ways that prevent its contestation never arises. Indeed, Hofstadter's attack on the curious jumps and leaps, on the hyperrationality of conspiracy theory, may actually be an attack against theory in general. How vast is the leap from social conflict and differentiation to the social contracts, original positions, and ideal-speech situations of normative political theory? How curious is the effort to vacate from the site of politics the lives, languages, and bodies that conflict and reproduce there? Much, too much, social and political theory leaves little room for mistakes and ambiguities, making attributions of rational choice willy-nilly.

The so-called distortions and imaginative leaps of conspiracy theory may be helpful tools for coding politics in the virtual realities of the techno-global information age. Not least because we've lost the conditions under which we can tell the difference: the increase in information brought about by global telecommunications disrupts the production of a normalized, hegemonic field of the normal against which distortions can be measured. The accusation of distortion is thus revealed as a play of power, one often made on the part of a dominant group against those who may perceive themselves as threatened, marginalized, or oppressed, as harmed by the devices of associations so inaccessible they may as well be secret. Would criteria for normal versus distorted help us deal with fears of government complicity in the impact of AIDS on black bodies in the face of the histories of denial and violation in which the Tuskegee experiments are embedded?

Turning the claims of conspiracy theory against those accustomed to using it as a dismissal, as an accusation, may enable the theorization of new types of political action, actions especially adapted to the multiple terrains of the information age. John Carlin describes the following war games played at the Department of Defense:

> The teams are presented with a series of hypothetical incidents, said to have occurred during the preceding 24 hours. Georgia's telecom system has gone down. The signals on Amtrak's New York to Washington traffic line have failed, precipitating a head-on collision. Air traffic control at LAX has collapsed. A bomb has exploded at an Army base in Texas. And so forth.
>
> The teams fan out to separate rooms with one hour to prepare briefing papers for the president. "Not to worry — these are isolated incidents, an unfortunate set of coincidences," is one possible conclusion. Another might be "Someone — we're still trying to determine who — appears to have the US under full scale attack." Or maybe just "Round up the usual militia suspects."[48]

Without theorizing conspiracy it may not be possible to confront political actions, to realize that struggles have already begun.

It may also not be possible to carry out political actions without conspiracy theory, without making links so as to create specific political images. E-mail, the Net, and the global web of media and communications enable a variety of different tactics for engagement — from "spamming," or sending out political messages as a sort of electronic junk mail, to hoax and alternative sites on the World Wide Web, to more covert and less legal forms of infiltration and subversion. Thanks to networked communication, images are not just for experts anymore.

Historians like Hofstadter write about conspiracy fears and paranoid styles from the presumption of a normal political and social field as one that is constituted by compromise, inclusion, debate, security, and constancy. The terms of politics, the players, the rules, and the ethical position of "each" of the two sides (for the options are necessarily binary) are clear and known. Subterfuge and secrecy can only be distortions in this world; they aren't necessary. This is a dangerous presumption today. Such a presumption covers over awareness of the invasive, the insecure, the illusory, exposed by abduction, accessible on the Net. "A good conspiracy is an unprovable conspiracy."[49]

Virtual Connections

Underlying some interpretations of abduction is an idea about the nature of truth. Some abduction researchers share this idea, regardless of

whether they have negative or positive appraisals of the phenomenon of abduction. This idea about truth, moreover, can be found in a variety of conspiracy theories. It can also be found in discussions of the Internet. The
idea is a notion of fundamental interconnectedness.

Abductees appear to link every odd or uncomfortable occurrence in
their lives. They connect missing computer files with missing fetuses. They
connect gazes from strangers sitting across a room with phones that ring
once and then stop. They connect the emotions they feel when seeing a
picture of a big-headed Gray with enormous black eyes with their inability
to remember details from their pasts. Beth Collings finds that none of the
conventional explanations offered for abduction — "coincidence," "lucid
dreams," or "faulty human memory" — can "justify the whole." "Until
something better came along, something that could explain *all* the connecting events, we had no choice but to continue as we had been," she
writes, "examining each unexplained event, comparing notes on shared
memories, talking candidly with family and friends, and keeping an open
mind."[50] Because the events are connected, one explanation has to account
for all of them. The truth will explain what it is that makes the connection
possible; that the connection is possible, is, in fact, already there, is assumed from the outset. The fact of connection, in other words, establishes
the primary criterion for accepting a claim to truth.

The researchers concerned with the negative aspects of abduction, with
the pain and suffering abductees experience and the frightening implica-
tions of the breeding project, also presume a fundamental interconnectedness. In addition to arguing for the necessity of a full and comprehensive
explanation, for a truth that can account for all the various experiences of
the abductees, Hopkins and Jacobs accept the possibility of a breeding project involving humans and extraterrestrials. Hybridity, though not yet explicable, is not baffling. With technology, anything is possible; anything is
knowable, eventually. Jacobs points out that this theory does not depend
on the genetic compatibility of humans and aliens, hypothesizing that the
hybrids are in fact products of genetic engineering.[51] His laboratory explanation supports an account of deep alien-human connection; it makes possible his contention that humans and aliens are interconnected to such an
extent that the connection results in progeny, a hybrid species or race.

Hopkins's recent research on the Linda Cortile case connects the abduction of a Manhattan housewife out of an upper-story apartment to
numerous witnesses from around the city, prominent politicians in particular.[52] On November 30, 1989, Cortile phoned Hopkins about an experience she had the night before, an experience she suspected was an abduc-

tion. She remembered a tingly feeling in her legs and a head with large black eyes. She and Hopkins had worked together uncovering other abduction memories for several months, so they decided to use hypnotic regression to learn more about the experience. Under hypnosis she described how four or five black-eyed beings paralyzed her, carried her into her living room, and then accompanied her out her twelfth-floor window in a beam of light. Once in their craft, she is examined. The aliens are especially interested in Cortile's nose and spend some time sticking an instrument in her right nostril. Three years later, in February 1991, Hopkins receives a letter from two men who identify themselves as "Police Officers Dan and Richard." The letter describes how, back in November 1989, around three in the morning, while sitting in their patrol car underneath an elevated portion of FDR Drive, they saw a large, reddish oval hovering over an apartment building. They got out binoculars to see it better and observed a woman in a white nightgown escorted by small ugly creatures float up into the craft in a beam of bright light.

As he traces out the various links surrounding this complicated case, Hopkins marvels over the aliens' theatricality. Cortile's abduction seems as if it were staged, for Dan and Richard were not the only witnesses. Indeed, the abduction seemed to have occurred at precisely that time when an important political figure would witness it. Hopkins links Linda's abduction to the fall of the Berlin Wall earlier that month and to the Czech general strike. He notes that Lech Wałęsa was in New York City on the very day of the abduction and speculates that other powerful politicians could have been involved in secret diplomatic meetings.[53]

Moreover, Hopkins discovers an intricate "cosmic micro-management" that brings Linda together with two other people, people that she didn't realize she knew, people with whom she had been abducted all her life. Hopkins concludes that the aliens are so intertwined in human lives that they arrange some human relationships. This he refers to as "controlled pairing." Like David Jacobs, Hopkins stresses that abductions affect families, occurring in successive generations. Abductions rarely happen only once. They are part of a lifetime. Abduction is continuous, permanent. "It's very much like an assembly line," says Jacobs.[54] Each abduction is connected to another; they are all part of something larger, something that connects humans and aliens, earth and outerspace.

John Mack, the most prominent of the positive interpreters of abduction, presents the most extensive vision of interconnection. He reports that his work with abductees reveals the aliens' preoccupation with the fate of the earth, especially with human destruction of the environment.[55] Mack writes: "Nothing in my work on UFO abductions has surprised me as much as the discovery that what is happening to the earth has not gone unnoticed elsewhere in the universe. That the earth itself, and its potential destruction, could have an effect beyond itself or its own environment was altogether outside the worldview in which I was raised. But it would appear from the information that abductees receive that the earth had value or importance in a larger, interrelated cosmic system that mirrors the interconnectedness of life on earth."[56] Drawing from what he has learned from abductees. Mack conceives environment as "more than nature or our physical ecology. It refers to the entire context of life itself." He posits that "the aliens seem to be concerned with our 'environment' in this total sense."[57] He stresses the tapestry metaphor that one abductee used to characterize the universe.

For Mack, the fact of interconnection at the heart of abduction provides a critical standpoint from which to assess the problematic conception of truth in Western scientific paradigms. Dream and waking states, spirit and material worlds, religious and physical phenomena merge, intersect, connect. Abduction, he thinks, is part of an experience designed to help or enable humans to reconnect a world, a truth, a reality, fragmented by Western rationality and science. This means that abductees in particular undergo a process through which they shed their feelings of separateness and move toward wholeness and unity. "They shed their identification with a narrow social role and gain a sense of oneness with all creation, a kind of universal connectedness," Mack finds.[58]

Nigel Clark argues that a vision of ultimate interconnection, of "unimpeded message flow," links radical ecology with cyberculture.[59] He explains that a "tenet of unity or wholeness" forms the basis for depth ecology's critique of Western society's separateness from nature. The Gaia hypothesis is but one version of a general emphasis on interconnection that runs through much of contemporary ecoculture. Clark notices a similar ideal in the writings of Douglas Rushkoff and other self-proclaimed voices of cyberculture: "Again, the benevolent spectre of universal interconnectivity is invoked. In this context it is the structures of ownership and control of the mode of information which must be subverted, in order that human subjects might reassert their community."[60] Abduction runs both theses. Whereas specific narratives within the ufological community stress one theme or the other, the overall program employs both versions of the ideal of ultimate interconnection. Abduction extends the idea of interconnectedness that is so prominent in contemporary society.

Of course, notions of interconnection, wholeness, and unity are not new. Non-Western cultures have offered various understandings of universal connection. Western theory has, from time to time, embraced ideals of wholeness, as in, for example, cyclical notions of history or medieval Christian conceptions of the oneness of reason, creation, and the revealed will of God. Some forms of mysticism, spiritualism, Rosicrucianism, and witchcraft continue to embrace a belief in the ultimate unity of all things. What makes the current emphasis on interconnection different, however, is that it is coupled with a scientific understanding of the world. That is to say, it is not primarily religious or mystical (although there are mystical strands and communities in cyberculture as well as in ecoculture). Instead, the supposition of interconnection is grounded in scientific notions of experiment, testing, reason, and proof. It is part of what Max Weber understood as a disenchanted or rationalized and intellectualized vision of the world. For Weber, disenchantment did not mean that everything about the world was already known. Rather, the world was in principle knowable, not subject to mysterious forces.[61] For the most part, this is the notion of interconnection at work in abduction as well. Abductees and abduction researchers are committed to the reassuring view that answers, interpretations, explanations for the phenomena are out there; all they have to do is find them.

If abduction is, as I've suggested, a symptomatic expression of the supposition of interconnection running through some contemporary currents of American culture, what is it symptomatic of? Put somewhat differently, what does it tell us about the presumption of interconnection? At the very least, it tells us that the problems of anomie and atomism that occupied sociologists in the 1950s and 1960s may have given way to a new set of issues around the ways people are connected to one another and to their environments. This, I think, is evidenced by current preoccupations with privacy. On the Net these preoccupations stress personal information and tracking technologies that monitor the sites we visit, products we buy, and messages we send. In the home, these preoccupations often center on sexual activities and the limits of state interference.

More specifically, however, there is something troubling about a presumption of interconnection: namely, it covers over how connections are created and maintained. This has been a key problem with some conspiracy theory as it elides the transition from fact to fact, failing to make clear just how a link is established. But I want to begin with a more everyday illustration. The sense of interconnection is in part a product of buttons. That is to say, many different activities in contemporary life employ the same user interface: buttons.[62] I can open my garage door, type this sentence, call out for pizza, and change channels on the television with one and the same motion. The differences among these activities are covered over by the ubiquity of buttons. Similarly, an idea like "We are all connected" deflects attention from those who are in fact not connected, those who may be homeless or left alone with no one to care for them. Furthermore, it forestalls inquiry into the various types and degrees of interconnection. What connection might mean, and in what contexts, is left up to the imagination, a lot like the reproductive dimensions of cybersex. This might open up a terrain for freedom, but at the same time it may very well close off inquiry into hierarchies of power.

If we take interconnections between people as given, we displace attention from the variety of ways connections are produced. This mind-set explains, in part, some of the derision heaped on conspiracy theory, but also, I think, some of the problems in political theory as well: the failure to keep in play the myriad links constituting the networks of information, capital, opportunity, desire, and DNA. Our connections may be products of a system, integrating us like so many PCs. They may be as insignificant or potentially significant as Internet links. We may be interconnected through proximity, inhabiting contiguous spaces in apartment buildings, shelters, or neighborhoods. We may be connected face-to-face. Traditions may link us. So may MTV or our choice of footwear. Although available to be filled in by notions of community, interconnections between people in no way presuppose or bring with them connotations of mutuality, responsibility, or support. If we presume that we are all already connected, do we rely on systems instead of one another? Do we forgo opportunities of mutual reliance or system interrogation?

Some people wonder how abductees can go on about their everyday lives if they really believe that aliens are abducting them, taking their eggs and sperm, and creating a hybrid race. In today's America, what other choices do they have? Abductees have to keep going; they have to continue relying on a system they don't trust, a system they fear, if they are to work, survive, and care for their families in whatever limited terrestrial way they can. The helplessness, the feeling of overwhelming entrapment and resulting passivity is part of abduction. An overarching mentality of interconnection might very well bring with it paranoid fears. For we may be connected in ways we don't understand, in hidden ways that don't work to our advantage. The challenge, then, is not just to assume the connection but to make the link, to uncover the secrets, to discover the unknown dimensions of the networks not only linking us but fabricating us together.

A crucial dimension of the presumption of interconnection is that *everything* is interconnected — everything, not just people. The differing levels of reality, as Mack's research shows, shift and converge to redefine common understandings of the real. In America, we are already familiar with the moves between the experiential and the televisual — from Dan Quayle's concern with Murphy Brown's position as an unwed mother to Murphy Brown's response. Who is fictional and in what context? Like those concerned with sex and violence on television, Ziauddin Sardar is worried about the incest and bestiality on alt.sex.stories. "It has nothing to do with intimacy, tenderness, or any other human emotion," he writes.[63] Why, I wonder, is this a problem for fictional or virtual encounters? Perhaps because we no longer make distinctions between the real and the virtual. Fantasy life, in all its permutations, is becoming real life and bringing with it heretofore unconceived challenges of governability. Already we react to screens as if they were people.[64] If we are accustomed to embracing the not-real as precisely that terrain upon which we can release what is often constrained in interactions with others, in relationships whose claim to reality is important, then how are we to govern ourselves once the boundaries between the two collapse?

In its current setting in a techno-global information society, the presumption of interconnection relies on a certain excess in the technologies of truth. It is a product of the sense that the world is a knowable place and of the rise in the various means available to know the world. The abductees employ all sorts of surveillance devices, all manner of lights and buzzers and recorders and transmitters, knowing that when something is triggered, a series of effects signifies an alien presence. These devices are so reliable that even their failures signify an alien presence. Interconnection is also the product of simultaneity; the collapse of space is also a collapse of time. As Vivian Sobchak observes, this has led many of us to feel as if we have "no time."[65] One sign of abduction is missing time. Interconnection is a dimension of the overall excess characteristic of contemporary consumption-oriented entertainment culture. Anything we have is connected to something we lack. Anything we see is connected to something we haven't yet seen. What we haven't seen is connected to what we don't have, and we know this. We are driven to see, to know, and to have more, to trace out those connections, to find the links to the hidden surprises that await. As with the capitalist mode of production, the information society relies on the link between excess and lack, on our inability to find satisfaction even when we have more than we can imagine.

Abduction may not offer the best interpretation for the experiences of Leah Haley, Beth Collings, Anna Jamerson, Karla Turner, and Katharina Wilson. It may not describe what actually happened to those who have been hypnotized by Budd Hopkins, John Carpenter, David Jacobs, and John Mack. It does tell us, though, that we no longer have the criteria for figuring out what the best explanation might be, what it might look like or entail. What happens to our everyday approaches to truth when reality isn't, when we try to amass information our relation to which is fragmented and unclear, when answers are lacking, either in availability or capacity to satisfy? The answer, abduction.

5
The Familiarity of Strangeness

"Removal of aliens who enter the United States illegally
. . . is an all-too-rare event . . ."*

The major media event of the last week of April 1997 began with
the discovery of thirty-nine bodies in a large house in Rancho Santa Fe,
California. Early reports from traditional media identified the bodies as
belonging to Web designers, white men in their twenties and thirties. They
were members of a group called Heaven's Gate. More reliable information,
some of it coming off the group's site on the World Wide Web, explained
that they had left their bodies in order to rendezvous with the spacecraft
traveling in the tail of the Hale-Bopp comet. Further investigation cor-
rected the early misidentifications: the bodies belonged to men and women

---

*From "Bill Summary: Major Provisions of H.R. 2202," *Congressional Digest* (May
1996), p. 141.

the majority of whom were in their forties and fifties. Most had spent much of the past twenty years following the teachings of "Do," Marshall Herff Applewhite, who with "Ti" (Bonnie Lu Nettles, who died in 1985) taught that UFOs would take the prepared to the level above human.

Much of the commentary in traditional media focused either on why the people "committed suicide" or on the dangers of the Internet. Net commentary trashed traditional media, pointing out that Jonestown didn't need the Web and that the Heaven's Gate group understood themselves not as dying but as leaving their bodies. Neither worried much about the UFOs and aliens so central to the group's beliefs. Aliens have already been assimilated into everyday life in America at the millennium. A primary vehicle for this assimilation has been the alien abduction narrative.

Over the past decade, stories of alien abduction have worked their way into the mainstream culture. Although abduction accounts have been part of UFO literature since the case of Betty and Barney Hill was documented in the mid-1960s, and have appeared every once in a while in the popular press, sustained attention to abduction in the mainstream media began in 1987. That was the year of the televangelism scandals, the Iran-Contra hearings, Wedtech, and the stock market crash. It was the year Japan was thought of as a major economic threat: Japanese goods had become favorites of American consumers and the Japanese purchased Rockefeller Center.[1] It was in effect the year when Reagan's presidency ended and the actor-president's legacy began. As Haynes Johnson notes, "Under his reign all lines blurred: news and entertainment, politics and advertising."[2] In 1987 two nonfiction books on alien abduction made best-seller lists, Whitley Strieber's *Communion* and Budd Hopkins's *Intruders*.

Since 1987 thousands of abductees have come out, legitimated by Harvard professor John Mack's work and authorized through the shift from consensus reality to virtual reality. On-line and face-to-face support groups are available to help abductees access, process, and create home pages for their experiences. By the mid-1990s the abduction narrative is established enough for the *New York Times Magazine* to satirize abductee meetings and put "World leader in alien abductions" at number four on a list of "What's Right with America."[3] The *New Yorker* can publish alien abduction cartoons, confident that readers will get the joke. Abduction is a regular occurrence on network TV. *Chicago Hope* and *ER* have run plot lines involving women pregnant with alien babies. The main character on the sitcom *Grace under Fire* was abducted by aliens, as were Joe and Spence on *Ellen*. Even better is Fox's *Beyond Belief*, where the audience is asked to decide which fantastic tales are based on fact and which are only fiction. Facts, fantasies, and tales of aliens, specifically those abducting humans, resonate and recombine in the American social at the end of the millennium.

If we think about science fiction, the prevalence of alien images in popular media is not surprising. Just as Cold War invasions responded to fears of communism and nuclear war, so do some prominent contemporary aliens click on current insecurities around technology, otherness, and the future. The most obvious link is between the space alien and the noncitizen. The 1997 hit summer comedy *Men in Black* was based on it. The MIBs — "Jay," played by Will Smith (one of the heroes in *ID4*) and "Kay," Tommy Lee Jones — work for Immigration and Naturalization Services, Division Six. The film opens with an Anglo man attempting to sneak a truckload of Mexicans into the United States. One of the Mexicans is really an alien. After catching the alien, Kay lets the Mexicans cross the border as he sarcastically commends the border guards for protecting America from such dangerous aliens. Later in the film, we learn that most resident aliens live in New York, leading ordinary, assimilated lives. We also discover that Newt Gingrich is an alien. Jay asks if most aliens are cab drivers. Kay answers: "Not as many as you would think." At Intergalactic Customs, American officials question arriving aliens: "Are you bringing in any fruits or vegetables?"

The tension in the 1996 summer film *The Arrival* also relies on the association between aliens and immigrants. All but two of the aliens are morphed into Mexican bodies (one of the two exceptions adopts the body of an African American boy). Some of the Mexican aliens have worked their way into American research institutes and corporations. Most work south of the border in a huge plant that is destroying the environment. Moreover, in a bizarre replication of Leonard Jeffries's "sun people/ice people" theory, the aliens are trying to make the planet hotter; ice can kill them. By making the aliens Mexican and human, within the United States and across the border, the film reverses colonialist history. White Americans are victims of a secret invasion. Will they be able to resist?

Reinforcing the link between aliens and immigration anxieties is the lack of an actual "arrival" in the film. The aliens are already here. And since they are not defeated at the end of the film, we realize there is nothing we can do about it. True, the alien presence is revealed to a computer-wielding SETI researcher, played by Charlie Sheen, but he has to act alone. He can't trust anyone. When he does, he is either betrayed or put in greater danger than he was in before. Collective action, cooperation, trust: all are too risky. The individual, here figured yet again as the white hero-scientist, is alone before the alien, unmediated. *The Arrival*, then, channels anxieties around security, otherness, and immigration into a story of extraterrestrial invasion. The audience can express its squeamishness about aliens without experiencing guilt over racism or political incorrectness.

This link between space alien and noncitizen appears in nonfiction (and nonscience) contexts as well. Peter Brimelow relies on it in *Alien Nation: Common Sense about America's Immigration Disaster*.[4] Deploying the title of a 1980s science fiction film and short-lived television series, Brimelow constructs a history of America as pristinely white up until the 1960s in order to argue for restrictive changes in U.S. immigration policy. His articulation inverts that of the more politically correct science fiction version of *Alien Nation*. Both the film and the TV series use the encounter with the alien as a metaphor for U.S. race relations. Set in Los Angeles, the story revolves around the ability of escapees from a former slave colony to create a new life in America, focusing on the prejudices they encounter in the process. Finally, although ufologists generally resist the urge to play with alien ambiguities, their awareness of the immigration link is clear. When I met with the director of the Mutual UFO Network, Walter Andrus, at MUFON headquarters in Seguin, Texas, he told me that because of the proximity to Mexico, they referred to UFO occupants as "entities."

In the borderlands between science fiction and ufology, the tabloids also articulate cultural anxieties around otherness with alien images, as in the story of Newt Gingrich's meeting with an alien.[5] The tabloids, moreover, extend the link to otherness. For example, the "12 U.S. Senators Are Space Aliens!" article in the June 7, 1994, *Weekly World News* uses the language of outing. Various senators are "quoted" as saying that they are "surprised it took so long to figure it out," that "the cat's finally out of the bag," and that they wish they could have told friends and relatives themselves. Already in the open, Barney Frank is not named as a space alien.

Linked to immigration, sexuality, senators, and science fiction, the alien in contemporary American cultures can't be confined. In fact, precisely because the alien violates myriad borders, crossing from news to entertainment to tabloid spectacle, it can operate as an icon of the instability of formerly clear distinctions. At a time when talk of the future is ever present, the alien accesses a host of associations with technology, conspiracy, violation, and the changing face of the real. More specifically, alien abduction narratives highlight with particular effect concern about the future of the species. Indeed, given its ufological origins, the prominence of abduction in mainstream media already marks the boundary-blurring that the alien represents. Such narratives become as seductive as the alien abductors themselves once we realize that people truly believe this event is happen-

Truths from the hot sheets (The Weekly World News)

ing to them, to us. The themes of reproduction, the (in)security of existing children, and the odd, frightening hybrids in whom a future hope is invested arise out of testimonies to actual experience.

Abduction narratives provide a program for organizing suspicions about contemporary life, suspicions concerning boundaries, technology, and the morphed simultaneity of the local and the global. Alien abduction compiles what I've referred to as the "familiarity of strangeness" in millennial America, virtual America, and cyber-America where the meaningless "techno" prefix edges out clarity and certainty. As we've seen, the shift from outerspace to cyberspace is about coming home, about the fabrication of home space as a site from which global interconnections are possible, about the realization that the threats and horrors encountered there make us as vulnerable as any astronaut. To this extent, the homeward turn it not as reassuring as one might expect. Our images of comfort and security collapse. Abduction tells us that even at home, especially at home, there is no security, there is no protection, there is no control, not even remotely. Home is uncanny, the site of familiar strangeness.

My notion of the familiarity of strangeness thus learns from and extends the idea of "making the familial strange" which Lynn Spigel develops in her fascinating discussion of the interconnections between the space program and television.[6] Whereas Spigel focuses on the domestic sphere and on the disruptions of norms of family life effected by certain 1960s sitcoms, I address the strangeness of that which is familiar, that which is everyday, effected through stories of alien abduction.[7] Alien themes and images not only interpret the experiences of abductees but also, precisely because of their status as interpretations of reality, serve as concentrated, sensationalized, symptomatic accounts of the fears of the rest of us — the potential abductees.

"Behind the arguments over specific immigration policies are central social questions about the essence of American citizenship . . ." *

Accounts of alien abduction seem to follow a common script.[8] A woman, sometimes a man, is driving alone at night, or is in bed, about to fall asleep. Suddenly, there is a bright light, the perception of small, moving figures, a feeling of paralysis. Arriving at her destination later than expected or finding her nightgown wrong-side out, she fears "something" has happened, something she cannot explain. Nosebleeds, scars that look like "scoop marks," and an awareness of "missing time" lead her to seek help. Through regression hypnosis she discovers that she has been abducted by small gray aliens with large black eyes. These abductions have occurred throughout her life. The aliens have taken her ova, implanted and extracted hybrid human-alien fetuses, and forced her to acknowledge these children as her own. Her human children are also likely to have been abducted. No one and nothing can protect her or her children from the aliens. And the whole scenario is so crazy that there is no acceptable language for talking about

*From the foreword to "Immigration Policy: Balancing National Interests," *Congressional Digest* (May 1996), p. 129.

"Desert Dreams." Jeffrey Westover writes, "I had a dream that involved viewing an abduction of a woman from an American southwest desert town and the subsequent implantation of something behind her left eye. I was allowed to view the proceedings to learn about why the 'aliens' are here and what their mission is about." (Jeffrey S. Westover ©1997)

or understanding what is going on.[9] There's no way to credibly express what has happened, unless one is willing to be sacrificed.

In this narrative, what happens to a woman is of global significance.[10] Her body, her ova, her DNA are the vehicles for humanity's encounter with another world, with the alien. Through her isolation and vulnerability she participates in an intervention that shatters commonsense notions of reality. Abducting her throughout her life, the alien is familiar, though she doesn't know it. Major events, events constitutive of who she is, have occurred behind her back. Local and global merge in abduction.

Like a bumper sticker, lapel ribbon, or big-eyed Gray, the slogan "Think Globally, Act Locally" shows up in a variety of locations in the nineties. Popular with left-wing orientations to social justice such as feminism, antiracism, and multiculturalism, it fits seamlessly in advertisements for Coke, Benetton, and IBM. Although it suggests an eco-friendly sense of responsibility, in the climate of privatization and the devolution of federal programs to city and state agencies, the idea of acting locally all too easily mutates into a market-minded individualism. Whose "local" is taken for granted, presumed by the voices urging us to act. But are we to help build the walls to "protect" our communities (suspecting that the walls may produce more harms than they keep out, that they may lock many of us in, that they may shelter the very causes of harm)? Are we to shut down the polluting factories and make sure that the toxic chemicals are not in our backyards and, in the process, lose our jobs and foist more chemicals into the communities of those less able to organize against corporate interest?

Thinking globally loses its connection with social accountability, articulated now with transnational corporate capitalism and the expansion of Western media and communications systems.[11] It's easy to think globally if we're all wearing Nikes, watching MTV, and having a Coke and a smile. It's easy when ethnicity becomes fashion statement, accessory, hair extension. It's easy when we don't have to consider who makes our shoes and what they are paid. The slogan's vagueness makes it adaptable, eliding the complexities that arise when one begins thinking seriously about global interconnections and how they impact on local action.

What's missing are the links that connect some locals to some globals. What's missing is an awareness of the networks within which any given local and global is constituted. What's missing is a sense of possible webs of connection and the ways in which some links present themselves to those who access them as more viable, more attractive, than others. More often than not, firsthand experiences, true-life stories, and gut feelings become stand-ins for the local. As fragments of the everyday, they can be cut-and-pasted into most any setting. Whether mix, montage, or menu, multiple layers now *mean* global. But solutions for a small planet require more than ISDN and fiber-optic ATM networks.

If we try to imagine what "Think Globally, Act Locally" could mean in practice, terrorism comes quickly to mind. A bomb at the Olympics gets world attention while disrupting specific, situated lives and practices. The Internet provides less violent possibilities. I can communicate with friends in Germany and never leave my room. I can write letters, sign petitions, forward irate messages to politicians around the world. I can get news as soon as it happens. Although language differences may sometimes present hurdles, usually I can navigate the World Wide Web hindered only by server speeds and my own imagination. I can present myself as anyone, anywhere. On-line, I am a citizen of the world, a virtual alien. National borders can't contain me.

Popular envisionings of new communications technologies suggest all too frequently that the screen that connects a local and a global is all that separates the local from the global. Critics and advocates share this assumption, stressing either the nightmare/dream of the new world order/global village or the production of locals in terms of fragmentation (bad) or privatization-personalization (good). The networks that link together genes, people, information, and global capital are occluded. And with them are the opportunities for making new links, in that combined sense of discovering and creating which is also part of Net experience.[12] Not only are the terms and relations establishing the contours of a local erased, but how any given local is drawn, and drawn into a particular conception of global, is bracketed from interrogation. These too simple evolutions of local into global rely on missing links.

If some Internet experiences approximate the reality of thinking globally and acting locally, then the slogan points toward a mode of being human that is radically different from more situated and mediated accounts of people in community. Langdon Winner explains: "Worldwide computer, satellite, and communication networks fulfill, in large part, the modern dream of conquering space and time. These systems make possible instantaneous action at any point on the globe without limits imposed by the specific location of the initiating actor. Human beings and human societies, however, have traditionally found their identities within spatial and temporal limits. They have lived, acted, and found meaning in a particular place at a particular time."[13] For Winner, the morphed simultaneity of the local and the global made possible by networked computer interactions suggests an alien reality of dissolution, paranoia, and powerlessness. The abduction narrative compiles these themes, enabling them to float through mainstream society in a stigmatized, hence safe, form. For abductees, grappling with dissolution, paranoia, and powerlessness is constitutive of their abductee identity. Indeed, it is part of the way they live, act, and find meaning in particular places at particular times. As they search for missing time, they endeavor to find the connections that will explain what they experience, that will connect what happens in their particular lives with a larger reality. Their support groups, writings, therapeutic work, and conventions directly engage these themes as fundamental problems for the contemporary experience of the human. Few locations in mainstream culture confront so self-consciously the impact of the erasure of mediating structures, communities, and worldviews on the meaning of human being.

Thus, simultaneous with the erasure of some mediating structures, communities, and worldviews is the production of new ones, radically new ones. If the rise of radio and television occasioned a nostalgia for the sewing bees and storytelling of some people's mythologized frontier, then the emergence of a popular appropriation of computer and communications technologies results in a similar nostalgia for a similarly mythic experience as a public. Contrary to *Life*'s photographic imagination of the public, not everyone dwelling in America had the same relationship to the astronauts. Contrary to the official claims of science and law, not everyone accepts expert versions of the facts. We know that experts have produced aliens through the exclusions they effect in order to establish their own authority. We know about the military's assessments of the claims by UFO witnesses during the Cold War. We know about the production of national borders and constructions of racial phenotypes. And what we don't know, we can look for — and create — on the Net.

Conspiracy theory is a way to think globally and act locally. It draws us away from the essence of citizenship by reminding us that citizenship is always already being subverted, that the history of American citizenship can be traced as a history of the fear for democracy. Instead of construing citizens as credible spectators, conspiracy theory knows that we can't believe what we see on television, that everything has to be interpreted. The languages of science, law and, importantly, even therapy, aren't trumps or exclusive codes (though Javascript may well be). If we are to "believe," we have to ask more than just "in what?" Our reasonable paranoia distinguishes among the facts, how they are produced, and the contexts in which they are deployed. After all, we learned our skepticism from law and science. Conspiracy theory helps us think globally and act locally because it discards the myth of the public sphere as it searches through the variety of networks through which democracy at the millennium is practiced.

"The proposed changes respond to concerns that the United States has lost control of its borders . . ."*

Like fairy lore and religious mythologies, abduction stories describe the interventions of nonhuman folk in human lives. They are stories of border crossings, of everyday transgressions of the boundaries demarcating the limits of that define reality. As such, in the demystified societies of the present they provoke skirmishes with arbiters of the real, with science, law, and the press. Since in each of these areas criteria for truth have shifted from a stress on facticity to a stress on sincerity and reliability (a shift often inaccurately described as a move from objectivity to subjectivity), abduction stories have become therapeutized. Research on abduction is done by psychologists and therapists. Abductees understand their experiences as traumas. They need support and counseling. They require hypnosis. The struggle over the real, then, is a struggle over the subject, over the accuracy of the subject's memories, over the appropriateness of the subject's affect. Belief in aliens is positioned as the outcome of belief in the words of a person. What happened to the abductee? What did she experience? Do we, can we, trust her enough to accept her story of her experience?

One must be careful not to reduce the abduction phenomenon to some variation of the "We've become a nation of victims" line. While the notion of hypnotizing someone who has encountered a UFO requires a specific constellation of ideas about memory, trauma, and hypnosis,[14] and while the growth of interest in abduction on the part of the therapeutic community parallels the rise of work on ritual child abuse, clearly a critical assessment of therapy culture doesn't need or depend on something as odd as alien abduction. The fascination with aliens and abduction has a more complex link, one that concerns borders and boundaries. Abduction stands in for our lack of certainty about when (and when not) to believe the claims and results of therapists.

If criteria for reliability tend to the conventional — that is to say, if they tend to be linked with ideas of expertise, training, and power — then those who understand themselves as resisting the operations of power may simply

---

*From the foreword to "Immigration Policy: Balancing National Interests," *Congressional Digest* (May 1996), p. 129.

reverse these criteria, linking reliability with folk or experiential knowledge, with the words and claims of those who are not legitimated by institutions or degrees. To use a simple example, since I've been working on UFOs and alien abduction, I've spoken with a number of people who say they don't usually believe scientists or the government and who see no reason to change this view just because we're talking about aliens.

The will to believe the disempowered might have generated the construction of the "case" around the experiences of Betty and Barney Hill as they drove home late one night in New Hampshire in 1961. From the time their story was first published in *Look* magazine in the mid-sixties, it has held totemic status in the UFO community because of the credibility of the Hills' testimony. Back on the road after stopping for a bite to eat, the Hills noticed an odd light that Betty insisted was a UFO. She made Barney stop the car. He approached the brightly lit object and, looking through binoculars, saw approximately six uniformed figures. Barney ran back to the car, terrified that he would be "captured" (his word). A day or two later, the Hills reported their sighting and discovered that others had seen UFOs that same night. In the following months, Barney sought help from a psychiatrist because of stress, an ulcer, and emotional conflicts regarding his divorce from his first wife and his distance from his sons. A couple of years later, still troubled about the UFO sighting and the sense that they had forgotten what had occurred that night, the Hills began working with Dr. Benjamin Simon, a prominent Boston psychiatrist known for his use of hypnosis in treating military personnel for "shell shock." During the sessions, a story emerged about being taken aboard an alien craft and examined. Somehow, a local reporter got wind of the story and wrote a series of sensationalized articles for a Boston paper. To set the record straight, the Hills told their story to John Fuller, the author of another book on UFOs.

In his book, John Fuller emphasizes that Barney's initial therapy had little to do with the UFO experience. His job stress was the result of the fact that although he had a 140 IQ, he worked nights at the post office. Additionally, he and Betty were active in the NAACP, campaigning for civil rights throughout the Northeast. Betty came from an old New England family, although her mother had broken ranks and become active in the labor movement. Barney was African American.

In those few sections of the book that acknowledge race and the Hills' mixed marriage, Fuller stresses the success of their relationship and minimizes the problems they encountered. Once he concedes that "Barney, at times, shows concern about their rejection in public places: hotels, restaurants or meetings."[15] Fuller doesn't connect Barney's job situation with racist employment practices; he suggests that Barney likes the wages, that they compensate for the lack of challenge in his work sorting letters. In fact, Fuller's effort to downplay race is so strong that Barney Hill himself starts to fade: "All through his family background was a record of interracial relationships. His mother's grandmother was born during slavery, her father being a white plantation owner. . . . His father, though poor, was a good provider. He, too, reflected a mixed marriage; his paternal grandmother was fair — the daughter of white and colored parents. His grandfather was a proud Ethiopian freeman."[16] During therapy, Fuller explains, "Barney become more aware of the special conflicts and problems arising from being a member of a minority race."[17]

As written by Fuller, the Hills' story is not just about alien abduction. It is also about racial difference and the constitution of difference through difference's denial. The text produces Barney not as an African American, but as a racial hybrid, as more a product of mixings than a black American who experiences racism daily. Barney is detached from the history of slavery (his great-grandmother's mother is not mentioned; the father is a plantation owner), from the reality of racial discrimination, and from his own experiences (in the text acknowledging the pain of racism is a therapeutic product, not unlike the acknowledgment of abduction). Is it possible that his story escaped the confines of ufology because it commented on tensions around racial difference and mixed marriage in the United States during the 1960s, on the transgression of racial boundaries? Was it a way of thinking the unthinkable? Of using a stigmatized discourse to probe stigmatized practices? A reviewer at the time found that the few "pages describing Mr. Hill's emotions when he stops at a restaurant, a motel, or gas station with his white wife movingly demonstrate some of the Negro's problems in our society."[18]

In contemporary abduction narratives, hybridity refers to the offspring of humans and aliens. While not every abduction story stresses the breeding project, many abductees refer to it. The better-known accounts, the stories that, like the Hills', have aired as TV miniseries, appeared in the tabloids, or become best-sellers, always contain themes that concern sex, violation, breeding. These references to transgressive and invasive sexual acts by aliens suggest that part of fascination with abduction might rest on the narrative's capacity to probe the outcomes of "mixed" marriages, to comment or deal with the change in borders around human races.[19] The story of foreign invaders who steal people from their homes and breed with them, creating a new, hybrid race resonates with broader cultural experiences and concerns, propelling abduction out of the UFO subculture and into popular awareness.

So far, I've been suggesting that in American popular culture alien abduction provides a narrative that explores what happens when borders are crossed, when they no longer provide boundaries. I've considered both the formal status of abduction stories as challenges to the real and the textual telling of a particular story in light of the social position of the people involved. Once within the actual accounts of abduction, border crossings occur with abandon: aliens and people walk through walls, float through space; the aliens are sexless; alien machines extract ova and sperm in a sort of techno-sex; fetuses float in vats.

It is less the details than the very fact of the existence of abduction testimony that is important. Even with its bizarre, unbelievable content, the narrative testifies to what for many is the predominant sense of contemporary reality: insecurity. The borders that secure us have been violated, transgressed. Dissolution is part of our everyday experience. Inscribed in American culture during the second half of the twentieth century, the lines between black and white, home and work, Left and Right, dangerous and safe, shift and blur so that we are never quite sure where we are. Yet, as Thomas Dumm reminds us, politics in America has "consisted of boundary maintenance."[20] Maybe that is why when we hear a story of alien abduction and we can't believe it, we feel reassured. The story sets up the boundary we think we need at a place that surely must be secure(d). The stigma of the alien protects us from facing insecurity even as it enables us to think insecurity to its limits.

As a thematization of insecurity, the abduction narrative presents an extreme version of a classic ufological theme: the inability of the government to protect us. From its early years in the Cold War up through today, ufology has attributed the paucity of physical evidence of flying saucers to a vast cover-up, explaining that the nation's political, economic, and religious institutions would collapse if the alien truth were known. Alien technology is superior to that of humans — it can't be stopped (though, in some quarters of the UFO community, there was a great deal of excitement about Reagan's "Star Wars" defense plan). The abduction narrative extends this insecurity from the air above the nation to the bodies of its citizens. Even in our homes, our beds, our cars, we are not safe. Even when we think we are safe, we're not. Our bodies can be violated without our knowledge, our DNA stolen in a galactic version of the Human Genome Project. Somehow our time is "missing." Horrible things happen to us that we can't remember. We cannot protect ourselves. We cannot protect our families.

In many ways, alien abduction stories evoke the trauma of child sexual abuse. These are accounts of lifetimes of abuse, of violations that occur when one is helpless and vulnerable, when one should feel safe and secure. Functionally, however, the narratives differ. Though familiar, the alien is not family; the alien remains strange. The site of abuse is the same, but the abusers differ. The image of the family is protected, although the actual family is violated. So instead of seeking help from the state, legal remedies or juridical intervention, the abduction narrative blames the state for its failure to protect; indeed, for its complicity with violation. Although the family cannot really help with protection, it can be taught — in some cases, with proper therapeutic intervention — to provide support. Alien abduction reveals security to be a myth and a misplaced hope. Aliens respect nothing: no rights, no protests, no borders. They violate at will, stealing the future as they steal identity itself or, at any rate, identity as configured in scientized millennial technoculture — DNA. Human bodies, as Richard Dawkins says, are little more than disposable soma for genetic reproduction.

Typical mainstream cultural responses to notions of extraterrestrial life focus on fundamental transformations of history or culture. As we've seen in reactions to the announcement of possible life in our solar system, the reality of the alien is supposed to stimulate a sort of species-consciousness: ethnic and sexual differences collapse as humanity begins to understand itself as a whole. The borders between Protestants and Catholics, say, seem trivial when Earth is in the shadow of fifteen-mile-wide saucers or teams of Grays systematically mining human DNA. Given the rise in nationalisms and ethnic hatreds since the end of the Cold War, it may seem quite reasonable that more and more people may take comfort in stories that evoke a global humanity.

But, as I've stressed, this universal humanity is configured within the familiarity of strangeness, within an apprehension of the foreign that calls into question the very possibility of reality. This contradiction suggests the impossibility of thinking an idea like that of a global citizen. The world is an unimaginable community. This idea is inscribed in popular culture by the all-too-often-used-in-titles term "Alien Nation." The alien is always foreign, an other. An alien nation would be a nation of foreigners, of those who are always outside the nation. An alien nation is not just without nationalism; it is without nationality. It is a nonnation, an antination. *ID4*, the film Bob Dole found patriotic and nonviolent although millions died, the

White House exploded, and the Statue of Liberty was left lying in the dirt, expresses this idea. Even as the president (Bill Pullman) appealed to American sentiments, he displaced the idea of nations: "From this day on, the Fourth of July will no longer be remembered as an American holiday, but as the day that the world declared in one voice that we will not go quietly into the night."[21]

Despite the unimaginability of a global community, in the United States we are repeatedly reminded that somehow we have become or entered one. Biologists study our genes, reiterating an unmediated sense of species. The computer industry celebrates the Internet as the results of millions of individual computers. Declaring the mediating mainframe to be a relic of the past, the industry attempts to screen out the networks that power the webs of connections. Apparently, we are all connected in a world wide web, a borderless information economy. If the hype around push technology is believed, the links will become even less visible: browsers such as Netscape will disappear ("The browser becomes invisible by becoming ubiquitous. It submerges inside other programs, removing itself from our consciousness") as media are pushed into our lives through myriad linked-communications technologies ("networked push media can — and will — bombard you with an intensity that invitational media never muster. . . . There are times you want the content to steer you").[22] Through systems and exchanges that we neither see, understand, nor control, we are linked into a multinational, multicultural vastness of numbing complexity. We have more facts at our fingertips than we can integrate. The state has been decentered. Citizenship means less than economic position and access to information. Those who don't quite get it try to secure the borders and keep out the aliens.

Analee Newitz reads the abduction narrative as "a cautionary racial fable for our multicultural times." Explaining the moral of the fable, Newitz writes:

> Official policies on extraterrestrials hold that when they come, they'll give us fair warning and essentially try to befriend us. I would suggest that the alien abduction story, real or imagined, clues us in to the fact that most people on Earth aren't really convinced by the "official" position of multiculturalism. The multicultural position goes something like this: when the non-whites finally come into their own, they will not be ruthless colonizers like white people were. But the alien abduction story teaches us that what we fear most is that white people are *not* the only people or beings who might try to take over and rule the world.[23]

She concludes: "In the new world order, we need to admit that *all* people can be dangerous. Danger doesn't always wear a white face — it may not even wear a human face."

"H.R. 2202 extends current wiretap and undercover investigation authority to the investigation of alien smuggling, document fraud, and other immigration related crimes . . ."*

Budd Hopkins is a New York artist who has become one of the most prominent of the abduction researchers. Hopkins's book *Missing Time* disconnected aliens from their craft, his research having indicated that people who had not even seen a UFO may have been abducted by aliens.[24] Missing time — i.e., not being able to connect one set of experiences with another — replaced lights in the sky as an alien signifier. And Hopkins's work on the "Kathy Davis case" is said to have uncovered the purpose behind abductions: the breeding project. He prefaces his account of that case with "a note to the reader" in which he describes himself as a skeptic. "I'm so skeptical," he writes, "that I find it beyond me to deny the possibility of anything."[25] *The X-Files* catchphrase "Trust no one" expresses a similar idea. The similarity between these two ideas stems from their position at the front of the information wars. Both concern an inability to access reliable networks, to find meaningful connections. If anything is possible, then our friends could be our enemies; what we think is true might be a lie; what we think is fantasy could be real. Such a swirl of possibilities implies that paranoia is a — perhaps the only — sensible response to this absence.

Fabricated through the process of colonizing terrains of truth previously held by religion, science in the West used claims of skepticism to distinguish its approach to the real. Some scientists today collapse the distinction between a skeptical approach and the institutionalized practices of science. Carl Sagan, for example, writes as if the scientific orientation to the world were by definition skeptical.[26] Moreover, he presumes that this orientation constitutes scientists as defenders of democracy. This presumption leads him to articulate belief in abduction, magic, or God with threats to democratic decision-making. For Sagan, all nonscientific belief is infused with the vestiges of traditionalism. Consequently, all nonscientific belief has to be understood as reinforcing traditional relationships of power.

*From "Bill Summary: Major Provisions of H.R. 2202," *Congressional Digest* (May 1996), p. 141.

In a society where scientists are in fact quite influential, where their research is funded by corporations, where their opinions can sway juries, where the applied results of their findings can level cities, Sagan's implication that scientists occupy a progressive, even populist, political position seems nostalgic, even naive. Ironically warning that "skepticism challenges established institutions," Sagan writes: "If we teach everybody, including, say, high school students, habits of skeptical thought, they will probably not restrict skepticism to UFOs, aspirin commercials, and 35,000-year-old channelees. Maybe they'll start asking awkward questions about economic, or social, or political, or religious institutions. Perhaps they'll challenge the opinions of those in power. Then where would we be?"[27] Of course, he doesn't worry that students might start asking awkward questions about scientific institutions. He doesn't worry that they could challenge the opinions of scientists. Sagan isn't as skeptical as Hopkins because he, Sagan, works within a worldview that he doesn't question. He works within a worldview that he accepts as already proven, as already valid. Consequently, Sagan's last question is disingenuous. He doesn't even know where we are now, when people are skeptical to the point of paranoia. Sagan's scientific skepticism relies on mediations that have already collapsed.

Sagan supposes that abduction represents a threat to democratic decision-making. He is right, but for the wrong reasons. Abduction is not a threat because it's traditional, but because it exposes the limits of a democracy based on a unitary conception of reality. Abduction reveals that contemporary practices of liberal democracy fail to remain neutral before competing conceptions of the real.

Already in 1977 Langdon Winner realized that the predominant orientation to the world in Western technologized societies was religious rather than scientific.[28] Contemporary societies are so complex that people can neither formulate a coherent picture of the world as a whole nor comprehend the workings of basic items they use every day. As Winner writes, "Under these circumstances, all persons do and, indeed, must accept a greater number of things on faith."[29] Given the vast increase in complexity, in the workings of technology in our lives, and in the crises of trust that have impinged on American society over the past few decades, it is hardly surprising that a new skepticism toward religious thinking — this time that which masks itself as science — has emerged. Key processes in our everyday lives are alien, unintelligible. And whom can we trust either to explain these processes or to oversee them so as to guarantee that they won't hurt us? Is there an ozone hole? Rush Limbaugh thinks the ozone hole is a liberal, tree-hugging plot against corporate freedom. Someone recently told me that even NASA scientists aren't sure there is an ozone hole. James McDonald, one of the first scientists to notice the effects of certain emissions on the ozone layer, was discredited because of his work in ufology.[30] These days I use a lot of sunscreen.

Contrary to the idea that interest in UFOs indicates ignorance or misplaced religiosity, conspiracy thinking and paranoia flourish in ufology thanks to a pervasive skepticism. No one and nothing can be trusted. There is no overarching conception of reality. Most people working on abduction acknowledge the problems of hypnosis and the uncertain status of the memories uncovered in regression therapy. Some think that the memories are implanted by the aliens, that they are staged as a kind of theater, that they function as screen memories or symbols that the abductee can handle, or that they are part of a huge disinformation campaign.[31] Others stress the limits of the abduction narrative, reminding the community that much is occluded by such a narrative and that more research is necessary on the psychic and psychological dimensions of the experience. Still others think that the government might be involved — somehow. The various facts reported by abductees, be they dreams, memories, or thoughts that came to them — again, "somehow" — swirl in and out of contexts. They themselves have no set meaning. The meaning of abduction comes from the various possible ways of articulating the facts.

Paranoia flourishes within the abduction narrative as well. Many abductees report evidence of alien implants. Their bodies are evidence. They note lumps, small incisions, nosebleeds, odd images on X rays. At the 1996 MUFON symposium, I saw video footage of surgery on a toe. The surgeon removed what was described as an implant. These implants are thought to serve as tracking devices. Implants enable the aliens to find abductees no matter where they are. A complex system of global surveillance is thus inscribed on abductees' bodies.

Throughout this book, I've sought to link paranoia with a sensible response to real virtuality that is produced through excesses in the technologies of truth.[32] It might seem that I am talking simply about facts or information, about that surplus of data which is already a fact of life on the electronic frontier. But the deluge of information leads to paranoia only if some of it could be true. That is to say, the abduction narrative in particular and ufology more generally result not from skepticism alone, but from the conviction that "the truth is out there."

In the face of deep skepticism, this conviction is reassuring. Conservative deployments in the information wars would have us think that most, if not all, problems of American culture can be attributed to lefty relativism.

As if looking for patient zero, the former NEH chair Lynne Cheney pinpoints a more exact origin: Foucault's *I, Pierre Rivière*.[33] She rearticulates academic debates on the conditions of truth with orthodox communist constructions of history, claiming that American culture now finds itself deeply entangled in the presumption "that there are no true stories, but only useful ones, no overarching principles, but only the interest of the moment."[34] Cheney, like others who have brandished the argument William Bennett aimed at Stanford during its curriculum debate in the 1980s, misreads American culture because of her polemical treatment of theory. Alien abduction tells us that there are so many stories that could be true, so many stories that apparently fulfill our criteria for truth, that we can't choose among them. We have principles. We just don't know where or how to apply them. As Agent Scully told Agent Mulder, "I've heard the truth. Now what I want are the answers."

In abduction, what is hidden is true, what is revealed is true, what we know is true, what we don't know is true.[35] Abduction thrives on the notion that we should always believe the victim; that the authenticity of experience signifies the reality of the experience. But, at the same time, if aliens are behind this, we can't trust them. Alien reality is always virtual reality. With a technology limited by our imagination, aliens can stage experiences no one will believe. The abductees know this. Perhaps the rest of us do, too, but don't want to. So, we confine the strange to the familiar (strange) discourse of ufology.

Perpetually blue-screened, the facts of the computer world can be pasted into the contexts of myriad truths. Can we trust someone who claims to be HIV-negative? Do we use the criteria of sincerity and familiarity to decide, or the standards of a science we don't understand? Will more information help us decide? How much more? A friend of mine tested positive once and negative twice in the space of two weeks. He feels okay about his odds but isn't exactly secure having his life reduced to statistical chances. In some states, hospitals test newborns for HIV. Often they don't tell the parents. Do they track these children? Is the information on the Internet? Can we rely on any answer we get to these questions? Part of the pleasure of ufology is the seduction of the unknown, the pleasure of working in the vertigo of unlimited connection. Though often advisable and more frequently unavoidable, one risk of paranoia is titillation, the simultaneous result of too much and too little information. Is there something "to do" about the sexual roulette played by some young gay men today?

"With a population of 500 million or more, our problems, of course, will be much, much greater. With twice as many people, we can expect to have at least twice as much crime, twice as much congestion, and twice as much poverty . . ." *

In addition to providing a program that processes the growing sense of dissolution and paranoia in a millennial American where the replication and recombination of digitized locals produce the virtually global, the alien abduction narrative images the passivity with which all these contemporary effects are received. The agents in abduction are always alien. The aliens are behind the processes to which and through which the abductee is subjected. The abductee is just the material. She is paralyzed, taken, probed, examined, returned, traumatized, hypnotized. Everything is accounted for in passive voice, the voice of a new generation.

Passivity might be a good idea, a means of survival. Confronted with dissolution, insecurity, surveillance, and paranoia, the best response could well be not to respond at all, to wait and see what happens. The problem is that too much happens. With permanent media, passive resistance is no resistance at all. The Internet gives us information ceaselessly. Everything seems to happen at the same time, so what has happened is old news; and the future, well, the future is now. Thomas Dumm puts it better when he speaks of the contemporary situation as one "when time has become empty of meaning, when perspective flattens."[36] Passivity makes sense if we lack perspective, if we lack even the possibility of perspective because all possible points from which to assess our situations have collapsed into one another. Passivity makes sense when truth presents itself as our *other* option, when truth demands that we leave our bodies and prepare for the level above human.

Winner points out that "passive monitoring of electronic news and information allows citizens to feel involved while dampening the desire to take an active part."[37] The abduction narrative is a program for thinking about what happens when we no longer even feel involved, when too much happens for us to sustain any longer the illusion that *we* make it happen. All abductees can do is watch it happen and try to remember. And even when

* Statement from Representative Anthony C. Beilenson (D–Calif.) included in "Pro & Con: Should Legal and Illegal Immigration Be Considered as Separate Measures?" *Congressional Digest* (May 1996), p. 149.

they remember, they realize that memories, like the computer effects in *J.F.K.* and *Forest Gump*, can be blue-screened onto different truths. In some abduction accounts the entities are referred to as the Watchers. In all accounts they are noted for their all-seeing black eyes.

The sense of powerlessness that abduction processes has as much to with the dissolution of boundaries as it does with simultaneity. When we think globally, we don't know who our neighbors are, we don't know whom to trust. Thanks to the Internet some of us know more people in countries on the other side of the globe than we do in our own buildings or on our own streets. We don't trust anyone; we put our faith in things, in computers and technology. Our friends are f.r.i.e.n.d.s and they'll be there for us (at least on Thursday evenings). Indeed, the new American stories — as featured in NBC's collection of must-see sitcoms — are not about action. They don't have heroes. Nothing happens. And the fact that nothing happens is what is supposed to connect the actors to the audience. The audience identifies with the characters on *Seinfeld* because nothing ever happens to any of us. Whether on TV or in front of it, we all just watch, just as we've been doing for years and years and years. Even these boundaries don't mean very much. Just as in previous incarnations of reality TV, people in the "real world" continue to be videoed for MTV or diagnosed on *Ricki!*

Slavoj Zizek's discussion of the "theft of enjoyment" can help us understand not just the thematization of passivity in the alien abduction narrative but also the way the abduction program as a whole disrupts the fantasy of global citizenship.[38] In his analysis of nationalism, Zizek suggests that we impute to the other an "excessive enjoyment," always suspecting the other of attempting to steal ours. He writes: "What we conceal by imputing to the Other the theft of enjoyment is the traumatic fact that *we never possessed what was allegedly stolen from us*: the lack ('castration') is original."[39] In abduction, the alien takes away our agency, and the sense of security and certainty upon which our agency was predicated. This theft of agency is manifest not just in the power of the alien to paralyze us and abduct us at will, but also in its technological superiority and prenicious breeding project. Because of its expertise, it takes away our pride in technological achievement. Because of its genetic investigations, it abducts our children, our ability to determine, or at least to influence, our future.

Zizek's formulation reminds us that the abduction narrative functions to conceal the fact that our agency was an illusion, just like our security and certainty. The technology has been controlling us, developing, spreading, replicating with its own momentum, a momentum no one of us can comprehend. We might have thought that our genes are all we have, but since we can't really be said to own or possess them (they constitute us, or so we are told), their theft by aliens marks our contradictory and ambiguous relationship to our own biochemistry.

The alien steals a security we never had. Describing the complexity of abductees' emotional lives, Budd Hopkins explains:

> We get through life partly by the fact that we can read another's face, we can read their body language, we can get some sense of emotion. All of those things are denied us during contact with aliens. There's really no way we can tell what they understand about us. Their understanding might be incredibly subtle in some ways, but miss on some other major things. There's no way to know. . . . One man I've worked with who is an abductee said to me, "Budd, when I was standing there with them, if I could have thought of them as enemies and cranked myself up with hate, I would have somehow handled the whole thing better. But," he said, "it was the ambivalence of not knowing what this is, the total confusion. This isn't an enemy, it isn't a friend, it's not like me. What is it? I can't read it." He said the confusion added to his sense of helplessness.[40]

The aliens steal our security, our ability to tell friend from enemy. They take away our capacity to establish borders, boundaries. Deep down, of course, these borders have been illusions. Some things never really fit. So, while it is often thought that the alien is that which is completely other, the abduction discourse exposes the alien as that which reminds us that nothing is completely other (and everything is somewhat other), that the very border between "like" and "unlike" is illusory.

Why is this a statement about global citizenship? Throughout this chapter, I've pointed to problems with imagining the global. If the alien steals our agency, security, and certainty, it steals the conditions, the fictions, necessary for imagining citizenship. Even the most minimal sense of citizenship implies a notion of meaningful action, of choices that matter, of a capacity to influence outcomes. Citizenship suggests a relationship with governing institutions upon which citizens can rely, a relationship that they can trust. To be a citizen is to be able to expect a certain degree of protection. We — and here I mean any we that is or has been used to refer to citizens as a collective — have never had the agency, security, and certainty that any alien who violates our borders is thought to steal.

Since Zizek views the relationship to the "Thing, toward Enjoyment incarnated" as the element that holds a given community together, my use of enjoyment to disrupt the idea of global citizenship might seem paradoxical. In my example, is not the fantasy of the alien's theft precisely that enjoyment which binds together a global community? Of course not. Even as it suggests the conflation of local and global, abduction relies on networks. As a discourse of paranoia it erases the very links upon which it relies, the links through which it generates new and shifting connections. Alien abduction is not a Thing. It does not bind together a global community; it produces and is produced by specific networks of people and information. The excesses produced by digitizing the technologies of truth tell us that it could be a Thing, while our resulting paranoia reminds us that it can't because nothing can.

If agency is a fiction, then passivity is, too. The aliens might steal both our agency and our passivity, but the abductees testify to their experiences nonetheless. They use their experiences to produce meanings, meanings that within some networks, at some sites, are accepted, transmitted, and respected as credible testimonies, as knowledge. Passivity is a description of some actions within the context of a televisual public that hails some of us as citizen-spectators. In a different context, from the alien perspective of cyberia, we are not passive. We produce knowledge as much as we consume it; indeed, the result of consumption is a new production. When we work the networks, we make connections, creating and discovering new links, new sites, resituating and reconnecting old links, old sites. The extraterrestrial perspective envisions not global citizenship but the differentiated interactions of Netizens as what is "post."

In the techno-global information age, the only citizens are those who try to contain the rest of us with their borders, sciences, traditions, and truths. Such antidemocrats continue to buy into the fictions of security and identity. They continue to think that they can draw up borders to keep the aliens out. They continue to think that some of us are explorers, and the rest of us explored, coloring some of our journeys as invasions and infections. Post citizenship, we've lost the easy ability to label friend and enemy, credible and incredible, that enabled Cold War citizens to search and destroy the enemies within. We've also lost the ability to identify and redress some harms. As aliens, as Netizens, as those situated in myriad networks of information, opportunity, capital, DNA, and desire, we have trouble making claims to inclusivity, fairness, and equity. We can make a claim to freedom and, given our history of slavery, this is hard enough. There is no escape key, but we can always try a new connection. We have no duty to watch television, or even to be wired. We're already connected. Space is passive, cyberia is not. Abduction is passive, abductees are not.

"A credible policy sets priorities regarding the categories of unauthorized aliens that require urgent attention . . ."*

I've focused on the pervasiveness of dissolution, border crossing, hybridity, and blurred boundaries. America at the millennium is cyberia. Television is a tabloid. *Sixty Minutes* blends in with *Sightings*. The *New York Times* puts flying saucers on its front page, above the fold. Of course, a significant number of people, presumably those older than the wired Generation X, still won't admit that the distinctions have collapsed. They still want to appeal to authoritative sources, to get their news from reliable media. These people don't recognize that they've already lost key ground in the early wars of the information age. They don't get it: many of us reject their so-called reliable sources. We rely on networks of truths, on multiple sites of information.

In an otherwise compelling analysis of the differing assessments of the O. J. Simpson trial, John Fiske includes a discussion of tabloid readers as the "information poor." Of course, *Men in Black* wasn't out yet, so he didn't have its evocative treatment of tabloids as hot sheets, as sources for truth. Nonetheless, the assumption that the "information poor" is a coherent category, or one that can be contrasted with, say, Fiske readers, undermines Fiske's theorization of information-age politics. He describes the "information poor" as those "who feel that official knowledge denies them access to its means of production, represses truths it does not wish them to know, and excludes their truths from its category of the legitimate. For the information poor, the fluid skepticism by which they control their own movement between belief and disbelief is a survival tactic in a society in which the information economy is as unequal in its distribution of resources as the financial economy."[41] Fiske doesn't realize that in the complex technocultures of late capitalism, we are all information poor. "Fluid skepticism" becomes sensible paranoia. Official knowledge, moreover, smears into entertainment, rumor, and lies while corporations and individuals produce their own versions of knowledge and truth.

Some of us at the millennium still want truth; that is to say, we want

*From "Immigration Policy Assessment: US Commission on Immigration Reform," *Congressional Digest* (May 1996), p. 140.

other people to accept the truth that we already have. We want to be able to appeal to a set of reliable criteria that will enable us to explain why we accept statistics on alien immigration but reject those on alien abductions. Or we want to believe that the extraterrestrial aliens are real, maybe even that they're here. So when we access sites like Eon-4 on the Internet, a serial site devoted to documenting the continuing story of a long-term extraterrestrial contact project, we presume the information we get isn't "real." But the delicious sense of hacking into a secret database seduces us into unleashing our hopes and fears. And we enjoy the seduction, we want to believe, we want a reality.

This experience of the willful suspension of disbelief is hardly new. We have done it ever since we learned to tell, and listen to, stories. But although the experience is familiar, the context in which it occurs today is strange. As the formative years of ufology make clear, when hopes and fears are unleashed in a contained area, they may contribute to collective opportunities for celebration, change, or critique. That is not the only possibility, though. In an alien context, in a context where the field of intelligibility has shifted to the point of dissolution, releasing hope and dreams can contribute to the production of virtuality, to the experience of powerlessness. Detached from the networks of power and information within which they are produced, facts and desires, like computer identities and DNA, are recombinant. At any given moment we can believe what we want, what we fear. We can establish the truth or rightness of almost anything. All we need are a few neat arguments, like a theory version of Photoshop. Academically or philosophically familiar, these ideas are now the widespread, popular experience of everyday American life in the information age.

Deployable in the struggles for social justice and for the expansion of freedom, in the context of the globalization of commercial entertainment media, communications and computing technologies, and private multinational corporations, virtual recombinant reality more readily facilitates surveillance, insecurity, and passivity. When we trust no one, mediating stories and relationships dissolve. Instead of opportunities for collective or community action, we find ourselves alone facing the alien. We continue to dream of truth, reassured that its out there. We are hardly cyborgs. We saw the *Challenger* explode. We are inscribed by the mysteries of technology, kicking the computer as if it will recover its lost memory. We continue to long for citizenship and security, chastised by the link to conspiracy theory. Our hope participates in abduction.

There might have been a time when it was important to defend democracy on the basis of reason or to appeal to the somehow general will of a somehow unified public. That time has passed. Welcome to the twenty-first century. Stories of rational persons making decisions freely and equally as they talk together in a public sphere no longer command much mindshare. Feminist, antiracist, and queer movements have successfully eliminated a number of the brackets necessary for constituting the public as a sphere. Environmental, AIDS, medical, and welfare activists have similarly challenged scientific and juridical authorities, politicizing a variety of social locations and dismantling the presumptions of elite knowledge, elite objectivity. It's been centuries since communities met face-to-face. It's been ten years since the deregulation of television. The illusion of even a televisual public has collapsed. People have options besides watching TV. Now we can write our own programs and build links to others who are more than spectators.

Millennial America is an alien nation, a nation of aliens, a nation that is alien. In 1996 the House considered legislation aiming to reform American immigration policy, legislation that sought to shore up the borders between aliens and citizens. H.R. 2202 "makes enforceable the grounds for denying entry or removing aliens who are or are likely to become a public charge."[42] Like a sacred fetus or unholy child, the alien is a product of dependency. Citizens are agents, independent, in control. Anyone who is independent, who steals or disrupts American agency, perhaps by taking jobs or benefits, is alien. The alien morphs into an abductor, the one who acts, who violates our safety, our border, our home, taking what is not its own. With such a naturalization process, the alien becomes a citizen, dissolving the distinction between the two and transgressing the borders that constitute the nation.

H.R. 2202 also wants to ensure that American business remains competitive in world markets. For this, America needs "access to skilled foreign workers." At the same time, the bill wants to protect American workers from abusive and fraudulent practices that permit "illegal aliens to gain employment." So it establishes pilot projects "for employers to verify through a simple phone call or computer message an employee's authorization to work. The system will work through existing databases, and not require creation of any new government database. The system also will assure employers that the employment eligibility information provided to them by employees is genuine."[43] "The system" can meet the contradictory demands of international capital and American workers. Think globally, act locally by relying on existing networks of surveillance. Systems provide assurance, establishing who is a genuine worker-citizen and who is not. Again dependency is linked to the alien, although now American workers need protection. The skillful citizen has ventured beyond the nation. Since citizenship is articulated with agency, the United States seems to be a nation of passive, dependent aliens. Citizens are part of a global community, but one that remains insecure, undefined, in need of surveillance, dependent on the alien and, hence, alien and unimaginable itself.

Despite or perhaps because of the excesses of privatization, the pervasive sense of millennial America is that nothing is "ours," nothing is safe, secure, protected. Violence, abuse, poverty, and neglect disrupt familiar images of home. Some respond with vigorous interest in *Home Improvement* or Martha Stewart's complicated domestic projects, both explicit in their stress on the need to build and repair homes. Technology promised to save us time, to give us access to information. Like Hopkins's abductees, many of us today are missing time. Since what happens happens now, by the time we have assessed "now" it is "then." We have too much data, but not enough to make any decisions because we are uncertain about the contexts and networks into which we might integrate this information. Enabled by technology we become aliens, connected outside the state. Just as often, we're abducted by this same technology. To think of ourselves as cyborgs ignores our inability to program, format, evaluate, and contextualize information.

Our neighbors are aliens. Assimilation has been discredited as an ideal, and multiculturalism hasn't become much more than a marketing strategy. Peaceful coexistence demands mental changes, accommodation, tolerance. Better to forget the neighbors, go inside, and enjoy cyber-citizenship on the World Wide Web. What happens to me — alone, isolated, vulnerable — is of global significance.

Alien abduction narrates the predominant experience of the familiarity of strangeness in the techno-global information age. Unlike metaphors of colonization that presuppose borders to be penetrated and resources to be exploited, abduction operates with an understanding of the world, of reality, as amorphous and permeable. Colonization, moreover, brings with it the possibility of anticolonial struggle, of emancipation and independence. Abduction recognizes the futility of resistance even as it points to other possible freedoms. There may be nothing we can do about the aliens, but we can still write our experiences, link them to others, and build networks of community. The colonial connotes history. Abduction warps space and time. Whereas colonization implies an ongoing process with systemic limitations, abduction involves the sense that things are happening behind our backs, things have been done to us that we don't remember and probably couldn't bear if we did. To fight colonization, we take control. We don't fight abduction; we simply try to recovery our memories, all the while aware that they could be false, that in our very recovery we participate in an alien plan.

Postscript
Commemorations, July 1997

Roswell, New Mexico

Taking pictures of my silver Gray alien backpack at the site of the alleged crash in July 1947 of an alien craft, I started to think that I was participating in the celebration of the fiftieth anniversary of nothing at all.

Of course, it didn't seem like nothing. The town of Roswell, New Mexico, put a lot of effort into "UFO Encounter '97." Most of the shops lining Main Street decorated their windows with full-scale drawings of Grays. Some had alien dummies and dolls. Others had balloons with large black eyes. You could buy alien piñatas, kites, shoes, aliens in jars, refrigerator aliens, alien puppets, alien Christmas tree ornaments, alien artificial insemination kits. You could buy alien *everything*. There must have been two hundred different alien T-shirts. Though fond of the alien Elvis T-shirt, I chose the "Kokopaliens," a nice combination of the Southwest Native

Roswell, New Mexico, July 1997

American figure of the flute-player, Kokopelia, and a Gray. Dehydrated from the desert heat, I drank "alien agua" and "UFO H_2O." Runners participated in the 5K/10K "alien chase." Approximately ten floats competed for prizes in the alien "crash and burn extravaganza" parade sponsored by the Jaycees. Roswell's two UFO museums sponsored lectures and book signings by important ufologists. The Church of Christ featured alternative speakers testifying to the Christian message of abduction. A scientist from San Diego claimed that he had indisputable proof that a fragment of debris from the Roswell crash was extraterrestrial. He didn't make himself available for questions, though.

Although some commentators in traditional media cynically dismissed the entrepreneurial efforts of the Roswellians, an ironic move given the media's own commercial embrace of the alien, the economic aspects of the occasion didn't bother me. I liked them. It seemed a very American sort of commemoration. But I worried about some of the vendors left with hundreds of alien T-shirts. A young woman who had cleverly created ornaments out of eggs — dyed green, blown-out, and featuring an aluminum-foil alien suspended in the middle — was depressed that they weren't selling. A boy, probably about ten, sold me alien stickers for just under ten cents apiece, explaining that any lower would be "below cost." One seller complained that the event organizers let too many people in, that it was too

Roswell, New Mexico, July 1997

competitive to make any money. I didn't tell him that I thought his T-shirts were boring.

Other vendors were more optimistic. A woman who hadn't sold many of her dehydrated water kits, which also had matching T-shirts, thought they would do well on the Internet. This was her first entrepreneurial effort, she explained. She had learned a lot and seemed invigorated, empowered. A postcard artist told me that the "UFO Encounter" weekends Roswell had been holding around the Fourth of July since 1995 — for the 1997 celebration was the fiftieth anniversary of the saucer crash, not the town's first alien event — had given him the opportunity to get his work out. They had stimulated his creativity and provided him with an audience.

So, amidst the celebratory atmosphere of a small-town festival, it didn't seem like an anniversary of nothing. After all, it was on TV, and on the radio, and on the Net. There were more reporters than tourists at the "crash and burn extravaganza" parade. They wanted pictures of alien freaks, of folks in costumes, of people who made themselves into opportunities for the rest of us to laugh, secure in our own normality, our own good sense and rationality. I watched as a group that appeared to be making a documentary for the BBC interviewed a woman wearing a large Dr. Seuss–style hat covered with Grays. The correspondent eagerly asked her why she was there. What did he expect, I wondered? A sincere exposition on the historical significance of the crash of an alien saucer in the United States? A wild-eyed tale of abduction? The woman shrugged and said her husband had wanted to come.

The media didn't create Roswell. It wasn't just a media event. Some people had come to New Mexico to remember. Fifteen dollars bought a tour of the crash site. Well, "a" crash site. Sitting in one of the lectures sponsored by the UFO Enigma Museum I learned from the man next to me that there was a "new" site, and that this new site was the "real" site. It was much harder to find than the one folks could tour because it was on government land and not clearly marked. "Tour" may not be the best word for what goes on at the "old" site, either. A school bus takes visitors deep into the Corn ranch, the one where Mac Brazel found some strange wreckage in 1947. The bus stops at a makeshift clearing. I say makeshift because I had trouble telling the difference between the surrounding desert and the clearing where visitors receive a one-page flyer on the event. A couple of Stonehenge–like obelisks, recently donated, and a picturesque early-model car mark the entrance to a long path. Several hundred yards down the path, two more obelisks and a commemorative stone designate the point from which tourists can view the rocky cleft where the saucer came to rest. The marker, a rough-hewn stone inscribed in a runic font, reads (unpunctuated): "We don't know who they were. We don't know why they came. We only know they changed our view of the universe. This universal sacred site is dedicated July 1997 to the beings who met their destinies near Roswell, New Mexico, July 1947." When enough people arrive, a guide under a large umbrella retells a history of the crash and cover-up.

An anonymous donor had supplied a wreath to signify the deaths of the aliens. An American flag several yards away indicated the site where the surviving alien had sat as the military came to sweep away evidence of the event. Why an American flag? Because it was the Fourth of July, Independence Day? Because all Americans are originally aliens? Because America claims aliens and others for itself, consuming, absorbing, appropriating them? As the marker says, the spot had been sacralized, I think by a group of Native American dancers. I saw several Mexican or Mexican American tourists wearing "illegal alien" T-shirts featuring Grays in sombreros.

Among those visiting the crash site was a large family. They were much like other American families visiting important sites from American history, sites like Gettysburg which my family visited when I was seven. The father looked like retired military. He had the physique, self-presentation, and hat that suggest military; I guessed the Air Force. With him were five kids, from about ten to late teens. The family, the father, had invested in

Roswell, New Mexico, July 1997

this trip. It cost fifteen dollars a person, although children thirteen and under got in free. The kids listened attentively as their father described what had happened at this site outside Roswell in 1947. He told of two saucers, an electrical storm, the possibility of a midair collision or American missiles. He described the long debris field, the alien bodies, the rapid quadrating-off of the site. The family had already visited the International UFO Museum and Research Center, so they had seen the headlines from various American newspapers dated July 8, 1947, headlines that mentioned the crashed wreckage of a saucer found in New Mexico. In 1947, "flying saucer" didn't yet mean an alien-powered craft, but it was still strange, still unexplained. By July 9, though, the story was explained, or covered up. The military announced that it was just a big mistake, only a weather balloon. The wreckage was disposed of and the case closed until witnesses started talking to UFO researchers in the 1970s.

For a couple visiting from Phoenix, it wasn't the anniversary of nothing. They had been planning on hosting a barbecue until they heard about the Air Force's most recent "final report" on Roswell. They decided that if the Air Force was willing to make up wild stories in order to cover up the truth of Roswell, well, there just must be something to it. So they decided to come see for themselves.

The Air Force report, which got widespread attention throughout the television media and fueled furious activity on the Net, attempts to provide an explanation for the claim that alien bodies were found at the Roswell crash site.[1] The report follows up on a previous "final word" on the matter that the Air Force published in 1994. This latest final word revised the weather balloon explanation, admitting that it had covered up the truth. The truth was that the wreckage was part of an array of high-altitude balloons used to spy on the Soviet Union. The project involved secret, classified research carried out under the code name "Mogul." The 1997 report responds to criticism that the Mogul explanation could not account for eyewitness observations of alien bodies.

The response relies on dummies. Apparently, throughout the 1950s, the Air Force used anthropomorphic dummies in high-altitude parachute tests. Although dummies were not used in New Mexico in 1947, the report suggests that Roswell witnesses may have linked together memories of the recovery of the material from Mogul balloons with memories of dummy recoveries.[2] To back up its findings, the Air Force draws directly from witness testimony cited in several UFO books that specifically mentions dummies and plastic dolls.[3] One of the most popular T-shirts in Roswell features Grays with the caption "We're No Dummies."

Perhaps it seemed like the anniversary of nothing because there was commemoration without narrative. That is to say, there were lots of details about bodies and sites and wreckage, lots of stories from highly credible witnesses, but no coherent narrative account of the events that we were supposed to be remembering. UFO researchers debate over when the crash was supposed to have happened: Late June, July 2, July 4? Was there one crash? Two? More than that? Some suggest that there were crashes all over the Southwestern desert. Were there alien bodies? What happened to the wreckage? In a book published to coincide with the Roswell anniversary, Colonel Philip Corso claims to have headed a military operation that used the alien wreckage to back-engineer important technological discoveries, discoveries that were then leaked to American scientists and corporations that would appear to have developed the innovations themselves. These originally alien technologies include computer microchips, integrated circuits, and fiber optics.[4] The book made the *New York Times* best-seller list.

Everyone, including the Air Force, agrees that something crashed and that the identity of that something was initially covered up with the weather balloon story. A number of different folks in Roswell told me that although they couldn't say what happened, "good people," "respected members of the community," and "folks people speak highly of" claimed to have seen something, so they believe them. The links connecting agreed-upon truths, an excess of detail, and the failure of narrative produce a site wherein multiple remembrances become possible. What they share is a sense of doubt and mistrust as suspicion fills in the gaps in the script. The commemorations, in their variety and excess, thus seem to precede the event they celebrated. Because the event can't be fixed or narrated, it appears to be more like an effect of the tourists, media, and T-shirts that mark it as having happened.

Listening to Whitley Strieber read letters sent to him from other abductees, I wondered if the anniversary of nothing covered over real anniversaries. If part of the impetus behind Roswell was a compulsion to remember, and in remembering to call into account, what other elements in an American history might be linked to this alien story? Strieber's presentation relied on a variety of connections to named events in that American history credited as public. He inscribed Roswell within a history of the Cold War, reminding the audience that in 1947 Roswell Army Air Field housed the 509th Air Group. The 509th was solely responsible for deliveries of the atomic bomb. It was, in other words, the locus of "the bomb," the United States' nuclear core. Is it possible that remembering Roswell is a traumatic repetition of America's nuclear past, of our continued complicity in the deaths of those we render aliens? Beneath the commemorative T-shirts and ashtrays, might Roswell stand for the hidden, secret, and denied costs of the Cold War?

Strieber declared, to great applause, "Where secrets start, the Republic stops." He tied Roswell to Nazis via "Operation Paperclip," the program that brought in Wernher von Braun and the other rocket scientists crucial to the success of NASA. For Strieber, however, Operation Paperclip was less an instrument for the success of the American space program than it was an element of a history that continues to elude narrative, a history of black budgets, experiments on civilian populations, and a community of secrets that during the Cold War came to stand in for the U.S. government. It was a sign that the Republic, the American ideal, had come to an end, occupied now by Nazis and those willing to work with Nazis.

Perhaps because it was the Fourth of July, Strieber's final link was to the American Revolution. Interpellating a community through his declaration, he heralded "a second American revolution," this one in ideas. Those willing to hear him, those willing to resist an authority that claimed a monopoly on truth, were hailed as new revolutionaries. Their independence, moreover, was established not with reference to the alien, not with respect to an asserted reality, but to the possibility that "the truth is out there." The revolution, in other words, involves continued iterations of uncertainty

Roswell, New Mexico, July 1997

("we don't know," "we aren't sure," "we don't have solid evidence") voiced even by someone who claims to have been abducted by aliens. Truth was projected into the future, not something that could be claimed now, not something that could justify a claim made in its name. Roswell, then, was a reenactment of that original resistance which constituted America. As such, it, and ufology with it, became — if only for a brief moment in a darkened auditorium — central to the myth or the rhetoric of a populist reclamation of democracy.

Perhaps the Roswell anniversary occupies that site in the popular culture of American democracy that can't be occupied by the anniversary of the CIA. Like Roswell, the Central Intelligence Agency pinpoints its origins to July 1947. Like Roswell, it is enmeshed in conspiracy and innuendo, in hints, cover-ups, denials, and half-truths. It implicates and is implicated in the Cold War. Both are outside the ideal and civil speech of the public sphere; both remain part of the hidden underside of liberal democracy. The stigma attached to UFOs and conspiracy theory, the stigma that embeds Roswell in the popular subculture, provides a fire wall that continues to block access to the CIA. Even at a time when the agency seems ever less significant, concern with its crimes and attention to its secrets carry a hint of paranoia that reflects more on the one seeking to investigate the CIA than on the agency itself. It's hard to talk about spooks, black budgets, and covert actions without sounding crazy. We can talk about Roswell because in so doing we deliberately enter a stigmatized site. We can't talk seriously, to be sure; but we can talk, jokingly, laughingly. We can't even joke about the CIA.

Several weeks after the Roswell anniversary, an AP wire service report was posted on the Internet, announcing that the CIA had lied about its interest in UFOs. Not surprisingly, the report was picked up by much of the mainstream press. The report drew from a study by Gerald K. Haines, "CIA's Role in the Study of UFOs, 1947–1990," published in the unclassified CIA journal *Studies in Intelligence* and available on the World Wide Web.[5] Haines notes that "the idea that the CIA has secretly concealed its research into UFOs has been a major theme of UFO buffs since the modern UFO phenomenon emerged in the late 1940s." Consequently, his report "chronologically examines the Agency's efforts to solve the mystery of UFOs, its programs that had an impact on UFO sightings, and its attempts to conceal CIA involvement in the entire UFO issue."[6] The report acknowledges that the cover-up charges were true and that the cover-up itself was completely counterproductive: it led to ever greater mistrust of the agency. Haines provides details about a CIA-sponsored panel on UFOs that met in January 1953. Noting the panel's conclusion that UFO reports might induce "hysterical mass behavior" harmful to constituted authority and might well clog communication channels, he writes:

> To meet these problems, the panel recommended that the National Security Council debunk UFO reports and institute a policy of public education to reassure the public of the lack of evidence behind UFOs. It suggested using the mass media, advertising, business clubs, schools, and even the Disney corporation to get the message across. Reporting at the height of McCarthyism, the panel also recommended that such private UFO groups as the Civilian Flying Saucer Investigators in Los Angeles and the Aerial Phenomena Research Organization in Wisconsin be monitored for subversive activities.[7]

Just because you're paranoid, it doesn't mean they're not out to get you. Flying saucers threatened the culture of containment. The CIA did approach UFO witnesses and investigators. I wonder if they sent Men in Black. As Karla Turner suspected, the government has tried to encode UFO messages in popular entertainment media — even Mickey Mouse is involved.

To be sure, if the Haines report is to be believed, and as soon as it was posted ufologists were debunking it as still more disinformation, the messages didn't involve a pact with the aliens. The CIA's continued investigation of UFOs uncovered no evidence of extraterrestrial activity. What had to be kept quiet was its use of high-altitude spy planes, the U-2 and the SR-17. Witnesses reporting UFOs were catching glimpses of a top-secret government reconnaissance project. "Air Force BLUE BOOK investigators aware of the secret U-2 flights," Haines notes, "tried to explain away such sightings by linking them to natural phenomena such as ice crystals and temperature inversions."[8] The witnesses were credible, after all.

More than an anniversary of nothing, then, Roswell may be a celebration of conspiracy thinking, a festival re-creating that paranoia, justified and not, which has been central to American political histories. Given the globalized technoculture of late-capitalist societies, many find that doubt and mistrust are primary features of democracy at the millennium. As Haines concludes: "Like the JFK assassination conspiracy theories, the UFO issue probably will not go away soon, no matter what the agency does or says. The belief that we are not alone in the universe is too emotional and the distrust of our government is too pervasive to make the issue amenable to traditional scientific studies of rational explanation and evidence."[9] An editorial, "Some Thoughts on a More Glorious Fourth," from the *Patriot Forum*, a paper in the small Maine town of Castine, expresses a similar sentiment. Rejecting the Air Force's dummy explanation, the editorial observes: "Add to this one-among-many blatant, arrogant examples of government duplicity (e.g. Watergate, Iran Contra, etc) and it is little wonder that the average citizen grows more and more cynical about the federal government as a reliable source of information. Indeed, whether there were aliens in Roswell or not is not the issue, rather it may be this cynicism as much as anything that has led to the celebration in Roswell."[10]

Can we rely on traditional scientific explanations? Are there any reliable sources of information? Can the reliability of the sources be detached from the information and, if so, does the reliability of the information then come to inhere in the networks in which it is used, deployed, and disseminated? James Earl Ray seems about to be released from prison. Ballistics evidence — scientific, technical, forensic information — indicates the possibility that the bullet that killed Martin Luther King Jr. did not come from Ray's gun. Out of eighteen bullets tested, twelve have a distinctive marking. The death bullet is like the unmarked six. What does it mean to continue to believe that Ray is an assassin? Can one find Ray guilty and also accept that others whose accusations have been backed up by "scientific" evidence (say, O. J. Simpson) are innocent? There is still no solution, no answer, no explanation for the explosion that downed TWA Flight 800. We still don't know who planted a bomb at the 1996 Atlanta Olympics.

Throughout the summer of 1997, national news shows aired videos of mysterious lights that were hovering in a straight line over Phoenix, Arizona, the previous March. Some have claimed that the lights were part of a military test of experimental flares. Others have analyzed the "infrared signatures" and argued that they couldn't be flares. That same year, within the space of two months, the Air Force and the CIA — the U.S. government — published official reports on UFOs. Coincidence?

Grand Rapids, Michigan

At the MUFON 1997 international symposium in Grand Rapids, Michigan, held the week after the Roswell celebration, there was the strong suggestion that even if the Roswell anniversary did commemorate something, it was insignificant given the evidence of abduction. Abduction, many at the symposium agreed, designates more than an event; it constitutes an intervention in human lives and history.

The symposium was based at the Amway Grand Hotel. Other groups using the hotel for conventions or occasions were Amway itself and the

"Daughters of Job." One of the high-school-age women in the latter group described it to me as "Masonic." All three groups, Amway, Mason-girls, and UFO researchers, looked at the others suspiciously, as if they were freakish, cultlike. Demographically, they looked pretty much the same, although MUFON was somewhat more racially diverse and the Daughters of Job had significantly more teenage girls.

The theme of the MUFON symposium was "The Fiftieth Anniversary of Ufology." The sessions focused on the trajectory of UFO research since 1947. An important exception was the paper from Jan L. Aldrich, a UFO researcher from Connecticut. In his author biography published in the symposium proceedings, Aldrich describes himself as "retired from the U.S. Army with over 25 years in the field artillery and seven overseas tours." Despite his many overseas tours, he "has had no significant UFO experiences."[11] Aldrich's paper recovers the details of a forgotten history of UFOs in order to contextualize both the Roswell incident and the originary story of Kenneth Arnold's June 1947 sighting of nine flying disks near Mount Rainier in Washington State. It opens up the ufological past, rooting it in a history that is neither distinctly American nor inscribed within the Cold War. Accordingly, Aldrich stresses a variety of stories that appeared in European newspapers prior to the Arnold story. Moreover, he links them to a history reaching back to World War II. The effect of Aldrich's paper, especially given the tone of the rest of the symposium, was to lessen the hold of Roswell and specific past events on the audience and to draw our attention to the patterns, and terrors, of the abductions surrounding us all right now.

The first speakers were Beth Collings and Anna Jamerson. I recognized them immediately from their picture in *Connections*. The man who introduced them emphasized that their names are not real, that they use pseudonyms. Anna and Beth described some of the same events that are in their book. They didn't say anything about the naked man in the white cowboy hat or the giant bee. Anna told the audience about the "thought bombs" the aliens had implanted, one of which was to have gone off in February 1997, giving her new, important information. February came and went, and nothing happened. I was impressed that she revealed this failure of prophesy. But then I noted how she linked her story within the larger abduction theme that "the aliens lie." By revealing the failed prophecy, Anna added to her credibility even as she reinforced the abduction narrative. Beth cried at one point. They were both serious, appropriate to the import of their claims. Sociologist Alan Hill, also observing the meeting, told me that Anna and Beth's performances were among the most convincing he had seen. Each performed the role of abductee well, especially given that the script remains in flux. They weren't "New Age-y"; they didn't talk about the aliens' life-style. Anna, however, did say she thought she was being trained to navigate a spaceship. Still, overall, each was able to produce a credible persona that claimed for itself the right to be recognized, heard, and respected. They took questions from the audience.

For the most part, the first day was devoted to abduction. David Jacobs, the Temple University historian, announced: "The abduction phenomenon has changed everything."[12] Jacobs urged the audience to forget Roswell and refuse conspiracy theory. Research on both, he argued, had been a fruitless waste of time. He stressed the importance of disentangling ufology from anything that hinted of "New Age." UFOs are about science and evidence, not past lives and spiritual enlightenment. Abduction, Jacobs claimed, produces precisely that evidence: "Abductions have provided what was impossible to obtain with sighting reports: evidence of alien motivation, intent, and purpose. The abduction phenomenon has allowed us to enter inside the objects rather than simply observing the outside shells of the objects. It has also allowed us to enter into the minds of aliens."[13] Jacobs was not exactly clear as to the content of these alien minds. He didn't elucidate precisely their motivation, intent, or purpose. Yet he did hint that their purpose has more to do with human physiology, with reproduction, with sex, than with technology. The big alien secret, the truth of the alien, it seems, has to do with sex, a sex that in nearly all accounts of abduction is presumed to be straight and procreative even when conjoined with the alien.[14]

Jacobs's interpretation of the alien agenda could be a galactic version of the legal theorist Catharine MacKinnon's "victim feminism."[15] Humans are those who are subject to aliens, who are used by aliens, who cannot and need not consent to aliens, who are repeatedly violated and abused by aliens. Jacobs writes: "The evidence is now quite strong that we have been invaded by aliens and [that] abductees are subject to their abilities. They have not made formal contact because they did not want to. They have remained secret because they want to. They have been engaging in a systematic physical exploitation of humans because of a specific agenda that advances their designs. Humans do not figure into the equation as partners."[16]

Jacobs also encouraged research on abduction because of the respect it has brought to the UFO community. Although he emphasized the need for more academic contributions to the study of abduction, contributions that he thought should come from tenured members of the academy, less susceptible to "ridicule and scorn," he noted that the achievements of ufology had been reached for the most part without any support from academia, the government, or the media. Precisely because of the efforts of ufologists and abduction researchers, a phenomenon that one would expect to have been rejected as "wild and absurd" is actually accepted; in many circles, abduction is not dismissed out of hand. Jacobs interprets this acceptance, the consideration of abduction as a possibility in a variety of media and socio-cultural locations, triumphantly: "We have withstood intensive ridicule and scorn for decades and emerged, not quite victorious, but still struggling for the truth."[17] Respect equals redemption.

Budd Hopkins was the final speaker of the evening. He sealed the symposium's stress on abduction, marking abduction as the central issue of ufology. Furthermore, he strengthened the negative thread of abduction interpretation that Jacobs, Collings, and Jamerson had introduced. Hopkins, in other words, rejected any and all claims about good, benevolent, transformative, eco-aliens. Indeed, without mentioning his name directly, Hopkins took direct aim at John Mack, linking Mack with the Heaven's Gate suicides. Hopkins argued that "for anyone to accept the idea that we must bypass our fellow humans and look to the UFO occupants as the final source of ecological wisdom and spiritual growth is, unfortunately, to take a step along the same path."[18] The ecological message of abduction is, of course, the spin Mack puts on abduction, the meaning he sees underlying the phenomenon. For Hopkins, any such positive spin is rooted in deception — not simply in the self-deception of the abductee or the researcher, but in the deliberate duplicity of the aliens.

Hopkins also attacked Richard Boylan, the psychiatrist who at the 1992 abduction conference held at MIT said that he would sooner trust an alien than the military. (Hopkins refrained from mentioning that Boylan lost his license. He did, however, link Boylan's political beliefs to the militia movement.) Agreeing that the military has a shocking record of lies and deceit, Hopkins nonetheless offered the following test: In one corner of a room stands a Gray with its large black eyes. In the other corner, representing the military, is Colin Powell. To whom should a young mother entrust the care of her baby for a three-day period?[19] In the MUFON audience, Powell won.

As he argued against transformative and positive interpretations of abduction, Hopkins continued his praise of the strength of abductees. For him, mistrust of the government and the aliens needs to be kept separate from "suicide cults" and "right-wing, racist militias." Reasonable and healthy mistrust is linked with a morally appropriate humanism, one that stresses the right to know what is happening to us and our families. The latter, on the other hand, is implicated in the aliens' habit of lying to people, of telling abductees that they, the aliens, are really their parents; it is part of the disavowal of life and humanity found in some religions. In this context, then, the abductees came across as even more heroic: "More than any of the rest of us — more, even, than our voluntary astronauts and cosmonauts — abductees possess an understanding of the richness and mystery of our universe in ways that are more profound and more intimate than any of us has known."[20] Whatever transformation might be part of abduction for Hopkins stemmed from the opportunity to take not an alien perspective, but an extraterrestrial one like that which has animated the ecological and spiritual concerns of some of the astronauts, and which has been part of a capacity to think globally.

Mars.com

Roswell shared front-page space with news of the *Pathfinder* Mars landing. In fact, they quickly became linked together, especially on the Internet. Like millions of others, I received an E-mail message that parodied official explanations for the Roswell story, headlined "Mars Air Force Denies Stories of UFO Crash." The message continued: "A spokesthing for Mars Air Force denounced as false rumors that an alien space craft crashed in the desert, outside of Ares Vallis on Friday. Appearing at a press conference today, General Rgrmrmy the Lesser stated that 'the object was, in fact, a harmless high-altitude weather balloon, not an alien spacecraft.' General Rgrmrmy the Lesser stated that hysterical stories of a detachable vehicle roaming across the Martian desert were blatant fiction, provoked by incidents involving swamp gas."

At various sites on the World Wide Web, people speculated that, like the moon landing, the *Pathfinder* mission was a fraud. At www.marsconspiracy.com, I found pictures (presumably enhanced by Photoshop) claiming to present the truth behind the mission. On each page was an official photograph available from the Jet Propulsion Lab, together with the caption "Take a look at what we found." Underneath, the "enhanced" pictures displayed a close-up of the JPL original, revealing part of a six-pack left on the "Martian surface," a large steam shovel, and the Death Star from George Lucas's *The Empire Strikes Back* undergoing construction. You could also "buy the gear NASA doesn't want you to have." On other sites, I found Mars photos featuring various types of aliens. These were playful, ironic iterations of more conspiratorial themes involving a government cover-up of life on Mars.[21] I learned that aliens may have been responsible for the failure of the previous American mission to Mars. In 1993, the Mars *Observer* simply disappeared right before it was supposed to have landed.

But these insertions of the *Pathfinder* mission into the UFO discourse didn't detract from the wider enthusiasm for the mission. Nearly 40 million people accessed Mars sites on the Web. People involved themselves with the trundling *Sojourner* and its adventures with rocks and parachutes. It was better than a videogame. If we can't all be astronauts, we can at least simulate Mission Control. NASA realizes that the astronaut lacks the iconic power it held for Americans in the sixties; and NASA knows that the key to future successes is the Internet, inviting people to participate in discoveries from where they are, from right there at home. Especially given the travails of the Russian space station *Mir*, and the dullness of the space shuttle astronauts, sending actual people to outerspace hardly seems worth the trouble. The *Pathfinder* mission shows, like the film *Apollo 13*, that the real action is terminal, at the screens behind the scenes.

Could it be a coincidence that *Pathfinder* landed on the Fourth of July, Independence Day? *Independence Day* featured the invasion of Earth; perhaps the techies and engineers at JPL had in mind a mini-invasion of Mars. Maybe NASA wanted to point toward a new world order, a global network that united people all over the globe. This time, instead of using computers to defeat the aliens, folks would use them to adopt their own extraterrestrial perspective. Enmeshed in the networks of information and virtuality that are technoculture at the millennium, we can make most any link plausible, even convincing. But will we find anyone to believe us?

Notes

INTRODUCTION

1. See Andrea Pritchard et al., eds., *Alien Discussions: Proceedings of the Abduction Study Conference* (Cambridge: North Cambridge Press, 1994).

2. Walt Andrus, "INDEPENDENCE DAY — ID4," *MUFON UFO Journal*, no. 339 (July 1996), pp. 9–12.

3. Karl Vick, "UFO Abduction Tales Not Quite So Alien: Mainstream Society Finds Space for Supernatural Storytellers," *Washington Post*, May 9, 1995, p. A1ff. A source at Disney (who spoke under condition of anonymity) told me that he could find no records pertaining to the decision-making process or the development of the attraction. He attributed the addition of the alien ride to Disney's efforts to "stay in touch with the Zeitgeist."

4. Glen Boyd, "Surfing for Saucers," *UFO Magazine* 11, no. 3 (May–June 1996), pp. 15–18.

5. Scott Mandelker, *From Elsewhere: Being E.T. in America* (New York: Birch Lane Press, 1995).

6. Budd Hopkins, "The Roper Poll on Unusual Personal Experiences," in Pritchard et al., eds., *Alien Discussions*, pp. 215–216.

7. George Gallup Jr. and Frank Newport, "Belief in Psychic and Paranormal Phenomena Widespread among Americans," *Gallup Poll Monthly*, no. 299 (August 1990), pp. 35–43.

8. See Bruce Handy, "Roswell or Bust," *Time*, June 23, 1997, pp. 62–67; and "Poll: US Hiding Knowledge of Aliens," CNN interactive (June 15, 1997), http://www.cnn.com/US/9706/15/ufo.poll/index.html.

9. *Weekly World News*, February 28, 1995.

10. Cover, December 1995.

11. "Sunday," *New York Times Magazine*, August 4, 1996, p. 13.

12. See the important collection edited by James R. Lewis, *The Gods Have Landed: New Religions from Other Worlds* (Albany: State University of New York Press, 1995).

13. I'm grateful to David Halperin for bringing to my attention the interesting work of one of his students at Chapel Hill, Andrea Richards. In an unpublished paper, "Exploring the Mothership Connection: Louis Farrakhan, Black Nationalism, and UFO Narratives," Richards analyzes the abduction claims of Louis Farrakhan, explaining that his experience is narrated not within traditional ufological themes but within the theology and eschatology of the Nation of Islam. Thanks as well to Craig Rimmerman for keeping abreast of the *New Yorker*'s coverage of aliens and for recommending Scott Heim's powerful novel, *Mysterious Skin* (New York: HarperCollins, 1995).

14. Langdon Winner, *The Whale and the Reactor* (Chicago: University of Chicago Press, 1986), p. 113.

15. My inquiry is indebted to the work of Michel Foucault. See his *Power/Knowledge*, ed. Colin Gordon (New York: Pantheon, 1980), and *Discipline and Punish: The Birth of the Prison* (New York: Vintage Press, 1979). As I use the term "discourse" to describe the discussions, communities, and practices connected with aliens and UFOs, however, I am following Lee Quinby's reworking of Foucault. Allowing that the parameters of a given field of statements cannot be fixed, Quinby provides an elastic conception of discourse that refers to the "conventions for establishing meaning, designating the true from the false, empowering certain speakers and writers and disqualifying others" (*Anti-Apocalypse: Exercises in Genealogical Criticism* [Minneapolis: University of Minnesota Press, 1994], p. xv). She stresses the constitution of a discourse within a social context "that establishes regularities or prescribed ways of speaking that allow and disallow statements" (p. xv). Together with elasticity, the stress on situatedness helps to account for the ways in which discourses proliferate and expand. Heretofore relatively closed discourses, in other words, can spread beyond their primary field of statements. They can colonize other discourses or infect them virally, a change in metaphor effecting an alteration in meaning that introduces the possibility of unpredictable discursive mutations. Some discourses may become parasitic on others, articulating elements of the host discourse to feed their own ends.

In addition to drawing from Quinby's conception of discourse, I also use Ernesto Laclau and Chantal Mouffe's analysis of a discursive structure as "an *articulatory practice* which constitutes and organizes social relations" (*Hegemony and Socialist Strategy* [London: Verso, 1985], p. 96). Here, as in other poststructuralist and cultural studies approaches, "articulation" is a term of art. An articulation establishes a link among elements that changes their identity (p. 105). Throughout this book, I have generally used the term "link" as an easier, breezier, cyberian synonym for "articulation."

16. William E. Connolly, *The Ethos of Pluralization* (Minneapolis: University of Minnesota Press, 1995), p. 100.

17. Jürgen Habermas writes: "The supposition of reasonableness rests on the normative sense of democratic procedures which should guarantee that all socially relevant issues can be thematized, treated with reasons and imagination and worked through to resolutions which — with equal respect for the integrity of each individual and each life form — suit the equal interests of all." Habermas, "Nachholende Revolution und linker Revisionsbedarf: Was heisst Sozialismus heute?" in *Die Moderne — ein unvollendetes Projekt* (Leipzig: Reclam-Verlag, 1990), p. 232 (my translation).

18. Elaine Showalter, *Hystories: Hysterical Epidemics and Modern Media* (New York: Columbia University Press, 1997), p. 12.

19. The term "consensus reality" is used by philosophers to denote a particular theory about the relationship between people's perceptions and descriptions of reality and the "stuff" that is "really" out there "in the world." They might contrast

this conception of reality with, say, a correspondence theory of reality. But "consensus reality" is also a term of art among ufologists and abductees who use it to refer to the notions of the real accepted by and acceptable to mainstream society. When I use the term, I have both meanings in mind.

20. The sort of conspiracy theory I'm advocating here has nothing to do with anti-Semitism. Despite the fact that American conspiracy theories have appeared across the political spectrum, targeting various enemies from the Ivy League Protestant establishment, the pope, communists, and, yes, Jewish bankers, many people mistakenly assume that all conspiracy theories are anti-Semitic. I am interested in the form of conspiracy thinking rather than in specific contents.

21. Grant Kester, "Access Denied: Information Policy and the Limits of Liberalism," available in the Articles/Papers section of Sarah Zupko's Cultural Studies Center on the World Wide Web (April 1997). An abridged version appeared in *Afterimage* 21, no. 6 (January 1994).

22. Here I am influenced by Bruno Latour's compelling discussion in *Science in Action* (Cambridge: Harvard University Press, 1987). Latour includes the example of UFOs to point to problems that arise when scientists think outside the "networks" that establish for them the conditions of inquiry, discussion, and proof. "For instance," he writes, "an astronomer will wonder why 'modern educated Americans still believe in flying saucers although they obviously do not exist.'" In this example, "it is implicitly assumed that people should have gone in one direction, the only reasonable one to take but, unfortunately, they have been led astray by something, and it is this something that needs explanation. The straight line they should have followed is said to be *rational*; the bent one that they have unfortunately been made to take is said to be *irrational*" (p. 183). Consequently, I am not trying to explain why people believe in UFOs. My interest is in what the attention to aliens and UFOs in contexts beyond the ufological tells us about contemporary American society.

23. "Push technology" refers to the elimination of the Web browser as media are pushed onto the screen without the user having to search for them. In 1997 early versions of this sort of technology were available from Pointcast, Backweb, and Active Desktop. In a typically enthusiastic embrace of this new technology targeted at a stockowning "you" burdened by disposable income, *Wired* writes: "Networked communications need interfaces that hop across nodes, exploiting the unique character of distributed connections. Technology that, say, follows you into the next taxi you ride, gently prodding you to visit the local aquarium, all the while keeping you up-to-date on your favorite basketball team's game in progress. Another device might chime on your wrist, letting you know that the route home is congested with traffic, and flashing the address of a restaurant where you can eat cut-rate sushi while waiting it out. At home on your computer, the same system will run soothing screensavers underneath regular news flashes, all while keeping track, in one corner, of press releases from companies whose stocks you own. With frequent commercial messages, of course." See "Push! Kiss Your Browser Goodbye: The Radical Future of Media beyond the Web," by the editors of *Wired*, March 1997, cover et seq.

24. Phil Cousineau, *UFOs: A Manual for the Millennium* (New York: Harper-Collins West, 1995), p. 179. Cousineau credits these "quick facts" to an analysis of a 1990 Gallup poll done by the *Center for UFO Studies Journal*.

25. "Antipolitics '94," *New York Times Magazine*, October 16, 1994, p. 37.

26. I'm indebted to Simon Critchley and Aletta Norval for convincing me on this point.

27. In her discussion of James Lovelock's Gaia hypothesis, Donna Haraway writes: "The signals emanating from an extraterrestrial perspective, such as the photographic eye of a space ship, are relayed and translated through the information-processing machines built by the members of a voraciously energy-consuming, space-faring hominid culture that called itself Mankind. And Man is, by self-definition, a globalizing and, therefore, global species. The people who built the semiotic and physical technology to see Gaia *became* the global species, in which they recognized themselves, through the concrete practices by which they built their knowledge." Haraway, "Cyborgs and Symbionts: Living Together in the New World Order," in *The Cyborg Handbook*, ed. Chris Hables Gray (New York: Routledge, 1995), p. xiv.

28. Warren Young, "The Machines Are Taking Over," *Life*, March 3, 1961, p. 108ff.

29. Constance Penley overlooks the importance of computers and cyberspace in her assessment of the continued utopian potential of NASA and outerspace. See her *NASA/Trek: Popular Science and Sex in America* (London: Verso, 1997).

30. Dennis Overbye, "And Will We Ever Return?" *Time*, July 25, 1994, p. 58.

31. Sharon Begley, "Next Stop Mars," *Newsweek*, July 25, 1994, pp. 42–47.

32. Kester's "Access Denied" appropriately places discussions of Net democracy in historical context, linking them with similar discussions of steam and electric power.

33. See the critical article linking the Internet with conspiracy theory by George Johnson, "Pierre, Is That a Masonic Flag on the Moon?" *New York Times*, November 24, 1996, p. E4.

34. For a thorough history of the Heaven's Gate group from the standpoint of the sociology of new religious movements, see Robert J. Balch, "Waiting for the Ships: Disillusionment and the Revitalization of Faith in Bo and Peep's UFO Cult," in Lewis, ed., *The Gods Have Landed*, pp. 137–166.

35. George Johnson, "Old View of the Internet: Nerds. New View: Nuts," *New York Times*, March 30, 1997, pp. E1, 6.

36. More complex assessments of the political and social meanings of networked computers have been common in genres of science fiction and cyberpunk, whether in film, literature, or comic books.

37. For accounts of the eclectic methodologies found in works often grouped together under the name "cultural studies," see the introductions to *Cultural Studies*, ed. and intro. Lawrence Grossberg, Cary Nelson, and Paula A. Treichler (New York: Routledge, 1992), pp. 1–16, and *The Cultural Studies Reader*, ed. and intro. Simon During (New York: Routledge, 1993), pp. 1–25. My understanding of my ap-

proach has also been greatly enhanced by Gil Rodman's detailed elaboration on the use of cultural studies for providing a specific enough account of a cultural phenomenon — one, that is, that doesn't explain away what makes a phenomenon interesting by subsuming it under, say, capitalism or postmodernism. The elements of cultural studies that he finds helpful for understanding the posthumous career of Elvis Presley are also what enable cultural studies to shed light on the UFO discourse: "its radical contextualism, its explicitly political nature, its commitment to theory, and its self-reflexivity." See Gilbert B. Rodman, *Elvis after Elvis: The Posthumous Career of a Living Legend* (New York: Routledge, 1996), p. 19.

38. See Julia Kristeva, *Strangers to Ourselves*, trans. Leon S. Roudiez (New York: Columbia University Press, 1991), and *Nations without Nationalism*, trans. Leon S. Roudiez (New York: Columbia University Press, 1993). The discussion of Freud's *Das Unheimliche* in the former details the psychoanalytic understanding of the "immanence of the strange within the familiar" (pp. 182–183). Priscilla Wald's compelling analysis of cultural anxieties as they appear in, draw from, and displace specific official narratives of nationhood and identity is also useful here. See Wald, *Constituting Americans: Cultural Anxiety and Narrative Form* (Durham: Duke University Press, 1995), especially her reflections on Freud's use of the uncanny (pp. 5–10). Wald writes: "Freud's *uncanny* recognition . . . turns on the discovery that the unfamiliar is really familiar (the stranger as self) but also that the familiar is unfamiliar (the self as stranger). . . . Ultimately . . . the uncanny sends us home to the discovery that 'home' is not what or where we think it is and that we, by extension, are not who or what we think we are" (p. 7).

39. My sketch of this normative model of the public sphere draws from Jürgen Habermas's conceptualization of the bourgeois public sphere in *The Structural Transformation of the Public Sphere*, trans. Thomas Burger (Cambridge: MIT Press, 1989). See also my critique of the public sphere in chapter 3 of *Solidarity of Strangers: Feminism after Identity Politics* (Berkeley: University of California Press, 1996), and in "Civil Society: Beyond the Public Sphere," in *The Handbook of Critical Theory*, ed. David Rasmussen (London: Basil Blackwell, 1996), pp. 220–242.

40. Examples include the contributions to Craig Calhoun's edited volume *Habermas and the Public Sphere* (Cambridge: MIT Press, 1992), to *The Phantom Public Sphere*, ed. Bruce Robbins (Minneapolis: University of Minnesota Press, 1993), and to *Public Culture* 7, no. 1 (Fall 1994).

41. See Zygmut Bauman's account of the stranger's disruption of the friend/enemy opposition. Arguing that strangehood cannot be reduced to problems of knowledge and interpretation, Bauman writes: "The strangers are not, however, the 'as-yet-undecided'; they are, in principle, undecidables. They are that 'third element' which should not be. The true hybrids, the monsters: not just unclassified, but unclassifiable. They therefore do not question this one opposition here and now: they question oppositions as such, the very principle of the opposition, the plausibility of dichotomy it suggests. They unmask the brittle artificiality of division — they destroy the world." See Bauman, "Modernity and Ambivalence," in *Global Culture*, ed. Mike Featherstone (London: Sage, 1990), p. 148.

42. For a thorough account of the paranoia and fear of conspiracy in American anti-alienism, see David H. Bennett, *The Party of Fear: From Nativist Movements to the New Right in American History* (Chapel Hill: University of North Carolina Press, 1988). I'm indebted to Marty Kelly for bringing this book to my attention.

43. In his introduction to *The Phantom Public Sphere* (pp. vii–xxvi), Bruce Robbins returns to Walter Lippman's critique of the public as an unattainable idea to consider what it means today for the public to be a phantom. In this context, Robbins challenges the equating of the political with the public in the sense of open. I, too, question the assumption that "making visible" is sufficient — or even necessary — for political action, suspecting that "truth" is always what is presumed to be seen or revealed. What makes the public a phantom is its opposition to the hidden. The public sphere is haunted by the possibility of the invisible, the closed, the secret, and the surreptitious. My concern is with the way that, through its very use, the concept of the public sphere compels disclosure even as it conceals its impossibility: there can never be a full disclosure because suspicion is generative. Put somewhat differently, the intersubjectivity that gives the public sphere its political character brings with it the limits and distortions of recognition.

44. I say "may" because, with aliens, conspiracy is in the air. In "The Clinton Haters," a cover article in the *New York Times Magazine* for February 23, 1997, Philip Weiss discusses the various conspiracies allegedly involving the Clinton White House. The cover announces that "no President has been put at the center of more conspiracy theories, nor been the object of more virulent accusations. What is it about Bill Clinton — and the nation he leads?" Yet, Michael Rogin points out the centrality of the former president, CIA director, Skull and Bones initiate, and Trilateralist George Herbert Walker Bush to conspiracy thinking. See Rogin, "'Make My Day!' Spectacle as Amnesia in Imperial Politics," in *Cultures of United States Imperialism*, ed. Amy Kaplan and Donald E. Pease (Durham: Duke University Press, 1993), pp. 499–534.

45. William Corlett, *Community without Unity: A Politics of Derridian Extravagance* (Durham: Duke University Press, 1989). Thanks to Tom Dumm for helping me understand the importance of this discussion of reassurance.

46. Here I am talking only about the UFO community in the United States. There are large and active UFO groups in England, Australia, and Brazil. A UFO museum and research center is under way in Japan. The Mutual UFO Network (MUFON) includes representatives from thirty-five different countries.

47. At present, I can't provide solid evidence for this statement. Gallup polls support the claim that sightings and belief appear throughout the U.S. population (although the percentage of college graduates who believe in UFOs is higher than the percentage of those with only a high school education). See Gallop and Newport, "Belief in Psychic and Paranormal Phenomena Widespread among Americans." UFO literature stresses the diversity among witnesses and abductees. MUFON's director Walter Andrus agrees with this assessment, although he acknowledges that the number of African Americans interested in joining MUFON tends to be low. At MUFON's 1996 International UFO Symposium, the audience seemed to be just

as I described. I've spoken personally with abductees from a variety of ethnic and religious backgrounds, including Mexican American, African American, Jewish, and Anglo Protestant.

Brenda Denzler's survey data on the 1996 symposium indicate that 83 percent of the participants were white. Her data confirm the Gallup poll results with regard to education: 63 percent of the participants had bachelor's degrees, and 11 percent had doctorates. Interestingly, 87 percent of the participants claimed to vote in regular elections. See Denzler, "Who Are We?" *MUFON UFO Journal*, no. 349 (May 1997), pp. 9–14.

48. Those of you reading this, don't worry; your secrets are safe.

49. See Tony Kushner, *Angels in America: A Gay Fantasia on National Themes* (New York: Theatre Commissions Group, 1993). In particular, I have in mind "Part One: Millennium Approaches." Also see David M. Jacobs, *The UFO Controversy in America* (Bloomington: Indiana University Press, 1975).

50. Lynn Spigel, "From Domestic Space to Outer Space," *Close Encounters: Film, Feminism, and Science Fiction*, ed. Constance Penley, Elisabeth Lyon, Lynn Spigel, and Janet Bergstrom (Minneapolis: University of Minnesota Press, 1991), p. 210. See also Walter A. McDougall, . . . *The Heavens and the Earth: A Political History of the Space Program* (New York: Basic Books, 1985).

51. Rogin writes: "The linkage of expansion to freedom instead of to the acquisition of colonies prepared the United States to see itself as the legitimate defender of freedom in the postcolonial Third World" ("Make My Day," p. 510).

52. In his account of narratives employed in the constitution of American national identity, Michael Shapiro explains that "responses to cultural anxieties have often taken the form of repeating the story of the winning of the West; the retelling of the myth of violent (yet sacred) expansion has been a dominant mode through which 'America' has performed its legendary national identity. Such textual performances, in which Americans are constituted (or reconstituted) in response to cultural anxieties about appropriate personhood, have been evident in various historical periods . . . in which America's mythic Western past was reaffirmed . . . [and are] especially pertinent to the politics of constructing the alien-other." NASA's construction of the astronaut-hero is one such retelling. See Shapiro, "Narrating the Nation, Unwelcoming the Stranger: Anti-Immigration Policy in Contemporary 'America,'" *Alternatives* 22, no. 1 (January–February 1997), pp. 1–34, quotation p. 28.

53. Elayne Rapping, *The Looking Glass World of Nonfiction TV* (Boston: South End Press, 1987), p. 79.

54. I'm drawing here from what Shapiro refers to as "the myth of vacancy at the place of settlement," a myth vital to the national identity of the biblical Israel and redeployed in America's fantasy of the wild, open West. See Shapiro, "Narrating the Nation," p. 25.

55. Paul Boyer, *When Time Shall Be No More* (Cambridge: Harvard University Press, Belknap, 1992), p. 265.

56. Showalter, *Hystories*, p. 196.

57. See my "Coming Out as an Alien: Feminists, UFOs, and 'the Oprah Effect,'" in *"Bad Girls"/"Good Girls": Women, Sex, and Power in the Nineties*, ed. Nan Bauer Maglin and Donna Perry (New Brunswick: Rutgers University Press, 1996), pp. 90–105.

CHAPTER 1. FUGITIVE ALIEN TRUTH

1. There are numerous ways to interpret not just *The X-Files* but also the series' connections to contemporary paranoia. For example, William Carey McWilliams finds that "in 1996 paranoia has taken a stride toward the mainstream: 48 percent of Americans, *Newsweek* told us, believe in UFOs and are convinced that the government is covering up the evidence, while 29 percent believe the government has been in contact with aliens. The TV Series 'The X-Files' (like the film *Independence Day*) symbolizes that rather creepy dimension of the national mood. It also tells us something about our politics: The heroes are people who work for the government. Americans may suspect officials of being in league with malign powers, but they also know, at least dimly, that government is the best hope they've got." McWilliams, "Clinton's Reelection: The 'X' Factor," *Commonweal*, October 11, 1996, p. 9. Given Mulder's antagonistic relationship to the rest of the bureau, I don't share McWilliams's interpretation of the series. Indeed, it seems to me that Mulder's hope rests less in the government than in the possibility of going directly to the people. See also the contributions to *"Deny All Knowledge": Reading the X-Files*, ed. David Lavery, Angela Hague, and Marla Cartwright (Syracuse: Syracuse University Press, 1996). Of course, the best place to find high-quality *X-Files* commentary is the Internet.

2. See Sarah Stegall's commentary on the episode: "Six Degrees of Separation," posted in 1996 at http://www.webcom.com/munchkyn*munchkyn@net.com.com. See also the introduction to Lavery et al., eds., *"Deny All Knowledge,"* pp. 13–20.

3. Bill Barker, *SCHWA* (Reno, Nev.: Schwa Press, 1993).

4. See John E. Mack, *Abduction: Human Encounters with Aliens* (New York: Charles Scribner's Sons, 1994).

5. See Whitley Strieber, *Communion: A True Story* (New York: William Morrow, 1987); Budd Hopkins, *Missing Time: A Documented Study of UFO Abductions* (New York: Richard Marek, 1981) and *Intruders: The Incredible Visitations at Copley Woods* (New York: Random House, 1987).

6. Although Hopkins's 1981 book, *Missing Time*, was the first to disconnect abduction from a UFO sighting (it reads missing time as a sign of an alien encounter), it was not the first published abduction account to receive widespread attention. The first, as I discuss below, occurred in the early sixties and involved a Massachusetts couple, Betty and Barney Hill.

7. A 1990 Gallup poll reported that 27 percent of its respondents believed UFOs had contacted Earth. This same poll reveals that although there has been a decline in belief in the reality of UFOs since 1978 (57% in 1978 vs. 47% in 1990), there has

been an increase in the number of people claiming to have seen a UFO (9% in 1978 vs. 14% in 1990). The *Time*/CNN poll taken in June 1997 has 8 percent of its respondents reporting to have seen a UFO and 22 percent believing that beings from other planets have contacted humans. "Poll: US Hiding Knowledge of Aliens," CNN interactive (June 15, 1997), http://www.cnn.com/US/9706/15/ufo.poll/index.html.

Results of a 1993 poll in Germany indicate that only 17 percent of Germans believe in the reality of UFOs, 19 percent of those living in the West and 12 percent of those living in the East. See the *Index to International Public Opinion, 1992–1993* (Westport, Conn.: 1995), p. 549. Additionally, a search of the *National Newspaper Index* indicates that mass-media attention to UFOs and aliens in 1995 (the year following the publication of Mack's book) was nearly twice that of 1990 (Menlo Park, Calif.: Information Access Company, 1995).

8. Karl Vick, "UFO Abduction Takes Not Quite So Alien: Mainstream Society Finds Space for Supernatural Storytellers," *Washington Post*, May 9, 1995, p. A16.

9. This posting was part of a series in which several members rambled and ranted about the Hollywood group known as the "Rat Pack." Some incorporated the Las Vegas performers Frank Sinatra, Dean Martin, Joey Bishop, Sammy Davis Jr., and Peter Lawford into various conspiracy theories involving the Kennedys, the Mob, and control of the government. Others worried about their treatment of Jerry Lewis or admired their cool ability to "walk into a party as if they were walking onto a yacht."

10. Travis Walton, *The Walton Experience* (New York: Berkley, 1978).

11. Neither Walton nor the announcers mention that the *National Enquirer* featured the Walton case in at least two issues (December 16, 1975, and July 6, 1976). They also forget to add that Walton and the six men who claimed to witness his abduction split the $5,000 prize they won from the tabloid for "1975's Most Extraordinary Encounter with a UFO." See Curtis Peebles, *Watch the Skies! A Chronicle of the Flying Saucer Myth* (Washington, D.C.: Smithsonian Institution Press, 1994), pp. 230–231.

12. See also Douglas Rushkoff's discussion of the T-shirt campaign by the media activist Nick Phillip, a campaign involving the production of T-shirts bearing the slogan "UFOs Are Real." Rushkoff quotes Phillip as saying, "It's the ultimate conspiracy, in a way, but its real value is on a metaphorical level. What an alien would represent in terms of dealing with our current paradigms — our understanding of what's possible. As we approach the next millennium, the rate of change is increasing dramatically. I think the UFO is an icon of that change. It's showing that we're moving through a period where we need more spirituality in order to answer the questions." Rushkoff, *Media Virus* (New York: Ballantine, 1994).

13. C. D. B. Bryan, *Close Encounters of the Fourth Kind: Alien Abduction, UFOs, and the Conference at MIT* (New York: Knopf, 1995), p. 155.

14. My stress on fugitivity grew out of reading Jacques Vallee's *Passport to Magonia: On UFOs, Folklore, and Parallel Worlds* (Chicago: Contemporary Books, 1993 [1969]). Vallee links the "fugitivity of UFO manifestations" with fairy tales,

theorizing that both are manifestations of a superior consciousness/entity intervening in human life from a parallel reality.

15. Elaine Showalter argues that alien abduction is but one strain of an epidemic of hysteria running rampant in America today. See her *Hystories: Hysterical Epidemics and Modern Culture* (New York: Columbia University Press, 1997).

16. Keith Thompson argues that the UFO phenomenon represents transitional or liminal experiences through which we come to appreciate the importance of the very process of questioning, of the search itself. See Thompson, *Angels and Aliens: UFOs and the Mythic Imagination* (New York: Addison-Wesley, 1991).

17. See Elaine Showalter, *Sexual Anarchy: Gender and Culture at the Fin de Siècle* (New York: Penguin Books, 1990) and Sally Ledger and Scott McCracken, eds., *Cultural Politics at the Fin de Siècle* (Cambridge: Cambridge University Press, 1995). Some of the discussions of American millennialism that take up UFOs and alien abduction include Hillel Schwartz, *Century's End: An Orientation Manual toward the Year 2000* (New York: Doubleday, Currency, 1996), esp. pp. 172–176, and Charles B. Strozier, *Apocalypse: On the Psychology of Fundamentalism in America* (Boston: Beacon, 1994), esp. pp. 235–237.

18. See Lee Quinby, *Anti-Apocalypse: Essays in Genealogical Criticism* (Minneapolis: University of Minnesota Press, 1994).

19. Gordon J. Melton, "The Contactees: A Survey," in *The Gods Have Landed: New Religions from Other Worlds*, ed. James R. Lewis (Albany: State University of New York Press, 1995), pp. 1–14.

20. See Théodore Flournoy, *From India to the Planet Mars: A Case of Multiple Personality with Imaginary Languages* (Princeton: Princeton University Press, 1994), in particular the introduction by Sonu Shamdasani which places Flournoy in the context of the formative years of psychology.

21. See Howard Blum, *Out There* (New York: Pocket Books, 1990).

22. Ibid., pp. 86–87.

23. See Paul Boyer, *When Time Shall Be No More: Prophecy Belief in Modern American Culture* (Cambridge: Harvard University Press, 1992).

24. See his self-published collection of papers delivered at various symposia during the late 1970s: Stanton Friedman, *Flying Saucers: Four Scientific Papers* (Fredericton, N.B.: UFORI, P.O.B., 1988).

25. Leon Festinger, Henry W. Riechen, and Stanley Schachter, *When Prophecy Fails* (Minneapolis: University of Minnesota Press, 1956).

26. See Jerome Clark, *The Emergence of a Phenomenon: UFOs from the Beginning through 1959* (Detroit: Omnigraphics, 1992), p. 77.

27. Mack, *Abduction*, p. 40.

28. Whitley Strieber, *Transformation: A Breakthrough* (New York: Avon Books, 1989), p. 53. See also Mack, *Abduction*; Thompson, *Angels and Aliens*.

29. Mack, *Abduction*, p. 415.

30. Quinby, *Anti-Apocalypse*, pp. xx–xxi.

31. For a thorough analysis of the cultural narratives of the Cold War, see Alan

Nadel, *Containment Culture: American Narratives, Postmodernism, and the Atomic Age* (Durham: Duke University Press, 1995).

32. David M. Jacobs, *The UFO Controversy in America* (Bloomington: Indiana University Press, 1975), p. 44.

33. Ibid., p. 50.

34. Ibid., pp. 57–60.

35. See Donald E. Keyhoe, *Flying Saucers: Top Secret* (New York: G. P. Putnam's Sons, 1960) and Donald H. Menzel and Ernest H. Taves, *The UFO Enigma: The Definitive Explanation of the UFO Phenomenon* (Garden City, N.Y.: Doubleday, 1977). The Condon report has NICAP claiming 12,000 members and APRO claiming 8,000. See Edward U. Condon, scientific director, *Final Report of the Scientific Study of Unidentified Flying Objects Conducted by the University of Colorado under Contract to the United States Air Force* (Board of Regents of the University of Colorado, 1968).

36. Jacobs, *The UFO Controversy in America*, p. 200.

37. Ibid. My summary of the Michigan sightings draws from Jacobs.

38. Quoted ibid., p. 202.

39. Quoted in Peebles, *Watch the Skies!* p. 175.

40. Quoted ibid.

41. Ibid., p. 183.

42. Jacobs, *The UFO Controversy in America*, pp. 232–233.

43. Condon, *Final Report*, p. 2.

44. U.S. House, *Symposium on Unidentified Flying Objects, Hearings before the Committee on Science and Astronautics*, 90th Cong., 2d. sess., July 29, 1968, no. 7, p. 83.

45. Jacobs, *The UFO Controversy in America*, pp. 108–131. Lewis, ed., *The Gods Have Landed*, provides an excellent bibliography of contactee pamphlets and publications from the 1950s as well as several insightful analyses of UFO groups as new religious movements.

46. Clark, *The Emergence of a Phenomenon*, p. 4.

47. Stephen J. Whitfield, *The Culture of the Cold War* (Baltimore: Johns Hopkins University Press, 1991), pp. 58–59.

48. In his history of Cold War America, Tom Englehardt concurs, viewing the ufologists as "almost the only group at the time to take on the national security state directly, assailing the secrecy that surrounded the government's UFO investigations and claiming a cover-up of information relating to the reality of space aliens." Englehardt, *The End of Victory Culture* (New York: Basic Books, 1995), p. 104.

49. U.S. House, *Unidentified Flying Objects, Hearing by the Committee on Armed Services*, 89th Cong., 2d sess., April 5, 1966, no. 55, p. 6047.

50. Condon, *Final Report*, p. 8.

51. John A. Keel, "The Flying Saucer Subculture" (New York Fortean Society, 1994), reprinted from the *Journal of Popular Culture* 8, no. 4 (1975), p. 886.

52. Englehardt, *The End of Victory Culture*, p. 104.

53. U.S. House, *Unidentified Flying Objects*, p. 6068.

54. Sydney Walker, "The Applied Assessment of Central Nervous System Integrity: A Method for Establishing the Creditability of Eye Witness and Other Observers," in U.S. House, *Symposium*, app. 2, pp. 152–175.

55. Ibid., pp. 166–167.

56. Ibid., p. 173.

57. U.S. House, *Symposium*, p. 194.

58. U.S. House, *Unidentified Flying Objects*, p. 6047.

59. U.S. House, *Symposium*, p. 107.

60. John Mack, "An Approach to Helping Abductees," in *Alien Discussions: Proceedings of the Abduction Study Conference*, ed. Andrea Pritchard et al. (Cambridge: North Cambridge Press, 1994), pp. 478–484; Deborah Bruce Truncale, "Alien/UFO Experiences of Children," in Pritchard et al., eds., *Alien Discussions*, pp. 116–126.

61. John G. Fuller, *The Interrupted Journey* (New York: Dial Press, 1966), p. 54. Fuller writes that Barney did not "associate his need for therapy with the UFO incident, feeling mainly that the conflict over his father–son relationship was at the base of his problem, the long distance to Philadelphia [where his first wife lived with their sons] making it impossible to be a devoted father." Parts of the book were serialized in *Look* magazine in 1966, and the book would become the basis for the 1975 television movie *The UFO Incident*, in which James Earl Jones plays Barney Hill.

62. Fuller, *The Interrupted Journey*, pp. 16–17.

63. "I became suddenly flabbergasted," Fuller quotes Barney Hill as saying, "to think that I realized for the first time that at the rate of speed I always travel, we should have arrived home at least two hours earlier than we did" (ibid., p. 45).

64. Ibid., p. 47.

65. Ibid.

66. Ibid., pp. 58–59.

67. See D. Scott Rogo's introduction to his edited volume *Alien Abductions: True Cases of UFO Kidnappings* (New York: New American Library, 1980), pp. 1–18.

68. Coral and Jim Lorenzen, *Abducted! Confrontations with Beings from Outer Space* (New York: Berkley Medallion Books, 1977), p. 142.

69. In his appendix to the Lorenzen book, R. Leo Sprinkle concludes (1) that "there are limitations in the effectiveness of hypnotic time regression procedures, and there is no guarantee that the procedures will produce a 'reliving' of earlier events in the life of the participant" and (2) that "many persons have the potential to utilize self-hypnosis or 'imaginative involvement' in order to recall earlier experiences, and these memories may not only provide reliable (repeatable, personal) information but possibly may provide valid (real, nonpersonal) information" (ibid., p. 216).

70. Ibid., p. 136.

71. Raymond E. Fowler, *The Andreasson Affair* (New York: Bantam Books, 1979), p. 210.

72. Ibid., p. 207. He adds: "In establishing the community reputation of a witness, one is basically concerned about honesty and basic human relations. Such in-

formation is obtained by questioning present friends, neighbors, teachers, ministers, and business associates." To establish Betty's credibility, he notes that she was a good homemaker who had married young and never completed high school. She had seven children before she was thirty years old. She was also a Pentecostalist who gave the aliens a Bible when they declined the material food she offered them.

73. Whitley Strieber, *Transformation*, pp. 267–269.

74. Hopkins, *Missing Time*, pp. 7–8.

75. Ibid., pp. 232–233.

76. Ibid., p. 12.

77. Edith Fiore, *Encounters: A Psychologist Reveals Case Studies of Abductions by Extraterrestrials* (New York: Ballantine, 1989), p. 257.

78. See Lawrence Fawcett and Barry J. Greenwood, *The UFO Cover-up: What the Government Won't Say* (New York: Simon and Schuster, 1992).

79. Budd Hopkins, "The Roper Poll on Unusual Personal Experiences," in Pritchard et al., eds., *Alien Discussions*, pp. 215–216. See also the critiques of the poll collected in the same volume.

80. See Vick, "UFO Abduction Tales."

81. In Pritchard et al., eds., *Alien Discussions*, p. 387.

82. Ron Westrum, "UFO Abductions as a Hidden Event," ibid., p. 533.

83. Jean E. Byrne, "Hypnosis as a Therapeutic Tool," ibid., p. 503.

84. Ibid.

85. Westrum, "UFO Abductions," p. 536.

86. Mack, "An Approach to Helping Abductees," p. 484.

87. See Michael D. Swords, ed., *Journal of UFO Studies* 1 (1989), p. 1.

88. Jenny Randles and Peter Warrington, *Science and the UFOs* (Oxford: Basil Blackwell, 1985), p. 68.

89. Ibid., p. 6.

90. Mack, *Abduction*, p. 20.

91. John Mack, "Studying Intrusions from the Subtle Realm: How Can We Deepen Our Knowledge," in *Ufology: A Scientific Enigma*, MUFON 1996 International UFO Symposium Proceedings (Seguin, Texas: Mutual UFO Network, 1996), p. 146.

92. Mack insists that any plausible explanation of alien abduction must account for the following:

1. The high degree of consistency of detailed abduction accounts, reported with emotion appropriate to actual experiences, told by apparently reliable observers.
2. The absence of psychiatric illness or other apparent psychological or emotional factors that could account for what is being reported.
3. The physical changes and lesions affecting the bodies of the experiencers....
4. The association with UFOs witnessed independently by others while abductions are taking place....
5. The reports of abductions by children as young as two or three years of age. (See Bryan, *Close Encounters of the Fourth Kind*, p. 418)

93. Pritchard et al., eds., *Alien Discussions*, p. 413.

94. Friedman, *Flying Saucers*, p. 11.

95. Ibid., p. 10.

96. Budd Hopkins, "A Response to NOVA: Science Is Not Always What Science Programs Do," *Houston Sky* (A Bimonthly UFO Newsletter for Houston-Area MUFON Members and Others), no. 9 (February–March 1996), p. 1 et seq.

97. Ibid.

98. Ibid., pp. 6–7.

99. Carl Sagan, *The Demon-Haunted World* (New York: Random House, 1995), p. 164.

100. Ibid., p. 166.

101. Ibid., p. 165.

102. See Linda Robertson, "Outing Exclusionary Economic Rhetoric," a paper presented at the Allied Social Science Association Convention, San Francisco, January 1996.

103. Leon Jaroff, "Did Aliens Really Land?" *Time*, June 23, 1997, p. 71.

104. Sue Woodman, "The Battle over Breast Implants," *New Woman*, December 1996, p. 96 et seq.

CHAPTER 2. SPACE PROGRAMS

1. The 1995 film, directed by Ron Howard, is based on a book by astronaut Jim Lovell, first published as *Lost Moon* and then reissued as *Apollo 13* (New York: Pocket Books, 1994).

2. Lee Quinby's analysis of home space stresses how the ambivalent set of meanings that home links together "fire up apocalyptic longing and anxiety." This might explain part of the appeal of road-trip stories in general and *Apollo 13* in particular. Her genealogy of home spaces, most specifically as it points to the feminization of a domestic private sphere in white middle-class homes in postwar America, provides a helpful description of the kind of home evoked by the film and in media coverage of astronaut lives throughout the prime years of the space program. Quinby explains that homes were defined as "places of affection for a nuclear family, which was owned by a comparatively absentee husband/father, overseen by a wife/mother, and enjoyed by 'legitimate' children until their maturity. The increased distances between where fathers worked and where they lived brought significant changes in home power/space" (*Anti-Apocalypse: Essays in Genealogical Criticism* [Minneapolis: University of Minnesota Press, 1994], p. 142).

3. Home is also quickly problematized. The first person at the party to speak is "bachelor astronaut" Jack Swigert. He is trying to impress a woman with a double-entendred account of how, as command module pilot, he slides a probe into a special hole in order to couple with the lunar module (LEM). Swigert demonstrates the procedure by inserting a beer bottle into a glass, suggesting that the woman think of herself as the glass and him as the bottle. In the book *Apollo 13* Lovell

explains: "At thirty-eight, Jack Swigert had previously been known mostly for being the only unmarried astronaut ever accepted into NASA corps. In the early 1960s — when image was all, and aptitude sometimes seemed to come second — this was unthinkable. But as the nation's attitudes loosened up in the late 1960s, so did NASA's. The tall, crewcut Swigert had the reputation — good-naturedly tolerated by the Agency — of a rambunctious bachelor with an active social life. Whether this was true or not was unknown, but Swigert did what he could to perpetuate the image. His Houston apartment included a fur-covered recliner, a beer spigot in the kitchen, wine-making equipment and a state-of-the-art stereo system" (p. 89).

Indeed, Swigert's status as the only unmarried astronaut contrasts with Lovell, who is married with four children, and Fred Haise, whose wife is pregnant with their fourth child. As the film progresses, the excesses and instabilities of Swigert's sexuality increase, adding to the tensions rising with the problems that beset the *Apollo 13* mission. A week before the launch, the third member of Lovell's crew, Ken Mattingly (Gary Sinise), is exposed to the measles. Swigert is showering when he receives the call from NASA that he is to take Mattingly's place. The woman showering with him is not the one he was flirting with at the party at the beginning of the film. Haise has little confidence in Swigert, as if the bachelor astronaut were some sort of homewrecker. Marilyn Lovell's loss of her wedding ring in the shower on the morning of the launch suggests as much, especially since, almost immediately thereafter, Swigert tells the medic helping him into his space suit: "I'm going to give them a ride they'll never forget."

This homoerotic note can be read into the excesses of straight masculinity apparently necessary in the intimate working relationship of a close and cozy spacecraft. It is sounded directly, however, when Haise tells Lovell, "It hurts when I urinate." He says, "I think ole Swigert gave me the clap." Not only is Swigert blamed for a problem, his sexuality is fingered, a sexuality capable of transmitting a disease to another man. After a brief pause, Haise continues: "He's been pissin' in my relief tube." In an age of AIDS, one cannot avoid linking sexual diseases passed between men with this line about equipment not supplied by NASA — especially given Hanks's Academy Award–winning role as a lawyer with AIDS in the film *Philadelphia*. Lovell responds, "Well, that will be a hot one at the debriefing for the flight surgeons. That's another first for America's space program." Perhaps this introduction of homoeroticism is what enables Lovell to embrace Haise as his fears and fever increase. Perhaps it has entered as the possibility that they will not return home, that the relationships and assumptions marking their previous conceptions of home have started to collapse.

4. My attention to urine in the film is indebted to Quinby's "Urination and Civilization: Practicing Pissed Criticism," in *Anti-Apocalypse*, pp. 115–134.

5. Quinby pays particular attention to the contemporary reconfiguration of the home through networks of electronic information circuitry, conceiving the phenomenon in terms of the "deployment of technopression" (*Anti-Apocalypse*, pp. 136–137).

6. See Scott Bukatman's *Terminal Identity: The Virtual Subject in Postmodern Science Fiction* (Durham: Duke University Press, 1993).

7. Walter Isaacson, "In Search of the Real Bill Gates," *Time*, January 13, 1997, p. 47.

8. Ibid., p. 46.

9. Walter A. McDougall, . . . *The Heavens and the Earth: A Political History of the Space Program* (New York: Basic Books, 1985), p. 399.

10. Loudon Wainright, "Apollo's Great Leap for the Moon," *Life*, July 25, 1969, p. 18D.

11. Http://www.feedmag.com/97.01best/97.01best/html.

12. Constance Penley, *NASA/Trek: Popular Science and Sex in America* (London: Verso, 1997), p. 15.

13. "Space: An American Necessity," *Life*, November 30, 1959, p. 36.

14. "Dawn of the Spaceman," *Newsweek*, July 11, 1960, p. 58.

15. McDougall, . . . *The Heavens and the Earth*, p. 7.

16. See ibid., pp. 141–156.

17. Ibid., p. 194.

18. Preliminary staff draft, "Organization for Civil Space Programs," February 22, 1958, pp. 1, 5 (NASA History Office), cited ibid., p. 171. McDougall provides a comprehensive history of the space program, documenting the impact of the Cold War, corresponding developments in reconnaissance and satellite technology, and military connections with space exploration. Since much of my concern is with the public image of the space program, I will not address its connection with secret military projects.

19. See McDougall, . . . *The Heavens and the Earth*, p. 346.

20. In his book *The Decision to Go to the Moon: Project Apollo and the National Interest* (Cambridge: MIT Press, 1970), John M. Logsdon writes: "This decision identified, for the world to see, a space achievement as a national goal symbolic of American determination to remain the leading power in the world" (p. 100).

21. Ibid., p. 122. I am not saying that the only reason Kennedy decided in favor of a moon program was image or prestige; but one factor among many, it is the one that interests me here. Logsdon provides a detailed analysis of this decision and American space policy more generally.

22. Quoted ibid., p. 128.

23. The sense of an audience was not restricted to the space program, however. The National Science Foundation sponsored a conference, "The Mass Media and the Image of Science," on November 6, 1959. In his remarks, the foundation's director, Alan T. Waterman, observed that the image of American customs in the minds of most Americans was that presented by the media. Consequently, he recommended that television consider replacing some of the "soap operas, shoot-'em-up Westerns, and other entertainment items" with science-related programming. He challenged the media to create "a climate of excellence" (not unlike that which had enabled the Soviet Union to achieve its technological successes), a climate "conducive to scientific and technological achievement." Yet, Waterman acknowl-

edged that the programs "must be entertaining enough to attract an audience, and thus, hopefully, to attract a sponsor." The space program would be fabricated so as to meet these demands. See Alan T. Waterman, "The Challenge of Excellence," Conference on the Mass Media and the Image of Science, Washington, D.C., November 6, 1959 (NASA History Office). For a discussion of the Kennedy administration's interest in and use of television, see also Daniel Marcus, "Profiles in Courage: Televisual History in the New Frontier," a paper presented at the 1996 annual meeting of the American Studies Association, Kansas City, Mo.

24. "Dawn of the Spaceman," p. 55 (note 14 above).

25. See Lynn Spigel, "From Domestic Space to Outer Space: The 1960s Fantastic Family Sit-Com," in *Close Encounters: Film, Feminism, and Science Fiction*, ed. Constance Penley, Elisabeth Lyon, Lynn Spigel, and Janet Bergstrom (Minneapolis: University of Minnesota Press), p. 209.

26. Don Myrus, *Keeping Up with the Astronauts* (New York: Grosset and Dunlap, 1962), p. 18.

27. "The Interpreters and 'the Golden Throats,'" *Newsweek*, October 8, 1962, p. 101.

28. Myrus, *Keeping Up with the Astronauts*, pp. 16–17. The film was *Frau in Mond* (1930); see McDougall, . . . *The Heavens and the Earth*, p. 26.

29. "Spoils of War: The Men Who Turned the Trick," *Newsweek*, February 10, 1958, pp. 32–34; "Reach for the Stars," *Time*, February 17, 1958, pp. 21–25.

30. "Spoils of War," p. 33.

31. "Reach for the Stars," p. 24.

32. "Changing Vistas — East, West, and South," *Newsweek*, October 8, 1862, pp. 25–26. See also "Spoils of War," p. 32: "When the Army set up the Redstone base in Alabama eight years ago, the Germans moved to Huntsville, where the grocery stores began stocking up with more sauerkraut."

33. "Changing Vistas — East, West, and South," pp. 25–26.

34. "Astronauts' Ordeal: Greater on the Ground?" *Newsweek*, October 8, 1962, p. 30.

35. Norman Mailer, *Of a Fire on the Moon* (Boston: Little, Brown, 1970), p. 66.

36. Ibid., p. 68. Mailer also describes the tension permeating a dinner gathering of astronauts, astronaut families, rocket designers, and corporate executives when the speaker introducing von Braun, who was to say a few words, went into historical detail: "There was an uneasy silence, an embarrassed pall at the unmentioned word of Nazi" (p. 74).

37. "The Nation: Space, a Man's Victory," *Time*, May 24, 1963, p. 17.

38. John Dille, "Those Seven — An Introduction," in M. Scott Carpenter et al., *We Seven* (New York: Simon and Schuster, 1962), p. 25.

39. "Changing Vistas — East, West, and South," p. 25.

40. "The Joyous Triumph of Apollo 13," *Life*, April 24, 1970, p. 29.

41. Warren R. Young, "What It's Like to Fly into Space," *Life*, April 13, 1959, p. 133.

42. Ibid., p. 140.

43. Ibid., p. 143.

44. Ibid., p. 146.

45. Ibid.

46. W. R. Lovelace II, "Ducklings, Probings, Checks That Proved Fliers' Fitness," *Life*, April 20, 1959, p. 26.

47. "Great Gordo," *Time*, May 24, 1963, pp. 17–21.

48. "His Flight Heralds an Era of Shrinking Time: Cooper's Trip and Einstein's Theory," *Life*, May 24, 1963, p. 38.

49. See William E. Connolly's discussion of territorialization in his book *The Ethos of Pluralization* (Minneapolis: University of Minnesota Press, 1995), pp. xxii–xxiv.

50. Allucquère Rosanne Stone, *The War of Desire and Technology at the Close of the Mechanical Age* (Cambridge: MIT Press, 1996), p. 40.

51. Dille, "Those Seven," pp. 3–4.

52. NASA Project A, Announcement no. 1, December 22, 1958 (NASA History Office, doc. VI-1). Michael Shapiro illustrates how previous visions of American expansion also used mission requirements as a means of exclusion. He points out that the sociologist E. A. Ross "thought that Jews make poor Americans because they are not fit to haul canoes through the wilderness." See Shapiro, "Narrating the Nation, Unwelcoming the Stranger: Anti-Immigration Policy in Contemporary 'America,'" *Alternatives* 22, no. 1 (January–February 1997), pp. 1–34; quotation, p. 30.

53. Dille, "Those Seven," p. 5.

54. Ibid., p. 4.

55. In his comprehensive study of the Apollo program, Andrew Chaikin notes that even after NASA lifted the test pilot requirement and began selecting astronauts on the basis of their scientific expertise, those who were not test pilots were considered "different" and were frequently grouped together with the scientists and doctors that the other astronauts considered to be nuisances or adversaries. See Chaikin, *A Man on the Moon: The Voyages of the Apollo Astronauts* (New York: Penguin, 1994), pp. 46–48.

56. Dille, "Those Seven," p. 7.

57. For a detailed account of differing versions of American ideals of manhood, see E. Anthony Rotundo, *American Manhood* (New York: Basic Books, 1993).

58. Dille, "Those Seven," p. 14.

59. Ibid., p. 13.

60. Clare Boothe Luce, "But Some People Simply Never Get the Message," *Life*, June 28, 1963, p. 31. Included with Luce's article are photographs and blurbs on the thirteen American women who had undergone astronaut training and met the standards set for astronauts. Unlike Tereshkova, all the American women were experienced pilots. One, Jerrie Cobb, had more than twenty years of flying experience and had set four world records. Indeed, an earlier *Life* feature on Cobb's training featured several large photographs of Cobb floating in a sensory-deprivation tank. The ad on the facing page used a skirted female cheerleader to demonstrate

that "Kotex is confidence." This was the only instance I found of an advertisement for "feminine hygiene" products accompanying the magazine's astronaut coverage. For more on NASA's failure to include women, see Luce's monthly column "Without Portfolio" in *McCall's*, May 1963, pp. 16, 163.

61. "The Interpreters and 'the Golden Throats,'" p. 101 (note 27 above).

62. Ibid.

63. Norman Mailer, "The Psychology of Astronauts," *Life*, November 14, 1969, p. 62. A revised version of this article later appeared in Mailer's *Of a Fire on the Moon*.

64. See also Tom Wolfe's discussion of the importance of emotions for astronaut imagery. Wolfe notes that, after the initial Mercury Seven press conference, the press was united in the conviction that "the public, the populace, the citizenry, must be provided with *the correct feelings!*" (*The Right Stuff* [New York: Farrar, Straus, and Giroux, 1983], p. 122).

65. "Astronauts' Ordeal," p. 30 (note 34 above).

66. Dora Jane Hamblin, "The Fire and Fate Have Left Eight Widows," *Life*, January 26, 1968, p. 61.

67. Dora Jane Hamblin, "The 'Magnificent Agony' of Wives Below," *Life*, November 1, 1968, p. 29.

68. Ibid., p. 30.

69. Hamblin, "Fire and Fate," p. 62.

70. Ibid.

71. Germaine Greer, *The Female Eunuch* (New York: McGraw-Hill, 1970), pp. 276–277.

72. Ibid., p. 277.

73. Hamblin, "Fire and Fate," p. 62.

74. Mailer, *Of a Fire on the Moon*, p. 48.

75. "Cult of the Astronaut," *Nation*, June 15, 1963, p. 149.

76. "Astronauts' Ordeal," p. 31.

77. "Heroes Must Be Pure," *Business Week*, April 14, 1962, p. 34.

78. Albert Rosenfeld, "Visions of the Lunar Voyage," *Life*, May 30, 1969, p. 51.

79. "A Divided Decade: The '60's," *Life*, December 26, 1969, p. 28.

80. Rosenfeld, "Visions of the Lunar Voyage," p. 50.

81. Mailer, *Of a Fire on the Moon*, p. 47.

82. Wolfe, *The Right Stuff*, pp. 178–193.

83. See Alan Shepard and Deke Slayton, *Moon Shot: The Inside Story of America's Race to the Moon* (Atlanta: Turner, 1994), p. 119.

84. Ibid., pp. 118–119.

85. Myrus, *Keeping Up with the Astronauts*, p. 15.

86. Donald Slayton, "We Believe They Should Leave the Flying to Us," *Life*, September 27, 1963, p. 90.

87. Carpenter et al., *We Seven*, p. 410.

88. Ibid., p. 413.

89. Kenneth Crawford, "The Politics of Space," *Newsweek*, October 8, 1962, p. 31.

90. John Young, "Well, Now That We're Here, What Do We Do?" *Life*, January 20, 1969, p. 43.

91. See Shapiro's discussion of the vacancy of the place of settlement in frontier narratives ("Narrating the Nation").

92. For discussions of the astronaut as cyborg, see Manfred E. Clynes and Nathan S. Kline, "Cyborgs in Space," in *The Cyborg Handbook*, ed. Chris Hables Gray (New York: Routledge, 1995), pp. 29–33. In their paper, first presented in 1960 at a symposium on spaceflight held at the Air Force School of Aviation Medicine in San Antonio, Texas, the authors discuss how man can adapt to the conditions of space travel by employing machine elements that aid in regulating the body's systems and needs. In this context, they introduce the term "cyborg," explaining that "the Cyborg deliberately incorporates exogenous components extending the self-regulatory control function of the organism in order to adapt it to new environments" (p. 31). See also Manfred E. Clynes, "Cyborg II: Sentic Space Travel," pp. 35–42 in the same volume.

93. "Moon Dream: It's Almost a Reality," *Newsweek*, October 8, 1962, p. 85.

94. Wolfe, *The Right Stuff*, pp. 20, 125, 126, 239.

95. Mailer, "The Psychology of Astronauts," p. 52.

96. See, for example, René, *NASA MOONED AMERICA!* (Passaic, N.J.: René, 1992). Also see "Then There Are Those Who Believe It's a Hoax," *Post-Standard* (Syracuse, N.Y.: reprinted from the *Washington Post*), July 20, 1994, p. A5.

97. Wolfe, *The Right Stuff*, p. 232.

98. Ibid., p. 261.

99. Ibid., p. 356.

100. Bruno Latour, *Science in Action* (Cambridge: Harvard University Press, 1987), p. 248.

101. Not all the Apollo astronauts were assimilated out of wonder. Edgar Smith, for example, carried out experiments in telepathy and ESP during the *Apollo 14* mission; and James Irwin (*Apollo 15*) underwent a conversion experience while walking on the moon. See Michael Quinn, "Neil Armstrong, You've Just Walked on the Moon — What Are You Going to Do Now?" *Time*, July 25, 1994, p. 17; also see Chaikin's "Epilogue" to *A Man on the Moon*, pp. 553–584.

102. Mailer, "The Psychology of Astronauts," p. 57.

103. Ibid.

104. Ibid., p. 58.

105. Chris Jones and Carla Cunningham, "Project Apollo Launches Oracle's E-Commerce Plan," *Infoworld*, December 16, 1996, p. 7.

106. Thanks to Leslie Feldman for bringing this commercial to my attention.

107. Shepard and Slayton, *Moon Shot*, p. 8.

108. Howard Rheingold, *Virtual Reality* (New York: Touchstone, 1991), p. 132.

109. See John Fiske, *Television Culture* (New York: Routledge, 1987).

1. Sharon Begley, "Down to Earth," *Newsweek*, October 7, 1996, pp. 30–36.

2. Ibid., p. 36.

3. Sharon Begley, "Next Stop Mars," *Newsweek*, July 25, 1994, p. 47.

4. Diane Vaughan, *The Challenger Launch Decision* (Chicago: University of Chicago Press, 1996), p. 12.

5. Constance Penley, "Space Out: Remembering Christa McAuliffe," *Camera Obscura* no. 29 (May 1992), p. 183. Another version of this article appears in Penley's *NASA/Trek: Popular Science in America* (London: Veso, 1997).

6. This refusal is a central theme in Penley's excellent analysis of the *Challenger* disaster.

7. Although this use of "interpellation" is best traced to Louis Althusser, "Ideology and Ideological State Apparatuses," in *Lenin and Philosophy*, trans. Ben Brewster (New York: Monthly Review Press, 1971), pp. 170–186, I want to flag Donna Haraway's gloss on the term in order not only to distance myself from Althusser's notion of ideology but also to accentuate the way in which the interpellation of the public does not fix the meaning or the content of the public. Haraway writes: "Interpellation is double-edged in its potent capacity to hail subjects into existence. Subjects in a discourse can and do refigure its terms, contents, and reach. In the end, it is those who mis/recognize themselves in discourse who thereby acquire the power, and responsibility, to shape that discourse" (*Modest Witness @Second Millennium. FemaleMan© Meets OncoMouse*™ [New York: Routledge, 1997], p. 50).

8. Penley, "Space Out," pp. 203–205.

9. Alan Nadel, "'I Never Bargain!' Justice Black and White for *The Fugitive* and Rodney King," a paper presented at the 1996 annual meeting of the American Studies Association, Kansas City, Mo.

10. Anna Jamerson and Beth Collings, *Connections: Solving Our Alien Abduction Mystery* (Newberg, Oreg.: Wildflower Press, 1996), p. xx.

11. David D. Yuan, "The Celebrity Freak: Michael Jackson's 'Grotesque Glory,'" in *Freakery: Cultural Spectacles of the Extraordinary Body*, ed. Rosemarie Garland Thompson (New York: New York University Press, 1996), p. 368.

12. Jamerson and Collings, *Connections*, p. xvi. I take the term "enfreaked" from David Yuan, who credits David Hevey for coining the term "enfreakment" ("The Celebrity Freak," p. 382).

13. Debbie Jordan and Kathy Mitchell, *Abducted! The Story of the Intruders Continues . . .* (New York: Carroll and Graf, 1994), p. vii.

14. Katharina Wilson, *The Alien Jigsaw* (Portland, Oreg.: Puzzle, 1993), p. 9.

15. See Thomas L. Dumm, *united states* (Ithaca: Cornell University Press, 1994).

16. Like some others who think about political and cultural theory, I thought for a while that the major problem was with "shared." That is to say, I was interested in the problem of how solidarity is possible when people don't share the same beliefs, traditions, or experiences; and, in my first book, I tried to provide an answer

based, in part, on the discourse ethics of Jürgen Habermas. See my *Solidarity of Strangers: Feminism after Identity Politics* (Berkeley: University of California Press, 1996). I now think that the problem goes deeper than I previously suspected; that even when people think they share beliefs and experiences, they may in fact and probably do have deeply conflicting interpretations of such beliefs and experiences.

17. See Nigel Clark's interesting discussion of ecology and cyberspace as well as notes to additional work on problems of representing nature: "Earthing the Ether," *Cyberfutures*, ed. Ziauddin Sardar and Jerome R. Ravetz (New York: New York University Press, 1996), pp. 90–110.

18. See Debbie Nathan and Michael Snedeker, *Satan's Silence* (New York: Basic Books, 1995).

19. Andrew Barry, "Television, Truth, and Democracy," *Media, Culture and Society* 15 (1993), p. 491.

20. See Jerome Clark, *High Strangeness: UFOs from 1960 through 1979* (Detroit: Omnigraphics, 1996). Clark mentions that Fish published her findings in the January 1974 issue of *Pursuit*, a journal of the Society for the Investigation of the Unexplained. He notes that, in December, the editor of *Astronomy* solicited opinions on the matter and that the debate, which included Sagan, continued for most of the following year.

21. See Clark, *High Strangeness*, p. 345. Clark also notes that the story of *Apollo 11*'s UFO sighting can be traced to a 1969 tabloid.

22. Lynn Spigel stresses that *Life* magazine's biographical spreads on the astronauts were part of a larger practice of mediating space technology through domestic practices and images. She describes how "national magazines mixed everyday situations with fantastic scenarios of space travel," and she quotes rocket scientist Wernher von Braun's remarks that "missile building is much like interior decorating." See Spigel, "From Domestic Space to Outer Space," in *Close Encounters: Film, Feminism, and Science Fiction*, ed. Constance Penley, Elisabeth Lyon, Lynn Spigel, and Janet Bergstrom (Minneapolis: University of Minnesota Press, 1991), pp. 217–218.

23. "He Brings It in 'Right on the Old Bazoo,'" *Life*, May 24, 1963, pp. 28–33.

24. Leah Haley, *Lost Was the Key* (Tuscaloosa: Greenleaf Publications, 1993), p. 26.

25. Ibid., p. 132.

26. Ibid., p. 51.

27. Ibid., p. 90.

28. Jamerson and Collings, *Connections*, p. 108.

29. Ibid., p. 112.

30. See C. D. B. Bryan, *Close Encounters of the Fourth Kind: Alien Abduction, UFOs, and the Conference at MIT* (New York: Knopf, 1995), pp. 200–230.

31. Jamerson and Collings, *Connections*, p. 123.

32. Ibid., pp. 123–124.

33. Ibid., p. 125.

34. Ibid., p. 129.

35. Ibid., p. 130.

36. Ibid., p. 131.

37. Ibid., p. 132.

38. Ibid.

39. Haley, *Lost Was the Key*, p. 90.

40. A memorial to Dr. Turner states: "Karla was a courageous investigator who was attempting to uncover the mystery of the very human, and therefore political, aspect of UFO abduction phenomena; that is, why are human beings seen in the company of nonhuman entities during UFO encounters of the fourth kind? Karla did not back off from her lectures and research when she was warned to. During a motoring trip with her husband last year, they encountered a UFO which approached so close that Karla became ill with radiation sickness. In a matter of months, Karla was stricken with cancer and became unable to continue her work. She died early this year." See Joan D'Arc, ed., *Paranoid Women Collect Their Thoughts* (Providence, R.I.: Paranoia, 1996), p. 70.

41. Karla Turner, *Into the Fringe: A True Story of Alien Abduction* (New York: Berkley Books, 1992), p. 91.

42. Ibid., p. 92.

43. Ibid., pp. 92–93.

44. Ibid., p. 106.

45. Bryan, *Close Encounters of the Fourth Kind*, p. 133.

46. Wilson, *The Alien Jigsaw*, p. 283.

47. Ibid., p. 284.

48. Ibid., p. 285.

49. Ibid.

50. This experience is strongly reminiscent of the "automatic writing" performed by mediums during the spiritualist movement at the turn of the nineteenth century. In fact, the markings on the body, the importance of trance, and the gendered dimensions of mediums and abductions suggest the possibility of a direct link between the two phenomena. While I hope to investigate this matter more thoroughly in the future, here I can only reference two key bridges between mediums and abductees: the contactee movement in the 1950s, out of which the New Age practice of "channeling" emerged, and the work of Théodore Flournoy with the medium Hélène Smith at the turn of the century. Smith's transmission of messages in Martian from Martians was written up by Flournoy in what was one of the first extensive case studies of multiple personality. See Sonu Shamdasani's excellent introduction to his edition of this fascinating work: Théodore Flournoy, *From India to the Planet Mars: A Case of Multiple Personality with Imaginary Languages* (1901; Princeton: Princeton University Press, 1994).

51. To be sure, the parallels can be extended in ways I can't go into here. A passage from Judith Lewis Herman, however, at least hints at some of the possibilities. She writes: "Because the truth is so difficult to face, survivors often vacillate in reconstructing their stories. Denial of reality makes them feel crazy, but acceptance of the full reality seems beyond what any human being can bear" (Herman, *Trauma*

and Recovery [New York: Basic Books, 1992], p. 181). See also Ian Hacking's insightful critique of the politics of memory, especially with regard to abuse, false-memory syndrome, and multiple personality disorder: *Rewriting the Soul* (Princeton: Princeton University Press, 1995).

52. Helen Daniels, "Truth, Community, and the Politics of Memory: Narratives of Child Sexual Abuse," in *"Bad Girls"/"Good Girls": Women, Sex, and Power in the Nineties*, ed. Nan Bauer Maglin and Donna Perry (New Brunswick: Rutgers University Press, 1996), p. 152.

53. This is not to say that they deny the incommensurable details. They don't. They are aware of them and occasionally present reports on them. My point is simply that the researchers have an interest as researchers in highlighting and publicizing a comprehensible account of their findings. See Thomas E. Bullard's eight-stage account of the structure of abduction reports: "UFO Abduction Reports: The Supernatural Kidnap Narrative Returns in Technological Guise," *Journal of American Folklore* 102, no. 404 (April–June 1989), pp. 147–170. See also David M. Jacobs's "common abduction scenario matrix," included as an appendix to his *Secret Life: Firsthand Documented Accounts of UFO Abductions* (New York: Simon and Schuster, 1992), p. 330.

54. Jonathan B. Imber, "Doctor No Longer Knows Best," in *America at Century's End*, ed. Alan B. Wolfe (Berkeley: University of California Press, 1991), p. 309.

55. See Howe's foreword to Karla Turner's *Taken: Inside the Alien-Human Abduction Agenda* (Roland, Ark.: Kelt Works, 1994).

CHAPTER 4. I WANT TO BELIEVE

1. See Andrea Pritchard et al., eds., *Alien Discussions: Proceedings of the Abduction Study Conference* (Cambridge: North Cambridge Press, 1994).

2. Leah Haley, *Lost Was the Key* (Tuscaloosa: Greenleaf Publications, 1993).

3. Ibid., p. 14.

4. Ibid., p. 15.

5. Ibid., p. 16.

6. Anna Jamerson and Beth Collings, *Connections: Solving Our Alien Abduction Mystery* (Newberg, Oreg.: Wildflower Press, 1996), p. xx.

7. Karla Turner, *Into the Fringe: A True Story of Alien Abduction* (New York: Berkley Books, 1992), p. 181.

8. Or Mississippi. Haley changes the name of the town and the military base. She also uses pseudonyms for everyone except UFO researchers.

9. Haley, *Lost Was the Key*, p. 30.

10. Ibid.

11. Ibid., pp. 34–45.

12. Ibid., p. 46.

13. Ibid.

14. For a thorough analysis of the difference between "old" and "new" talk

shows, the difference between, say, *Donahue* and *Sally Jesse Raphael*, see Jane M. Shattuc, *The Talking Cure: TV Talk Shows and Women* (New York: Routledge, 1997).

15. I am grateful to Shane Kenyon for insight on this point.

16. See the discussion in Herman E. Van Bolhuis and Vincente Colom, *Cyberspace Reflections* (Brussels: VUB University Press, 1995), pp. 106–107.

17. Thomas E. Weber, "Who Uses the Internet," *Wall Street Journal*, December 9, 1996, p. R6.

18. See Budd Hopkins, *Witnessed* (New York: Pocket Books, 1996). Hopkins includes an appendix in which he discusses Collings's and Jamerson's abduction experiences.

19. Ziauddin Sardar and Jerome R. Ravetz, "Introduction: Reaping the Technological Whirlwind," in their edited volume. *Cyberfutures: Culture and Politics on the Information Superhighway* (New York: New York University Press, 1996), p. 10.

20. James B. Twitchell writes that "since the advent of the remote-control operation, the viewer essentially makes up his own show out of a potpourri of sequences. Most critics don't understand this because they don't consume television as an ever-shifting carnival" (*Carnival Culture: The Trashing of Taste in America* [New York: Columbia University Press, 1992], p. 204).

21. See Mark Slouka, *War of the Worlds: Cyberspace and the High-Tech Assault on Reality* (New York: Basic Books, 1995), p. 149.

22. See Kurt Andersen, "The Age of Unreason," *New Yorker*, February 3, 1997, pp. 40–43.

23. These issues and concerns have been brought up in myriad ways in a variety of contexts. Among the numerous contributions in some of these areas are the essays collected in Linda Alcoff and Elizabeth Potter, *Feminist Epistemologies* (New York: Routledge, 1993); Bruno Latour, *Science in Action* (Cambridge: Harvard University Press, 1987); Sandra Harding, "Is Science Multicultural? Challenges, Resources, Opportunities, Uncertainties," in *Multiculturalism: A Critical Reader*, ed. David Theo Goldberg (Cambridge: Basil Blackwell, 1994), pp. 344–370; and Greg Sarris, "'What I'm Talking about When I'm Talking about My Baskets,' Conversations with Mabel McKay," in *De/Colonizing the Subject: The Politics of Gender in Women's Autobiography*, ed. Sidonie Smith and Julia Watson (Minneapolis: University of Minnesota Press, 1992), pp. 20–33.

24. Jon Katz seems to employ such an assumption when he writes, "But if you watch those screens and read enough, carefully enough, for long enough, the truth unfailingly struggles to break through, often in indirect and surprising ways" (*Virtuous Reality* [New York: Random House, 1997], p. 129).

25. Slouka worries: "By flooding the culture with digitally manipulated images, I'm saying, we risk devaluing *all* visual representations and, by extension, the reality they pretend to depict. Which is no small thing. Allowed to run unchecked, the crisis I am describing could come to have a profound effect on Western democratic culture. How? By knocking out one of the supporting girders of the liberal democratic state: the belief in universal access to reliable information and therefore, by implication, to truth" (*War of the Worlds*, p. 124).

26. Peter Ludlow, ed., *High Noon on the Electronic Frontier: Conceptual Issues in Cyberspace* (Cambridge: MIT Press, 1996). Ludlow gives the following example: "Suppose that Smith works for a Japanese auto manufacturer here in the United States. Is it appropriate that the U.S. government be able to spy on the communications between Smith and Smith's employer, particularly if the information being exchanged includes valuable trade secrets that might be of value to U.S. auto makers?" (pp. 176–177).

27. In his speculations on warfare in the information age, John Carlin suggests that issues such as military defense are implicated as well; see Carlin, "A Farewell to Arms," *Wired*, May 1997, pp. 51–54, 220–226.

28. My position here in no way assumes that television is a "monolithic totality." Rather, I agree with Elayne Rapping's point that television "succeeds more than other forums in hailing us as citizens with interests in common and in embodying a version of public debate on matters of common concern that has credibility and authority — in spite of questions about the quality of its mediation or its actual effects in terms of viewer behavior." See Rapping, *The Movie of the Week: Private Stories/Public Events* (Minneapolis: University of Minnesota Press), p. xxxi. For an analysis of the consolidation of television news that also stresses the production of the "well-informed citizen," see Michael Schudson, "National News Culture and the Rise of the Informational Citizen," in *America at Century's End*, ed. Alan Wolfe (Berkeley: University of California Press, 1991), pp. 265–282.

29. As Budd Hopkins recounts in *Witnessed*.

30. Katharina Wilson, *The Alien Jigsaw Researcher's Supplement* (Portland, Oreg.: Puzzle, 1993), p. 42.

31. Jamerson and Collings, *Connections*, p. 115.

32. Turner, *Into the Fringe*, p. 97.

33. Ibid., p. 119.

34. Pritchard et al., eds., *Alien Discussions*, p. 542. The UFO skeptic Phil Klass has featured several short articles on Boylan in his *Skeptics UFO Newsletter*. In the September 1995 issue, Klass points out that the California State Board of Psychology stripped Boylan, a former president of the Sacramento Valley Psychological Association, of his license. Klass writes: "The Board's investigation was prompted by lawsuits filed by two of Boylan's female patients who charged that he tried to convince them they had suffered UFO abductions. Boylan's treatment for female abducees was to join him in naked hot-tub therapy sessions" (p. 5). For a critical assessment of Klass, see my "Coming Out as an Alien: Feminists, UFOs, and 'the Oprah Effect,'" in *"Bad Girls"/"Good Girls": Women, Sex, and Power in the Nineties*, ed. Nan Bauer Maglin and Donna Perry (New Brunswick: Rutgers University Press, 1996), pp. 90–105.

35. Wilson, *Supplement*, p. 121.

36. Hopkins, *Witnessed*.

37. John Mack, *Abduction: Human Encounters with Aliens* (New York: Charles Scribner's Sons, 1994), p. 402.

38. Ibid., p. 411.

39. See Patricia A. Turner, *I Heard It through the Grapevine* (Berkeley: University of California Press, 1993), esp. pp. 180–201.

40. See ibid., pp. 151–163; and John Fiske, *Media Matters: Race and Gender in U.S. Politics* (Minneapolis: University of Minnesota Press, 1996), esp. pp. 191–216.

41. Jonathan Vankin, *Conspiracies, Cover-ups, and Crimes* (New York: Paragon House, 1991), p. 151.

42. Ibid., p. 232.

43. See David H. Bennett's *The Party of Fear: From Nativist Movements to the New Right in American History* (Chapel Hill: University of North Carolina Press, 1988).

44. S. Paige Baty, *American Monroe: The Making of a Body Politic* (Berkeley: University of California Press, 1995), p. 130. In her fascinating study of Marilyn Monroe and the inseparability of the political from the cultural in late twentieth-century America, Baty analyzes the conspiracy theories around the star's death. Baty understands conspiracy theory as a "cartographic" mode of remembering: "it seeks to bring history's hidden plots to light in the mass-mediated realm of public appearance" (p. 117). She explains: "Remembering here is equivalent to tracking, or mapping, history's hidden plots. The conspiracy narrative traces a seemingly random series of events and weaves them into a coherent 'secret plot.' Conspiracy narratives fix plots as a normative standard, producing narrative structures in which the world becomes more coherent but less open to the exigencies of spontaneous human action" (p. 119).

"Plot" may be a central feature of conspiracy theories around Monroe or perhaps of theories about assassinations and violent deaths more generally. It is less important, however, in the UFO discourse and, I would add, for conspiracy thinking in technoculture. The pleasure that conspiracy theory provides has less to do with coherence and meaning than with power and contestation. As Baty agrees, one who theorizes conspiracy holds a form of knowledge, an insight into the workings of history. But whereas Baty stresses the plot structure of this knowledge, I stress its character as evidence; that is, the specific bits and pieces the theoretician holds onto. The power of a conspiracy theory comes less from its narrative than from the evidence upon which it is built. Once a fact is established, verified, myriad links become possible. Ufologists, Kennedy assassination researchers and, I think, even biographers of Marilyn take great pains to produce evidence, and their quarrels and disagreements with official explanations stem from the failure of such explanations to account for the evidence.

45. Richard Hofstadter, "The Paranoid Style in American Politics," in *The Fear of Conspiracy*, ed. David Brion Davis (Ithaca: Cornell University Press, 1971), p. 3. For a thoughtful critique of Hofstadter, see William Chaloupka, "Conspiracy Thinking as a Mode of Political Culture," paper presented at the 1997 American Political Science Association Annual Meeting. For a compelling account of "political demonology" attentive to myriad deployments and manifestations of conspiracy thinking in American political culture, see Michael Rogin, *Ronald Reagan, the Movie* (Berkeley: University of California Press, 1987).

46. Ibid., p. 8.

47. Ibid., p. 6. See also the contributions to Richard O. Curry and Thomas M. Brown, eds., *Conspiracy: The Fear of Subversion in American History* (New York: Holt, Rinehart and Winston, 1972). For the most part, the contributors share with Hofstadter, who has an essay in the collection, the presumption that confidence in the political system and trust in the two-party process is politics as normal, that change is what has to be explained, and that no matter how frequent or pervasive conspiracy theory and political paranoia are in American politics, they are distortions of democracy.

48. Carlin, "A Farewell to Arms," p. 51.

49. Vankin, *Conspiracies*, p. 27.

50. Jamerson and Collings, *Connections*, p. 228.

51. David Jacobs, *Secret Life: Firsthand Documented Accounts of UFO Abductions* (New York: Simon and Schuster, 1992), p. 310.

52. Hopkins, *Witnessed*, pp. 3–21.

53. Ibid., p. 364.

54. Quoted by Patrick Huyghe, "The Secret Invasion: Does It Add Up?" *Omni*, Winter 1995, p. 60.

55. Mack, *Abduction*, p. 395.

56. Ibid., p. 413.

57. Ibid., p. 396.

58. Ibid., p. 409.

59. Nigel Clark, "Earthing the Ether," in Sardar and Ravetz, eds., *Cyberfutures*, pp. 90–110.

60. Ibid., p. 91.

61. See Max Weber, "Science as a Vocation," in *From Max Weber: Essays in Sociology*, trans., ed., and intro. H. H. Gerth and C. Wright Mills (New York: Oxford University Press, 1946), pp. 129–156.

62. I owe this insight to Shane Kenyon.

63. Ziauddin Sardar, "Cyberspace as the Darker Side of the West," in Sardar and Ravetz, eds., *Cyberfutures*, p. 26.

64. See Byron Reeves and Clifford Nass, *The Media Equation: How People Treat Computers, Television, and New Media Like Real People and Places* (Cambridge: Cambridge University Press, 1996).

65. Vivian Sobchak, "Democratic Franchise and the Electronic Frontier," in Sardar and Ravetz, eds., *Cyberfutures*, p. 81.

CHAPTER 5. THE FAMILIARITY OF STRANGENESS

1. Special thanks to Bernie Lanciaux for pointing this out to me.

2. Haynes Johnson, *Sleepwalking through History* (New York: W. W. Norton, 1991), p. 140. For similar assessments, see the contributions to Sidney Blumenthal and Thomas Byrne Edsall, *The Reagan Legacy* (New York: Pantheon, 1988).

3. Sam Johnson and Chris Marcil, "What's Right with America (61 Things)," *New York Times Magazine*, July 16, 1994), p. 55.

4. Peter Brimelow, *Alien Nation: Common Sense about America's Immigration Disaster* (New York: Harper Perennial, 1996).

5. *Weekly World News*, February 28, 1995.

6. Lynn Spigel, "From Domestic Space to Outer Space," in *Close Encounters: Film, Feminism, and Science Fiction*, ed. Constance Penley, Elisabeth Lyon, Lynn Spigel, and Janet Bergstrom (Minneapolis: University of Minnesota Press, 1991), pp. 205–236. See also Lee Quinby's genealogy of home space in *Anti-Apocalypse: Exercises in Genealogical Criticism* (Minneapolis: University of Minnesota Press, 1994). Quinby writes: "For apocalyptic-minded home dwellers, the home as uncanny, where the familiar turns strange, also comes from a rise in households of interracial and ethnic difference and/or gay or lesbian couples" (p. 143).

7. In her lyrical recounting of stories told in an abductee support group in Austin, Texas, Susan Lepselter also evokes the uncanny quality of abduction, emphasizing the shift of Earth and home into the realm of nature before the gaze of an extraterrestrial culture. See Lepselter, "From the Earth Native's Point of View: The Earth, the Extraterrestrial, and the Natural Ground of Home," *Public Culture* 9 (Winter 1997), pp. 197–208. Thanks to Elayne Rapping for bringing this article to my attention.

8. Thomas E. Bullard, "UFO Abduction Reports: The Supernatural Kidnap Narrative Returns in a Technological Guise," *Journal of American Folklore* 102, no. 404 (April–June 1989), pp. 147–170; David Jacobs, *Secret Life: Firsthand Documented Accounts of UFO Abductions* (New York: Simon and Schuster, 1992).

9. The relationship between the abduction script or narrative and the experiences of those who think of themselves as abductees is complex. As developed by Bullard and Jacobs (note 8 above), the script blends together the major published accounts of abduction with unpublished research. Consequently, individual cases may differ significantly from the script. Additionally, researchers differ in their interpretations of the phenomenon. And the script is culturally variable. For example, a Finnish participant in the abduction study conference held at MIT explained that there are "quite a lot" of encounters in Scandinavia "but we don't report them to the Americans." She continued: "We have three UFO organizations in Finland, 16 in Sweden, and 5 in Norway. . . . We don't think it [abduction] is something negative. Most experiences are very positive. But, they're not with little Grays. They are with totally different aliens. People report heads with two antennas, or heads divided, or abstract sort of features. They report the Nordic type of course [tall human-looking blonds prominent in British abduction stories]. Our phenomena may be due to our folklore; we consider it normal to have gnomes in the mountains, and have gnomes take children and bring them back, as they've done for thousands of years. We don't think there's something special." See Andrea Pritchard et al., eds., *Alien Discussions: Proceedings of the Abduction Study Conference* (Cambridge: North Cambridge Press, 1994), pp. 48–49.

10. Admittedly, since some abductees are men (Brenda Denzler's research indicates [E-mail communication] that the ratio of women to men is approximately 2:1), a more precise formulation would acknowledge that in abductions of men what happens to the abductee's sperm, his penis, is also of global importance. Since more than a few men already believe that their penises are globally significant, I didn't think a male-oriented statement would sound as odd or surprising as one focusing on women. An interesting component of men's accounts of abduction, however, is their sense of being raped and violated. Their abduction narratives tend to employ a language that feminizes themselves and their experiences. See my "Coming Out as an Alien: Feminists, UFOs, and the 'Oprah Effect,'" in *"Bad Girls"/"Good Girls": Women, Sex, and Power in the Nineties*, ed. Nan Bauer Maglin and Donna Perry (New Brunswick: Rutgers University Press, 1996), pp. 90–105.

11. For an interesting account of the connections between global media and the "bogus" notion of global citizenship, see Chris Carlsson, "The Shape of Truth to Come," in *Resisting the Virtual Life*, ed. James Brook and Iain A. Boal (San Francisco: City Lights, 1995), pp. 235–244. See also Thomas Dumm's discussion of the experience of shopping in a supermarket as exemplary of some of the tensions and confusions of local instantiations of commercial corporate globalism: *united states* (Ithaca: Cornell University Press, 1994), pp. 142–152.

12. My thinking about networks grows out of conversations with Lee Quinby.

13. Langdon Winner, *The Whale and the Reactor* (Chicago: University of Chicago Press, 1986), p. 115.

14. My thinking on this point has been informed by Ian Hacking's account of multiple personality disorder as a specific product of the politics of memory. See Hacking, *Rewriting the Soul* (Princeton: Princeton University Press, 1995).

15. John G. Fuller, *The Interrupted Journey: Two Lost Hours "Aboard a Flying Saucer"* (New York: Dial Press, 1966), p. 9.

16. Ibid., p. 55.

17. Ibid.

18. Harold Greenwald, "Forgotten Visit to a Flying Saucer," *Saturday Review*, December 31, 1966, pp. 22–23.

19. The Gray, however, is not marked only by color. It also has enormous black eyes and a fetuslike body. For an interpretation that emphasizes the eyes, see my "Coming Out as an Alien." Abductees have also reported other types of aliens without arousing much interest in the larger culture. These include Reptilians, Ancients (or Praying Mantis–like), and Nordics. See David Chance, *A Visual Guide to Alien Beings* (self-published, 1996).

20. Dumm, *united states*, p. 12.

21. Dean Devlin, Roland Emmerich, and Stephen Molstad, *Independence Day* (New York: Harper Prism, 1996), p. 148.

22. See the story by the editors of *Wired* that begins on the cover with this announcement: "We interrupt this magazine for a special bulletin — Push! Kiss Your Browser Goodbye: The Radical Future of Media beyond the Web" (*Wired*, March 1997, pp. 13, 17).

23. Annalee Newitz, "Alien Abductions and the End of White People," *Bad Subjects* 6 (May 1993), badsubjects-request@uclink.berkeley.edu.

24. Budd Hopkins, *Missing Time* (New York: Ballantine, 1981).

25. Budd Hopkins, *Intruders* (New York: Ballantine, 1987), p. xiii.

26. See Carl Sagan, *The Demon-Haunted World: Science as a Candle in the Dark* (New York: Random House, 1995).

27. Ibid., p. 416.

28. Langdon Winner, *Autonomous Technology* (Cambridge: MIT Press, 1977).

29. Ibid., p. 284.

30. James McDonald was a professor of physics and meteorology at the University of Arizona, where he served as scientific director of the Institute of Atmospheric Physics in 1956–57. In 1971 he testified before the House Committee on Appropriations about the effects on the atmosphere of the supersonic transport plane. McDonald argued that SST emissions would reduce ozone levels and could lead to an increase in skin cancer. During McDonald's testimony, Representative Silvio Conte of Massachusetts "pointed out that McDonald was an expert on UFOs and believed power failures in New York 'were caused by these flying saucers.'" That day and the next, spectators and representatives laughed at McDonald as Conte continued to challenge his credibility. Later that year McDonald committed suicide. See David M. Jacobs, *The UFO Controversy in America* (Bloomington: Indiana University Press, 1975), pp. 260–261.

31. In his public speeches, Budd Hopkins stresses that the aliens can't be trusted, that they persistently alter their shapes as well as the abductees' memories. Also see his *Witnessed: The True Story of the Brooklyn Bridge Abductions* (New York: Pocket Books, 1996).

32. Although I share neither Eli Sagan's conception of paranoia nor his account of selves and societies as proceeding through several stages as they develop out of and overcome paranoia, the connection he illuminates between paranoia and the fragility of the self is helpful. Considering the contemporary situation in terms of shifts away from unitary models of subjectivity toward more open and fluid possibilities, we can see how the reassurance of truth that paranoia offers might provide fragile selves with a momentary sense of stability, a temporary guarantee of coherence. See Eli Sagan, *The Honey and the Hemlock: Democracy and Paranoia in Ancient Athens and Modern America* (Princeton: Princeton University Press, 1991), p. 26.

33. Lynne V. Cheney, *Telling the Truth* (New York: Simon and Schuster, 1995).

34. Ibid., p. 195.

35. See Gilles Deleuze and Félix Guattari's account of the paranoid-interpretive ideal regime of significance in *A Thousand Plateaus* (Minneapolis: University of Minnesota Press, 1987). Such a regime "is defined by an insidious onset and a hidden center bearing witness to endogenous forces organized around an idea; by the development of a network stretching across an amorphous continuum, a gliding atmosphere into which the slightest incident may be carried; by an organization of radiating circles expanding by circular irradiation in all directions, and in which the individual jumps from one point to another, one circle to another, approaches the

center then moves away, operates prospectively and retrospectively; and by a transformation of the atmosphere, as a function of variable traits or secondary centers clustered around a principal nucleus" (p. 120). Since the center is purely abstract, referring to an infinity of other signs ("Lack or excess, it hardly matters"), Deleuze and Guatarri conceptualize its "substance of expression" as "faciality." "The face is the Icon proper to the signifying regime," they write, "the reterritorialization internal to the system" (p. 115). In abduction, and now throughout American popular culture, the face often appears gray with large, opaque, black eyes.

36. Dumm, *united states*, p. 148.

37. Winner, *The Whale and the Reactor*, p. 111.

38. Slavoj Zizek, "Eastern Europe's Republics of Gilead," in *Dimensions of Radical Democracy*, ed. Chantal Mouffe (London: Verso, 1992), pp. 193–207.

39. Ibid., p. 197.

40. See the interview with Hopkins in Michael Lindemann, *UFOs and the Alien Presence* (Santa Barbara, Calif.: The 2020 Group, 1991), pp. 164–165.

41. John Fiske, *Media Matters: Everyday Culture and Political Change* (Minneapolis: University of Minnesota Press, 1996), p. 271.

42. "Bill Summary: Major Provisions of H.R. 2202," *Congressional Digest* (May 1996), p. 142.

43. Ibid.

POSTSCRIPT

1. James McAndrew, Headquarters United States Air Force, *The Roswell Report: Case Closed* (Washington, D.C.: U.S. Government Printing Office, 1997).

2. McAndrew lists the conclusions of the new research: "Air Force activities which occurred over a period of many years have been consolidated and are now represented to have occurred in two or three days in July 1947. 'Aliens' observed in the New Mexico desert were probably anthropomorphic test dummies that were carried aloft by US Air Force high altitude balloons for scientific research. The 'unusual' military activities in the New Mexico desert were high altitude research balloon launch and recovery operations. The reports of military units that always seemed to arrive shortly after the crash of a flying saucer to retrieve the saucer and 'crew' were actually accurate descriptions of Air Force personnel engaged in anthropomorphic dummy recovery operations" (ibid., p. 3).

3. Ibid., p. 69.

4. See Philip J. Corso with William J. Birnes, *The Day after Roswell* (New York: Pocket Books, 1997).

5. See http://www.odci.gov/csi/studies/97/unclas/ufo.http.

6. Gerald K. Haines, "CIA's Role in the Study of UFOs, 1947–1990," *Studies in Intelligence* 1, no. 2 (1997), p. 1.

7. Ibid., p. 4.

8. Ibid., p. 6.

9. Ibid., p. 11.

10. "Some Thoughts on a More Glorious Fourth" (editorial), *Patriot Forum*, July 3, 1997, p. 4. Thanks to John Ackerman for providing me with a clipping of the article.

11. Jan L. Aldrich, "1947: The Beginning of the UFO Era," in *The Fiftieth Anniversary of Ufology: MUFON 1997 International UFO Symposium Proceedings*, ed. Walter H. Andrus and Irena Scott (Seguin, Tex.: Mutual UFO Network, 1997), pp. 179–194.

12. See David M. Jacobs, "UFOs at Fifty: Some Personal Observations," in Andrus and Scott, eds., *Proceedings*, pp. 16–30.

13. Ibid., p. 24.

14. I say "nearly" all accounts because of the exceptional case described by Ann Druffel and D. Scott Rogo in *The Tujunga Canyon Contacts* (New York: Signet, 1989). The researchers in this complex case of multiple abductions note that "some of the Tujunga close-encounter witnesses are members of the gay community. Those UFO entities concerned with the reproduction (and evolution) of the human race were possibly investigating to obtain details about this non-procreative life-style" (p. 232).

15. For the most explicit statement of this position, see Catharine MacKinnon, *Only Words* (Cambridge: Harvard University Press, 1993). Her account of women's lack of credibility in a pornographic culture that denies the legitimacy of their experiences reiterates the language of abductees and abduction researchers. She writes: "You cannot tell anyone. When you try to speak of these things, you are told it did not happen, you imagined it, you wanted it, you enjoyed it" (p. 3).

16. Jacobs, "UFOs at Fifty," p. 29.

17. Ibid., p. 27.

18. Budd Hopkins, "The UFO Phenomenon and the Suicide Cults—An Ideological Study," in Andrus and Scott, eds., pp. 246–257.

19. Ibid., p. 249.

20. Ibid., p. 257.

21. See Amy Harmon, "NASA Flew to Mars for Rocks? Sure," *New York Times*, July 20, 1997, p. E4. Her article, in the "Week in Review" section, was one of several involving themes of truth and conspiracy. A piece by Matthew L. Wald, "In the Air, No Mysteries Allowed," covered TWA Flight 800. Elaine Sciolino offered an article on military lies, "A Rigidly Flexible Notion of Truth." Finally, a discussion of congressional use of the immunity law, Stephen Labaton's "Playing the Immunity Card," was tagged "It Worked in Watergate."

Index

Central Intelligence Agency (CIA), 190–191

Challenger, 22, 68, 97, 99–102

Cheney, Lynne, 172

Citizens, 22; as audience, 11, 63, 68, 69–70, 97, 176; as Netizens, 69–70, 97, 176; UFO witnesses as, 40, 45

Citizens Against UFO Secrecy (CAUS), 52

Citizenship, 224n28; agency and, 179–180; astronaut as icon of, 69–70; credibility and, 39–40, 45; globalization and, 23–24, 167–169, 174–176; global thinking and, 160–163; noncitizens and, 23–24, 138, 155–156; public sphere and, 19. *See also* Democracy; Television

Clarion, 33–34

Clark, Nigel, 148

Clinton, Bill, 52, 204n44

Close encounters, 50–51

Close Encounters of the Fourth Kind, 112

Close Encounters of the Third Kind, 101

Cobb, Jerrie, 216–217n60

Cold War: containment culture, 34–38, 41–46, 162, 188, 190–191; formation of UFO community and, 22, 133; NASA and, 11, 214n18. *See also* Communism

Collings, Beth, 105, 134, 140, 146; *Connections*, 112–116, 121–122; at MUFON symposium, 193–194

Colonization, 12, 155, 168–169, 205nn52, 54; technoculture and, 180–181

Colorado study, 37, 44

Communism, 22, 70–74, 76, 90–91. *See also* Cold War

Condon, Edward, 38, 41

Connolly, William, 7

Consensus reality, 8, 15, 17, 19, 24, 30, 45, 57, 125, 137, 154

Conspiracy theories, 8, 94; as

American phenomenon, 142–143, 225n44; celebration of, 191–192; criticism of, 144–145, 150; as everyday politics, 13–14; globalization and, 162–163; interpretation and analysis in, 143–145; networks and, 145; as site for contestation, 8–9. *See also* Trust

Contactees, 33–34, 40–41, 121, 221n50. *See also* Abductees

Containment culture. *See* Cold War

Cooper, Gordon, 69, 76, 81, 83, 110, 111

Corlett, William, 17

Corso, Philip, 187

Cortile, Linda, 141, 146–147

Cousineau, Phil, *UFOs: A Manual for the Millennium*, 10–11

Crawford, Kenneth, 92

Credibility: of abductees, 59, 125, 210–211n72; audience and, 69, 72–77, 101–102; of government, 17, 36–38, 41–42, 118–119, 142; moral standing and, 42–45; scientific criteria, 54–61, 211–212n92; scientific/juridical discourse and, 44–45, 55; of space program, 72–77, 93–94; televisuality and, 73–74; therapy discourse and, 52–53, 163–164; of UFO researchers, 56–57; of UFO witnesses, 39–40, 42–43. *See also* Truth

Cronkite, Walter, 37, 63, 86

Cults, 14, 33, 40

Cyberspace: agency and, 176; hope and, 69–70; interconnections and, 148; outerspace, link with, 67–69, 96, 100, 102; passivity and, 135; as site of abduction, 135–136. *See also* Networks

Dean, Robert, 6

Democracy, 10, 120, 188–190; American fear for, 17, 162,

172, 177, 195–196; talk shows and, 132; in traditional media, 13–14; virtual reality and, 136–139. *See also* Skepticism

Parker, Calvin, 13, 50

Passivity, 180–181; in abduction narratives, 122–123, 135, 150, 173; Internet and, 68, 173–174; outerspace and, 68–70; technoculture and, 68–70; technology and, 173–177; theft of enjoyment theme, 174–176. *See also* Agency

Penley, Constance, 68, 99–100, 102

Phillip, Nick, 207n12

Popular cultures: as alien space, 132–133; outerspace images, 5–7, 11; paranoia and, 132–133

Project Blue Book, 37–38, 38, 191

Project Sign, 35

Public sphere: bracketing and, 137, 179; consensus and, 19, 137, 200–201n19; domestic space and, 80–84; illusion of, 8, 14–15, 204n43; Internet and, 137–139; networks as alternative to, 14–15, 102, 139; other and, 16–17; as unitary, 11, 16–18, 170

Quinby, Lee, 34, 200n15, 212n2

Race issues, 155–156, 164–166; multiculturalism and, 168–169; space program and, 71, 75, 81, 84–86, 92–93

Randles, Jenny, *Science and the UFOs*, 56–57

Rapping, Elayne, 20, 224n28

Rationality, 7–10, 15–17, 55–56, 200n17, 201n22

Reagan administration, 9, 100, 102, 154

Reality: contestation of, 123–124, 129; in cyberspace, 135–136; face-to-face

interactions, 136, 139, 175, 179; networks as shaping, 132–133, 137–138. *See also* Consensus reality; Experience; Truth; Virtual reality

Rheingold, Howard, 96

Right Stuff, The, 65, 77

Robbins, Bruce, 204n43

Rosenfeld, Albert, 90

Roswell, 3

Roswell, New Mexico, 60; Area 51, 3, 29, 55; crash site, 185–186; marketing aliens in, 182–184; museums, 3, 185, 186, 189. *See also* UFO sightings

Sagan, Carl, 55, 58–59, 110, 169–170; *The Demon-Haunted World*, 59

SCHWA, 26–30, 34

Science: dismissal of UFO community, 9, 18; domestic space, link with, 111, 120; skepticism and, 8–9, 11, 169–171

Scientific/juridical discourse, 22, 30, 42–46, 55–61; credibility and, 42–46; criteria for credibility, 54–61, 211–212n92; rights language, 53–54, 105; as site of resistance, 39–42; therapy discourse and, 51, 53

Scully, Frank, *Behind the Flying Saucers*, 36

Search for Extraterrestrial Intelligence (SETI), 58

Shapiro, Michael, 205n52, 216n52

Shepard, Alan, 12, 72–73, 91, 95–96

Showalter, Elaine, *Hystories*, 7–8, 23, 208n15

Simon, Benjamin, 49–50, 164

Simpson, O. J., 8, 13, 177

Skepticism, 24, 104; of audience for space program, 73–74, 77, 94–95; debunkers, 136–137; science and, 8–9, 59–60, 169–171. *See also* Paranoia

Slayton, Deke, 91, 96, 110

Slouka, Mark, 136, 223n25

insecurity and, 55; media and, 118–119. *See also* Conspiracy theories

Truth, 8; alien as icon for, 21–22; American relationship to, 30; anxiety and, 17–18; belief and, 177–178; as consensual, 45, 137; experience as, 52–53, 107–109, 172, 219–220n16; fugitivity of, 30–32, 54–55, 139, 171–172, 208–209n14; hypnosis and, 50–51; inaccessibility of, 22, 26; interconnections and, 146, 148; Internet and, 136–138, 223n25; military and, 35–36; networks and, 132–133; technoculture and, 139; as unitary, 17–18, 170. *See also* Credibility

Turner, Karla, 129, 140, 191, 221n40; *Into the Fringe*, 117–118, 121

2001: A Space Odyssey, 96

UFO community, 107; dismissal of, 9–10, 18; as microcosm of America, 18; originary moment, 22, 33, 133; as self-defensive, 16

UFO discourse: absence and, 46; containment culture and, 34–35, 42–46; deconstruction of, 30; dismissal of mainstream science, 59–60; evidence and, 31–32; knowledge and, 29–31; other and, 16–17; as participatory, 134–135; populism of, 34, 132; reflexivity of, 55–56; rights language, 53, 105, 196; scientific/juridical discourse and, 22, 30, 39–40, 42–46, 51, 55–61; as self-defensive, 16–17; as site of contestation, 8–10, 19, 20, 34–35, 41–42, 70, 162–164; skepticism as necessary to, 55, 59–60, 171; truth, concern with, 31–32; us, concept of, 18–19

Ufology, 6; agency and, 34–35; apocalypticism and, 33–34;

appropriation of dominant discourse, 42–46; as challenging military, 41, 209n48; as discourse of resistance, 39–42; factionalism in, 55, 123; skepticism and, 171; social stigma and, 6, 18, 60

UFO researchers, 35, 45–46, 57

UFO sightings, 13, 35–38, 36–37, 41, 43, 51. *See also* Roswell, New Mexico

Vaughan, Diane, 99

Virtual reality, 8, 96; paranoia and, 136–139. *See also* Consensus reality; Reality; Technology

von Braun, Werner, 74–76, 188, 215n36

Wainwright, Loudon, 67

Wald, Priscilla, 203n38

Wałęsa, Lech, 147

Walker, Sydney, 43–44, 45

Wall Street Journal, 1, 136

Walton, Travis, 30–31, 50, 101, 207n11; *The Walton Experience*, 31

Warranting, 84

Warrington, Peter, *Science and the UFOs*, 56–57

Washington Post, 1, 30

Waterman, Alan T., 214–215n23

Weekly World News, 4, 156

Westover, Jeffrey, 47, 106, 128, 159

Westrum, Ron, 53, 54

When Prophecy Fails, 33

Wilson, Katharina, *The Alien Jigsaw*, 105, 119–121, 135, 140

Winner, Langdon, 6, 161, 170, 173

Witnesses of UFOs: as citizens, 40, 45; credibility of, 36, 39–40, 42–43; as objects of medical research, 43–44. *See also* Abductees

Wolfe, Tom, 77, 91, 94, 95

Women: abduction narratives and, 22, 100–103; as astronauts, 98–99;

outerspace, link with, 101, 120. *See also* Breeding project

X Files, The, 3, 17, 23, 25–26, 29, 169, 172, 206n1

Young, John, 92
Young, Warren R., 78–79
Yuan, David D., 105
Žižek, Slavoj, 174, 176